Tolley
Employment
Handbook

by

Elizabeth A Slade QC MA *(Oxon)*
Deputy High Court Judge,
A Recorder of the Crown Court,
A Master of the Bench of the Inner Temple,
Honorary Vice-President of the
Employment Law Bar Association

Eighteenth Edition

by

members of
11 King's Bench Walk Chambers

and

Stephen Hardy, Senior Lecturer in Law,
University of Manchester

Members of the LexisNexis Group worldwide

United Kingdom	LexisNexis UK, a Division of Reed Elsevier (UK) Ltd, Halsbury House, 35 Chancery Lane, LONDON, WC2A 1EL, and 4 Hill Street, EDINBURGH EH2 3JZ
Argentina	LexisNexis Argentina, BUENOS AIRES
Australia	LexisNexis Butterworths, CHATSWOOD, New South Wales
Austria	LexisNexis Verlag ARD Orac GmbH & Co KG, VIENNA
Canada	LexisNexis Butterworths, MARKHAM, Ontario
Chile	LexisNexis Chile Ltda, SANTIAGO DE CHILE
Czech Republic	Nakladatelství Orac sro, PRAGUE
France	Editions du Juris-Classeur SA, PARIS
Germany	LexisNexis Deutschland GmbH, FRANKFURT, MUNSTER
Hong Kong	LexisNexis Butterworths, HONG KONG
Hungary	HVG-Orac, BUDAPEST
India	LexisNexis Butterworths, NEW DELHI
Ireland	LexisNexis, DUBLIN
Italy	Giuffrè Editore, MILAN
Malaysia	Malayan Law Journal Sdn Bhd, KUALA LUMPUR
New Zealand	LexisNexis Butterworths, WELLINGTON
Poland	Wydawnictwo Prawnicze LexisNexis, WARSAW
Singapore	LexisNexis Butterworths, SINGAPORE
South Africa	LexisNexis Butterworths, DURBAN
Switzerland	Stämpfli Verlag AG, BERNE
USA	LexisNexis, DAYTON, Ohio

© Reed Elsevier (UK) Ltd and Elizabeth Slade QC 2004
Published by LexisNexis UK

A CIP Catalogue record for this book is available from the British Library.

ISBN 0 7545 2707 7

Printed and bound in Great Britain by William Clowes Ltd, Beccles, Suffolk

Visit LexisNexis UK at www.lexisnexis.co.uk

List of contributors

Members of 11 King's Bench Walk Chambers

Andrew Blake BA, LLM, barrister – Holidays (27), Insolvency of Employer (29)

John Cavanagh QC, MA (Oxon), LLM (Cantab) – Unfair Dismissal I to III (50, 51, 52)

Akhlaq Choudhury BSc, LLB, barrister – Disability Discrimination (9)

James Cornwell MA (Oxon), MPhil (London), DPhil (Oxon), Dip Law, barrister – Discrimination and Equal Opportunities III (13)

Harini Iyengar MA (Oxon), BCL (Oxon), barrister – Time Off Work (46)

Seán Jones BA, BCL (Oxon), barrister – Discrimination and Equal Opportunities I (11)

Richard Leiper LLB, MJuris, barrister – Public Sector Employees (34), Transfer of Undertakings (49)

Jane McCafferty MA (Cantab) – Equal Pay (22), European Community Law (23)

Julian Milford MA, barrister – Continuous Employment (6), Redundancy I and II (35, 36)

Paul Nicholls LLB, BCL (Oxon), barrister – Collective Agreements (5), Contract of Emloyment (7), Employee or Self-Employed? (15), Engagement of Employees (21), Probationary Employees (33), References (37)

Nigel Porter MA, LLM, barrister – Introduction (1), Advisory, Conciliation and Arbitration Service (2), Codes of Practice (4), Disclosure of Information (10), Employees' Past Criminal Convictions (17), Human Rights (28), Pay I and II (31, 32), Temporary and Seasonal Employees (44)

Anya Proops MA (Cantab), PhD, barrister – Employee Participation (16), Foreign Employees (24), Vicarious Liability (53)

Clive Sheldon BA, LLM, barrister – Maternity Rights (30), Sickness and Sick Pay (41), Termination of Employment (45), Wrongful Dismissal (55)

Daniel Stilitz BA, MA, barrister – Strikes and Industrial Action (42), Trade Unions I and II (47, 48)

Holly Stout MA (Cantab), DipLaw – Discrimination and Equal Opportunities II (12), Equal Pay (22), Wrongful Dismissal (55)

Peter Wallington MA, LLM, barrister – Employment Tribunals I to III (18, 19, 20), Retirement (39), Working Time (54)

Other contributors

Gina Antczak FCA, CTA – Taxation (43)

Stephen Barc LLB, solicitor, senior legal editor, Butterworths – Children and Young Persons (3), Education and Training (14), Service Lettings (40)

Peter Cooke BSc, solicitor, partner in Salans – Directors (8)

Martin Edwards MA (Oxon), ACI Arb, Head of Employment Law at Mace & Jones – Restraint of Trade (38)

Stephen Hardy, LLB, PhD, FRSA, MCIArb, Senior Lecturer in Law, School of Law, University of Manchester – Health and Safety at Work I and II (25, 26)

Preface

The 18th edition of *Tolleys Employment Handbook* is witness to some significant changes both editorial and legal. Addressing editorial changes first, Peter Wallington has stepped down as General Editor. Peter's erudition, dedication and courtesy made him the perfect man for the job. This year, my colleagues have had to make do with something less than perfection but it is a testament to their own dedication that they have coped so ably. The team of writers has again expanded and now includes James Cornwell and Holly Stout both of whom have been engaged in the substantial restructure that has been effected to the discrimination chapters. Feedback from readers suggested that having separate chapters for sex, racial, religious and sexual orientation discrimination had lead inevitably to repetition and frequent cross-referencing. Three new chapters: Discrimination and Equal Opportunities I, II and III replace the former treatment of those areas.

1 October 2004 has seen a number of very important changes, including the new statutory disciplinary and grievance procedures set out in *Employment Act 2002, Part 3* and the new *Employment Tribunals (Constitution and Rules of Procedure) Regulations 2004*. The latter development has led to a substantial rewriting of the chapters on Employment Tribunals. The Courts have, as ever, been equally busy providing material for our contributors. There have been a number of landmark decisions this year including: *Dunnachie v Kingston Upon Hull City Council* [2004] UKHL 36 on the question whether compensation for injury to feelings is available in unfair dismissal cases; *McCabe v Cornwall County Council* and *Eastwood v Magnox* [2004] UKHL 35 on damages at common law for psychiatric injuries caused by breaches of a contract of employment; *Archibald v Fife Council* [2004] UKHL 32 on the question whether the duty to make reasonable adjustments imposed by *Disability Discrimination Act 1995* stretched to offering the employee an entirely different job; and *Lawson and Serco* [2004] EWCA 12 on the geographical jurisdiction of tribunals.

There are many other significant developments incorporated into this new edition. We have sought to state the law as it was at 31 October 2004 with later developments included wherever possible.

Feedback from readers has considerably assisted the development of the work. If you would like to contact the editorial team you may do so by emailing us at tolleysfeedback@11kbw.com.

Seán Jones

Contents

		PAGE
Table of Statutes		vii
Table of EU Legislative Material		xxix
Table of Statutory Instruments		xxxiii
Table of Cases		xlix
Abbreviations and References		cxxi
1	Introduction	1
2	Advisory, Conciliation and Arbitration Service (ACAS)	9
3	Children and Young Persons	15
4	Codes of Practice	25
5	Collective Agreement	31
6	Continuous Employment	35
7	Contract of Employment	47
8	Directors	79
9	Disability Discrimination	101
10	Disclosure of Information	133
11	Discrimination and Equal Opportunities – I	147
12	Discrimination and Equal Opportunities – II	191
13	Discrimination and Equal Opportunities – III	227
14	Education and Training	255
15	Employee or Self-Employed?	261
16	Employee Participation	271
17	Employee's Past Criminal Convictions	281
18	Employment Tribunals – I	287
19	Employment Tribunals – II	325
20	Employment Tribunals – III	381
21	Engagement of Employees	397
22	Equal Pay	399
23	European Community Law	443
24	Foreign Employees	459
25	Health and Safety at Work – I	471
26	Health and Safety at Work – II	497
27	Holidays	519
28	Human Rights	525
29	Insolvency of Employer	535
30	Maternity and Parental Rights	543
31	Pay – I	559

Contents

32	Pay – II	585
33	Probationary Employees	591
34	Public Sector Employees	593
35	Redundancy – I	601
36	Redundancy – II	615
37	References	625
38	Restraint of Trade, Confidentiality and Employee Inventions	629
39	Retirement	653
40	Service Lettings	669
41	Sickness and Sick Pay	677
42	Strikes and Industrial Action	687
43	Taxation	707
44	Temporary and Seasonal Employees	725
45	Termination of Employment	733
46	Time Off Work	747
47	Trade Unions – I	763
48	Trade Unions – II	785
49	Transfer of Undertakings	801
50	Unfair Dismissal – I	821
51	Unfair Dismissal – II	839
52	Unfair Dismissal – III	871
53	Vicarious Liability	895
54	Working Time	899
55	Wrongful Dismissal	921
Index		947

Table of statutes

PARA

Access to Health Records Act 1990 .... 10.1,
51.8
s 2–6, 8 .... 10.15
Access to Justice Act 1999
s 55 .... 20.26
90 .... 32.3
Sch 13
para 64, 66 .... 32.3
Access to Medical Reports Act 1988 ...... 10.1,
51.8
s 1 .... 10.15
3 (1) 10.15
4 .... 10.15
5 (1), (2) 10.15
8 .... 10.15
Administration of Justice Act 1982
s 10 (i) 41.16
Agricultural Wages Act 1948
s 3, 4 .... 27.7
11 .... 27.7
Agriculture (Safety, Health and Welfare
Provisions) Act 1956
s 3, 5 .... 26.27
25 (3), (6) 26.27
Air Force Act 1955 .... 34.2
Apportionment Act 1870 .... 27.8
s 2 .... 7.24, 31.22
5 .... 7.24, 31.22
7 .... 7.24, 31.22
Arbitration Act 1950
Pt I(ss 1–34) 2.6
s 4 .... 55.38
Arbitration Act 1975
s 1 .... 55.38
Arbitration Act 1996 .... 19.37
Armed Forces Act 1966 .... 34.2
Armed Forces Act 1991 .... 34.2
Armed Forces Act 1996 .... 22.2, 34.2
s 24 .... 22.4
Army Act 1955 .... 34.2
Asylum and Immigration Act 1996 ...... 11.12
s 8 (4)–(6B) 24.9
8A 24.9
Attachment of Earnings Act 1971 .... 32.11
s 1 (1)–(3) 32.1
5 (1) 32.1
6 .... 32.3
(2) 32.1
7 (1) 32.6
(2) 32.7
(4) (a), (b) 32.9
9 (2) 32.6

PARA

Attachment of Earnings Act 1971–contd
s 12 (3) 32.6
14 (1) (b) 32.7
15 (c) 32.7
16 (1)–(3) 32.2
23 (5) 32.8
24 (1), (2) 32.2
Sch 3
Pt I 32.4
Pt II
para 7, 8 .... 32.5
Betting, Gaming and Lotteries Act 1963 .. 7.5
Sch 5A 7.25
Capital Allowances Act 2001
s 262 .... 43.2
Child Support Act 1991 .... 32.1, 32.11
Child Support, Pensions and Social Security
Act 2000
s 74, 75 .... 43.17
Children Act 1989
s 3 .... 46.19
Sch 13
para 32 .... 3.3
Children and Young Persons Act 1933 ..... 3.2,
3.3
s 18 (1) 3.2, 54.3
(2) 3.3
(2A) 3.2
21 .... 3.3
23–26 .... 3.4
Children and Young Persons Act 1963 ..... 3.2,
3.3
s 37–42 .... 3.4
Children and Young Persons Act 1969 ...... 3.3
Chiropractors Act 1994
s 40 (2), (4) 17.4
Civil Jurisdiction and Judgments Act
1982 .... 24.11
Civil Jurisdiction and Judgments Act
1991 .... 24.11
Civil Liability (Contribution) Act 1978 ... 25.10
Civil Procedure Act 1997
s 1–4 .... 32.1
Companies Act 1985 .... 8.1, 10.1, 11.12
s 144 (3), (4) 8.18
234 .... 10.9, 9.15
(4) 16.3
246 (3) 8.23
247 (3) 8.23, 8.26
247A 8.23
303 .... 8.27
304 .... 8.27

Table of statutes

PARA

Companies Act 1985–*contd*
s 309 (1), (2) 16.2
310 (1) 8.18
    (3) (a), (b) 8.18
311 .... 8.25
312 .... 8.28
313 .... 8.31
314, 315 .... 8.32
316 (3) 8.28, 8.31, 8.32
317 (3) 8.7
318 (1), (4) 8.8
319 .... 7.3, 8.11, 55.14
    (1)–(3) 8.12
    (5) 8.12
379 .... 8.27
727 .... 8.18, 8.19
    (2) 8.19
Sch 6 .... 8.28
Pt I 8.22
    para 1 (1) (a) 8.22, 8.23
          (b) 8.22
          (c)–(d) 8.22, 8.23
          (2) (b) 8.22, 8.23
          (3) 8.22
        2 .... 8.23
          (1), (2) 8.22
        5 .... 8.22
        7 .... 8.26
        8 (1) 8.28
Pt II, III 8.22
Sch 7
    para 9 .... 9.15, 10.9
        11 .... 10.9, 16.3
Sch 7A 8.22
    para 6 (1) (d) 8.28
        13 .... 8.26
        14 .... 8.28
Companies Act 1989 .... 8.1, 16.3
s 137 (1) 8.18
Company Directors Disqualification Act
    1986 .... 8.1
s 2 (1) 25.38
Consumer Protection Act 1987
s 36 .... 25.21
Sch 3 .... 25.21
Contempt of Court Act 1981 .... 28.5
Continental Shelf Act 1964
s 1 (7) 11.12
Contracts (Applicable Law) Act 1990 .. 24.10
s 2 (2) 24.10
County Courts Act 1984
s 55 (1), (2) 13.12
69 .... 55.31
Courts and Legal Services Act 1990 ..... 13.18
Sch 17
    para 5 .... 32.3
Crime and Disorder Act 1998
s 31, 32 .... 26.26
Criminal Justice Act 1982
s 37 (2) 1.10

PARA

Criminal Justice Act 1982–*contd*
s 77, 78 .... 17.1
Sch 14
    para 36 .... 17.1
Sch 16 .... 17.1
Criminal Justice Act 1991
s 17 .... 1.10, 25.37
18 .... 1.10
Criminal Justice Act 1993
s 65 .... 1.10
Criminal Justice Act 2003
s 321 .... 46.5
Sch 33 .... 46.5
Criminal Law Act 1977
s 32 (1) 1.10
Criminal Justice and Public Order Act
    1994 .... 11.12, 26.26
s 126 .... 34.2
Sch 9
    para 11 (2) 17.6
Crown Proceedings Act 1947 .... 12.32
Data Protection Act 1984 .... 10.1, 10.13,
                                          10.15, 41.7
s 5 (1), (2) 10.12
21–23 .... 10.12
Sch 1
Pt I
    para 7 .... 10.12
Data Protection Act 1998 .... 10.1, 10.12,
                                          26.1, 37.6, 41.7
s 1 (1) 10.14
Pt II(ss 7–15) 10.14
s 7 .... 10.14
10 .... 10.14
12, 13 .... 10.14
s 14 .... 10.14
Sch 1 .... 10.14
Sch 3 .... 10.14, 17.8
Sch 8 .... 10.13
Deregulation and Contracting Out Act
    1994 .... 3.5, 18.11, 48.21,
                                          51.3, 54.1
s 20 .... 7.25
Sch 10
    para 1 .... 44.3
Disability Discrimination Act 1995 .... 1.6,
      9.1, 9.9, 9.22, 12.9,
      12.21, 15.1, 18.29, 19.9,
      19.18, 19.29, 21.1, 21.2,
      22.12, 23.7, 26.2, 33.1,
      37.4, 39.3, 39.6, 51.8,
                                          54.13
s 1 (1) 9.2, 9.6
    (2) 9.3
2 (1) 9.5, 9.7
    (4), (5) 9.6
3 (3) 9.4
Pt II(ss 3A–18D) 18.22
s 3A (1) 9.11, 9.12, 9.15, 39.9
    (a), (b) 9.15

PARA

Disability Discrimination Act 1995–*contd*
s 3A (2) 9.12
(3) 9.11, 9.15
(4) 9.10
(5) 9.10, 9.15
3B 9.21
4 (1) 9.19, 39.9
(2) 9.20, 9.24, 39.9
(d) 9.21
(3), (4) 9.24
(5) 9.21
(6) 9.24, 24.11
4A 9.13, 9.15
(1) 9.12, 39.9
(2) 9.12, 9.14
(3) (b) 9.15
4B (1)–(3) 9.25
4G 9.20, 39.9
4H 9.20, 39.9
(1) 9.14
4I 39.9
4J 39.9
(4) 9.20
5 (5), (6) 9.11
6 ...... 9.14, 9.15, 9.23, 23.6
(1) 9.15
6A–7D 9.24
8 (1)–(4) 9.34
(5) 9.34, 19.66
(6) 9.34
9 ...... 7.17
(1) 9.36
(2), (3) 9.37
13 (1)–(3) 9.26
14 ...... 9.26
14A (3) 9.26
14B 9.26
16 ...... 9.13
16A 9.17
16B 9.18
16C 9.27
17A 18.11
(1) 9.18
(1C) 9.15
(4) 9.18
(5) 9.20, 39.9
17B (1) 9.18
18 ...... 9.20
18A 9.26, 9.34
(2) 9.13
18B (2), (6) 9.14
18C 9.24
18D (2) 9.12
Pt III(ss 19–28) 18.13
s 53 ...... 4.12
(4)–(6) 4.13
53A (8), (8A) 9.32
56 ...... 19.8
(2) 9.35
(3) (a) 9.35

PARA

Disability Discrimination Act 1995–*contd*
s 56 (3) (b) 9.35, 19.9
57 ...... 9.29
(4) 9.27, 9.28, 9.30
(5) 9.30
58 (1) 9.27, 53.1
(2), (3) 9.28
(5) 9.27
59 (1) 9.24
(2A), (3) 9.24
55 (1)–(4) 9.16
61 (7) 9.3
(b) 9.8
(8) 9.3
64 ...... 34.2
(7) 9.24
68 ...... 24.11
(1) 9.17, 14.2
(2), (2A) 9.24
(4) 9.24
Sch 1
para 1 (1), (2) 9.2
2 (1)–(4) 9.2
3 (3) 9.7
4 (1), (2) 9.2
5 ...... 9.2
6 (1), (2) 9.7
(3 (a) 9.7
7 (1), (2) 9.8
(5) 9.8
8 (1) 9.7
Sch 3 ...... 18.11
para 2 (1), (2) 9.33
3 ...... 18.29
(1) 9.34
(2) 9.34, 18.29, 18.30
(3) 9.34
(4) 9.34
Sch 3A
para 2 ...... 19.33
Sch 4
para 2 ...... 9.34
Sch 6
para 4 ...... 9.15
Disability Rights Commission Act 1999 . 9.31
s 1–3 ...... 9.31
4 ...... 9.31, 18.11
5–7 ...... 9.31
9 ...... 9.31
Sch 3
para 23, 24 ...... 9.31
**Disabled Persons (Employment) Act
1944** 9.3, 9.8
Education Act 1996
s 8 ...... 3.1
Pt II Ch V (ss 101–126) 34.2
Pt III (ss 183–311) 34.2
s 558 ...... 3.1
559 (1)–(4) 3.3
560 (4), (5) 3.2

Table of statutes

PARA

Education Act 1996–*contd*
 s 579 (1) 3.1
Education (Work Experience) Act 1973
 s 1 .... 3.2
Employers' Liability (Compulsory Insurance)
 Act 1969 .... 25.1, 26.16
Employers' Liability (Defective Equipment)
 Act 1969
 s 1 (3) 25.6
Employment Act 1980 .... 30.1, 48.3
 s 20 .... 6.1
 Sch 2 .... 6.1
Employment Act 1982 .... 48.3
Employment Act 1988 .... 4.4, 48.33
Employment Act 1989 .... 3.5, 14.4
 s 3 (2) 12.3
 (3) 12.18
 8 .... 12.9
 10 (3) (b), (c) 3.5
 (4) 3.5
 11 (1), (2) 11.5, 12.12
 (5) 26.5
 12 (1), (2) 26.5
 Sch 3
 Pt III 3.4
Employment Act 2002 .... 2.9, 2.10, 4.2,
    7.4, 18.2, 18.6, 19.34,
    19.37, 30.27, 46.19, 51.4,
    51.10, 54.23
 s 17 (1) 30.20
 20 .... 30.11
 21 (1), (2) 30.16
 22 .... 18.3
 24 .... 18.3, 19.29
 26 .... 18.3, 18.10
 27 .... 18.3
 28 .... 18.3
 29 .... 18.19, 18.25, 50.15
 30 .... 7.5, 7.13, 7.23. 51.3
 (2) 7.17
 (3) 51.3
 31 .... 18.3, 54.22
 (2), (3) 52.13
 (4) 52.13
 (6) 51.3, 52.13
 32 .... 18.3, 18.5, 18.16, 18.18,
    18.19, 18.20, 18.23, 18.24,
    18.25, 18.30, 18.31, 19.10,
    50.15, 54.22
 (2) 50.15
 (3) 50.15
 (4) 18.19, 18.20, 50.15
 (5) 18.19
 (6) 18.19, 50.16
 (7) 51.3
 (8) 18.19
 33 .... 18.3, 18.16, 18.18, 18.20,
    18.23, 18.30, 19.10, 51.3
 34 .... 51.3, 51.4, 51.11, 52.13

PARA

Employment Act 2002–*contd*
 s 34 (3), (4) 52.5
 (6) 52.8
 35 .... 7.5
 36 .... 7.5
 38 .... 52.14
 (2), (3), (5) 52.13
 43 .... 46.2, 46.3
 51 (1) (a), (b) 51.3
 Sch 2 .... 7.23, 18.23, 50.15, 54.22
 para 6–9 .... 50.7
 Pt 3 .... 51.3
 para 14 .... 51.3
 Sch 3 .... 54.22
 Sch 4 .... 18.19, 18.32, 54.22
 Sch 5 .... 7.9
Employment Agencies Act 1973
 s 3–3D 44.3
 5 (2) 44.5
 6 .... 44.3
 13 .... 15.3
 (2), (3) 44.5
Employment and Training Act 1973
 s 2 .... 12.30
 8–9 .... 14.5
 10 .... 12.30, 14.5
 10A, 10B 14.5
Employment of Children Act 1973
 s 2 (2), (2A), (3) 3.3
Employment of Women, Young Persons
 and Children Act 1920
 s 1 (1), (2) 3.4
 3 (2) 3.4
 Schedule 3.4
Employment Protection Act 1975 .... 2.1,
    4.2, 16.1, 30.1, 31.23,
    35.1, 47.4, 47.19
 s 97 (5) 27.7
 Sch 9
 Pt I 27.7
Employment Protection (Consolidation)
 Act 1978 .... 1.6, 23.2, 23.7, 30.1,
    35.1, 50.1, 51.3
 s 8 .... 31.16
 140 (1) 50.19
 151 .... 6.1
 (3) 6.3
 Sch 3 .... 45.12
 Sch 9
 para 1 (5A) 13.7
 Sch 13 .... 6.1, 35.4, 35.13
 para 9 (1) (b), (c) 6.7
 17 (2) 6.9
 Sch 14 .... 31.34, 35.13, 45.15
Employment Relations Act 1999 .... 2.4,
    11.12, 30.1, 44.3, 47.11,
    47.19, 48.10, 52.7
 s 1 .... 16.13
 (2) 50.11, 51.3, 51.11

x

PARA

Employment Relations Act 1999–*contd*
s 5 .... 16.13, 47.38
10 .... 6.13, 20.1, 48.22,
  50.11, 51.3, 51.10
  (2) 48.22
  (4)–(5) 48.22
  (6) 46.2, 48.22
11 .... 18.11, 51.3, 51.10
  (1), (2) 48.22
12 .... 48.22, 51.2
  (3) 39.2
  (4) 6.13, 50.11
13 (4) 48.22
16 .... 6.13, 50.11, 50.17, 51.3
18 .... 50.20
  (1) 50.15
22 .... 31.10
23 .... 50.3
24 .... 47.25
28 .... 48.17
30 .... 16.1, 16.14
32 .... 24.10
  (3) 50.15
33 .... 52.16
  (1), (2) 52.15
34 (1) 52.14
  (4) 52.10, 52.14
37 .... 51.3
  (1) 52.10, 52.14
  (4) 48.4
Sch 1 .... 16.13, 47.19, 47.25, 50.11,
  51.3, 51.11
  para 30–31 .... 5.2
Sch 2 .... 48.18
Sch 3 .... 42.14
Sch 5 .... 6.13, 50.11, 50.17, 50.18,
  51.3
Employment Relations Act 2004
s 38 .... 20.1
Employment Rights Act 1996 .... 1.6, 6.1,
  9.22, 11.12, 12.33, 13.8,
  15.1, 18.11, 18.22, 23.6,
  23.7, 24.3, 24.11, 25.1,
  26.8, 29.1, 30.1, 31.14,
  31.23, 35.1, 50.1, 50.6,
  51.3, 51.8
s 1 .... 7.7, 7.9, 8.6, 8.8
  (1), (2) 7.4
  (3) 7.5
  (4) 7.5
    (d) (i) 27.8
    (ii), (iii) 7.6
  (e) 7.6
  (5) 7.5
2 .... 8.6
  (1) 7.5
  (2), (3) 7.6
  (4)–(6) 7.4
3 .... 7.4, 8.6

PARA

Employment Rights Act 1996–*contd*
s 3 (1) 7.5
  (2) 7.5, 7.23
  (5) 7.5
4 .... 7.9, 8..6
  (1) 7.7, 35.12
  (3) 7.7
  (6), (8) 7.7
5 .... 8.6
  (1) 7.8
6 .... 8.6
7 .... 7.5
7A (1) (c) 7.4
7B 7.4
8 .... 31.16, 32.9
9 .... 32.9
  (1)–(4) 31.17
11 .... 7.9, 18.9, 31.8, 31.20
  (1), (2) 7.9, 31.19
  (4) 7.9, 31.19
12 (1), (2) 7.9
  (3)–(5) 31.20
Pt II(ss 13–27) 7.17, 7.23, 18.11,
  19.29, 27.6, 31.6, 31.12,
  48.21
s 13 .... 7.9, 45.11
  (1) 27.6, 31.6, 31.8, 31.12
  (2) 31.6
  (3),(4) 31.6
14 .... 7.9, 31.6, 45.11
15 .... 7.9, 31.6
  (1) 31.6, 31.8
  (2) 31.6
  (5) 31.6
16 .... 7.9, 45.11
17 .... 7.9
  (1)–(3) 31.7
18 .... 7.9, 45.11
  (1) 31.7, 31.8
  (2) 31.7, 31.8
  (3) 31.7, 31.8
19 .... 7.9, 45.11
  (1) 31.7
20 .... 7.9, 45.11
  (1) 31.7, 31.8
  (2) 31.7
  (3) 31.7
  (5) 31.7
21 .... 7.9, 45.11
  (1) 31.7, 31.8
  (3) 31.7
22 .... 7.9, 45.11
  (1)–(4) 31.7
23 .... 7.9, 18.9, 31.8, 31.20,
  45.11
  (1) 31.8
  (3) 18.31, 31.8
  (4) 18.31
24 .... 7.9, 31.8, 31.20, 45.11

Table of statutes

PARA

Employment Rights Act 1996–*contd*

s 25 .... 7.9, 31.8, 31.20
  (1), (2) 31.8
  (3) 31.6, 31.8
  (4), (5) 31.8
26 .... 7.9, 31.8, 45.11
27 .... 7.9, 31.12, 45.11
  (1)–(3) 31.6
  (5) 31.6
Pt III (ss 28–35) 29.2, 29.5, 31.2
s 28 .... 19.29
  (1)–(5) 31.24
29 (1) 6.13, 31.25
  (2) 31.25
  (3)–(5) 31.26
30 (1)–(5) 31.27
31 .... 31.27
32 .... 31.27
34 .... 18.9
  (1)–(3) 31.28
35 .... 31.27
36 .... 7.25, 54.1
37 .... 7.25, 54.1
38, 39 .... 7.25, 54.1
40 .... 54.1
41 .... 54.1
  (2), (3) 7.25
42 .... 54.1
  (2) 7.25
43 .... 7.25, 54.1
43A 6.13, 16.10, 50.11, 51.3,
                                           51.11
43B 6.13, 26.9, 50.11, 51.3,
                                           51.11
  (1) (b) 10.18
  (2)–(4) 10.18
43C 6.13, 10.18, 26.9, 50.11,
                                     51.3, 51.11
43D 6.13, 10.18, 26.9, 50.11,
                                     51.3, 51.11
43E 6.13, 10.18, 26.9, 50.11,
                                     51.3, 51.11
43F 6.13, 10.18, 26.9, 50.11,
                                     51.3, 51.11
43G 6.13, 10.18, 26.9, 50.11,
                                     51.3, 51.11
  (2) (a)–(c) 10.18
  (3)–(4) 10.18
43H 6.13, 10.18, 26.9, 50.11,
                                     51.3, 51.11
43I 6.13, 50.11, 51.3, 51.11
43J 6.13, 10.18, 50.11, 51.3,
                                           51.11
43K 6.13, 50.11, 51.3, 51.11
43L 6.13, 50.11, 51.3, 51.11
44 .... 26.9
  (2), (3) 26.9
45 (1)–(8) 7.25
45A 54.23

PARA

Employment Rights Act 1996–*contd*

s 46 .... 39.10
47 .... 49.1, 49.18
47A 3.9
47B 10.17, 10.18, 19.29, 26.9
47E 46.19
48 .... 3.9, 7.25, 30.9, 31.12
  (1) 26.10
  (1A) 26.10
  (2)–(4) 26.10
49 .... 16.11, 26.10, 30.9, 31.12,
                                           54.23
50 .... 19.29, 46.5
  (4) 46.5
51 (1)–(3) 46.6
52 .... 19.29
  (1), (2) 46.7
53 .... 19.29, 29.2
  (1)–(6) 46.7
  (7) 46.8
54 (1), (2) 46.8
  (4) 46.8
55 .... 19.29, 46.11
  (1) 30.2, 30.3, 30.5
  (2) (a), (b) 30.3
56 .... 19.29, 29.2
  (1) 30.2, 30.3, 30.5
  (2)–(4) 30.4
  (5), (6) 30.5
57 .... 6.13
  (1)–(5) 30.5
57A 46.18, 50.18, 51.3
  (1)–(6) 46.17
57B (1)–(4) 46.18
58 .... 39.10, 46.12
  (1) 46.12
59 .... 39.10, 46.12
  (1)–(4) 46.12
  (6) 46.13
60 .... 39.10, 46.12
  (1)–(5) 46.13
61 .... 46.14, 49.1, 49.18
62 .... 49.1, 49.18
  (1) 46.14
63 .... 49.1, 49.18
63A (1) 3.7, 3.9
  (2)(c) 3.7
  (3) 3.7, 3.9
  (4) 3.7
  (5) 3.7
  (7) 3.7
63B (1) 3.7, 3.9
  (2) 3.7
  (3) 3.7
  (4) 3.7
63C 3.7
  (1)–(5) 3.8
Pt VII (ss 64–70) 29.2
s 64 .... 19.29

PARA

Employment Rights Act 1996–*contd*
s 64 (3) 31.29
   (5) 31.30
  65 (1), (2) 6.13, 31.30
   (3) 31.31
   (4) (a), (b) 31.31
  66 .... 22.4, 22.14, 30.23
   (1) 30.6
   (2) 30.6, 30.8
  67 .... 22.4, 22.14, 54.13
   (1), (2) 30.24
  68 .... 19.29, 22.4, 22.14, 30.25
  69 .... 22.4, 22.14
   (1)–(3) 30.25, 31.32
  70 .... 18.9, 22.4, 22.14
   (1)–(3) 30.25, 31.33
   (4)–(7) 30.24
  71 ..6.6, 30.8, 30.17, 30.18, 46.19, 50.4
   (4) 39.8
    (c) 30.20
   (5) 39.8
  72 .... 30.17, 30.20, 46.19
   (5) 30.20
  73 .... 6.6, 30.17, 46.19
  74, 75 .... 30.17
  75A, 75B 6.6, 46.19
  75C, 75D 46.19
  80 .... 2.4
  80A 46.19
  80B 46.19
  80C 46.19
   (1) 6.6
  80D–80E 46.19
  80F–80H 2.10, 46.19, 51.3
  80I 2.10, 46.19
  86 .... 29.5, 50.13, 51.3, 55.16,
                     55.27
   (1) 6.13, 45.7
    (a) 41.5
   (2) 6.13
   (3) 45.7, 55.16, 55.21
   (4) 6.13, 41.5
   (5) 6.13, 45.8
   (6) 35.4
  87 (1) 6.13, 45.12, 55.27
   (2) 45.12
   (4) 45.12, 55.27
  88 .... 45.12, 55.27
  89 .... 45.12, 55.27
  90 .... 45.12, 55.27
  91 .... 45.12, 55.27
   (1)–(4) 45.12
   (5) 45.12, 55.27
  92 .... 45.15
   (1) 45.14, 45.15
   (3) 6.13
   (4) 45.14
   (7) 6.6, 52.7
  93 .... 37.8

PARA

Employment Rights Act 1996–*contd*
s 93 (1)–(3) 45.15
Pt X (ss 94–134A) 50.20
s 94 (1) 50.3
  95 .... 49.20
   (1) 45.18, 50.4
    (c) 26.11
   (2) 50.5
  97 .... 6.1
   (1) 18.23, 35.4, 50.13
   (2) 6.6, 50.13
   (4) 50.13, 52.7
  98 .... 39.2
   (1) 51.1, 51.2
    (b) 44.7, 51.13, 51.14
   (2) 51.2, 51.14
    (d) 51.13
   (3) 51.5
   (4) 19.59, 20.17, 28.7, 33.2,
              51.4, 51.9, 51.11
    (b) 44.7
   (6) 33.2
  98A 52.5, 52.8, 52.13
   (1) 51.3
   (2) 51.4, 51.11
  99 .... 50.18, 51.3, 51.11
  100 .... 50.15, 50.18, 51.11, 52.10,
                 52.14
   (1) (a), (b) 52.8, 52.9
    (d), (e) 51.3
   (2)–(3) 51.3
  101 .... 51.3, 51.11
   (1)–(3) 7.25
  101A 51.3, 51.11, 54.24
   (1) (d) 50.18, 52.8, 52.9
  102 .... 39.10, 51.3, 51.11
   (1) 52.8, 52.9
  103 .... 49.1, 49.18, 50.18, 51.3,
              51.11, 52.8, 52.9
  103A 10.18, 19.29, 50.15, 50.18,
           51.3, 51.11, 52.10, 52.14
  104 .... 50.18, 51.11, 54.24
   (1)–(3) 51.3
   (4) 7.25
  104A 31.12, 51.3, 51.11
  104B 51.3, 51.11
  104C 46.19, 51.3
  105 .... 51.3, 51.11
   (1) 7.25
    (c) 51.3
   (3) 52.10, 52.14
   (4) 7.25
   (6A) 19.29, 51.3, 52.10, 52.14
   (7D) 51.3
  106 .... 30.22, 44.7
   (2) 51.14
   (3) 51.14
  107 .... 51.16
  108 (1) 6.13, 50.11

Table of statutes

PARA

Employment Rights Act 1996–*contd*
s 108 (2) 6.13, 50.11
    (3) 7.25, 30.7
      (b) 6.13, 50.11
      (c) 6.13, 50.11
      (d) 6.13, 50.11
      (dd) 6.13, 50.11
      (e) 6.13, 50.11
      (f) 6.13, 50.11
      (ff) 6.13, 50.11
      (g) 6.13, 50.11
      (gg) 6.13, 50.11
      (h) 6.13, 50.11
      (gh) 6.13, 50.11
      (hh) 6.13, 50.11
      (i) 6.13, 50.11
      (j) 6.13, 50.11
109 .... 12.8, 22.22
    (1) 39.2, 39.4, 50.14
      (a) 39.2
    (2) 7.25, 30.7, 39.2
110 .... 51.3
111 .... 18.23
    (2) 18.25, 50.2
    (3) 18.24, 18.32
112 .... 19.37
    (1) 52.1
    (5) 52.5
113 .... 19.37
114 .... 19.37
    (1) 52.2
    (3) 52.2
    (4) 52.4
115 .... 19.37
    (1) 52.3
    (2) 52.3
    (3) 52.4
116 .... 19.37
    (1) 52.2
    (2) 52.3
    (4) 52.3
    (5), (6) 52.4
117 .... 19.37, 52.15
    (1) 52.4
    (2) 52.4, 52.5
    (2A) 52.5
    (3) 19.66, 52.4, 52.5
    (4) 19.66, 52.4, 52.5
    (5) 19.66
    (7) 52.5
118 .... 19.37
    (1) 52.6
    (2), (3) 52.16
119 .... 19.37
    (2) 52.7
    (3) 52.7
    (4), (5) 52.7
120 .... 19.37, 52.9
    (1) 52.8

PARA

Employment Rights Act 1996–*contd*
s 120 (1A), (1B) 52.8
121 .... 19.37, 52.8
122 .... 19.37
    (1) 52.9
    (2) 52.9
    (3) 52.9
    (3A) 52.8, 52.9
    (4) 52.8, 52.9
123 .... 19.37
    (1) 52.11, 52.13
    (2), (3) 52.11
    (6) 52.13
    (7) 52.13
    (8) 52.5
124 .... 19.37, 48.16
    (1A) 10.18, 51.3, 52.14
    (3) 52.4
    (4), (5) 52.10
124A 52.13
125 (1)–(3) 52.17
    (4) 52.18
    (5) 52.18
    (6) 52.17
127A 55.30
127B 10.18
128 .... 18.9, 18.18, 51.3, 52.21
    (2)–(5) 52.21
129–132 .... 18.9, 18.18, 52.21
Pt XI (ss 135–181) 29.3
s 135 .... 35.2
136 (1) 35.6, 45.18
    (2) 35.6
136 (3) 35.6
    (5) 35.6
138 (1) 6.6, 35.6, 52.8
    (2) 35.6, 35.12
    (3) 35.6
    (4) 35.6, 35.12
    (5) 35.6
    (6) 35.6, 35.12
139 (1) 35.7
140 (1)–(3) 35.10
141 .... 52.8
    (1) 35.10, 35.12
    (2) 35.10
    (3) 35.10, 35.12
    (4) 35.10, 35.12
142 (1), (2) 35.6
145 .... 18.27, 35.4
    (5) 6.6, 35.4
146 (1) 35.6
    (2) 35.12
147 (2) 35.8
148 .... 35.8, 35.9
149 .... 35.9
150 (1), (3) 35.8
152 .... 39.2

PARA

Employment Rights Act 1996–*contd*
s 152 (1) (b) 35.9
153 .... 39.2
155 .... 6.13, 35.2, 35.4
156 .... 12.8, 22.22
    (1) 39.2
    (a) 35.10, 39.2
    (b) 35.10
157 .... 29.4, 35.10
158 .... 35.10, 35.13
159 .... 35.10
160 .... 35.10
161 .... 35.10
162 (1)–(3) 35.13
    (4), (5) 35.13
163 .... 18.9, 19.29
    (1) 35.14
    (2) 35.7
164 .... 18.22, 19.29, 29.4
    (1),(2) 18.27, 35.11
    (3) 18.27
166 (6), (7) 29.4
167 .... 6.12, 29.4
170 .... 18.9, 29.7
Pt XII (ss 182–190) 29.3
s 182 .... 15.3, 29.5
183 (3) 29.5
184 (1) (a) 29.5
    (2) 29.5
185 .... 29.5
186 .... 29.5
188 .... 18.9, 29.7
189 .... 29.5
191 .... 34.2, 34.3, 55.43
192 .... 34.2
193 .... 34.6
196 .... 50.15
    (1) 45.8
    (2), (3) 31.8, 31.18
    (5) 50.15
197 .... 50.15, 50.20
    (1) 50.15
198 .... 7.4, 7.8
199 .... 7.8, 45.8, 50.15
    (2) 31.18, 35.10, 50.15
    (4) 31.18
200 .... 50.15
    (1) 31.18, 34.2
    (2) 34.2
201 .... 50.15
202 .... 34.6
203 .... 7.25, 19.33, 19.35, 45.7,
                                                              52.22
    (1) 2.4, 7.17, 19.32, 31.8,
                                      35.14, 45.2, 50.19
    (2) 2.4, 7.17, 31.8, 35.14,
                                              50.15, 50.20
    (f) 19.33
    (3), (4) 19.33

PARA

Employment Rights Act 1996–*contd*
s 205 (2) 31.8
206 (4) 18.9
Pt XIV (ss 210–235) 46.14
s 210 .... 6.1 , 35.13, 50.12
    (1)–(3) 6.2
    (4) 6.5, 6.12
    (5) 6.5
211 .... 6.1, 35.13, 50.12
    (1) 6.3
    (2) 6.3, 6.5, 35.4, 35.13
    (3) 6.3, 6.11
212 .... 6.1, 35.13, 50.12
    (1) 6.6
    (3) 6.6, 6.7
    (a) 6.7
    (b) 6.7, 44.8
    (c) 6.7
    (4) 6.6
213 .... 6.1, 35.13, 50.12
214 .... 6.1, 6.12, 35.13, 50.12
    (2) 35.13
215 .... 6.1, 6.5, 6.12, 50.12
    (1) (a) 6.10
    (2) (a), (b) 6.10
216 .... 6.1, 6.5, 6.12, 35.1,
                                                35.13, 50.12
    (1)–(3) 6.10
217 .... 6.1, 6.5, 6.12, 35.13,
                                                             50.12
218 .... 6.1, 35.13, 50.12
    (2) 6.9
    (3)–(5) 6.9
    (6) 6.9
    (8)–(10) 34.2
219 .... 6.1, 6.6, 35.13, 50.12,
                                                               52.4
220 .... 31.32
221 .... 27.4, 31.12, 31.32, 31.34,
                                      35.13, 45.15, 52.7
    (2) 31.35, 31.36
    (3) 31.35, 31.36
222 .... 31.34, 31.35, 35.13, 45.15,
                                                               52.7
223 .... 31.34, 35.13, 45.15, 52.7
    (1), (2) 31.35
    (3) 31.36
224 .... 31.34, 31.37, 35.13, 45.15,
                                                               52.7
225 .... 31.12, 31.34, 31.38, 35.13,
                                                     45.15, 52.7
226 .... 31.12, 31.34, 35.13, 52.7
    (2) 45.15
227 .... 31.12, 31.34, 35.13, 45.15,
                                                     48.16, 52.7
    (1) 47.38, 48.22, 52.7
    (a) 52.15
228 .... 31.12, 31.34, 35.13, 45.15,
                                                               52.7

Table of statutes

PARA

Employment Rights Act 1996–*contd*
s 229 .... 31.12, 31.34, 35.13, 45.15,
                                                    52.7
230 (1) 35.3, 50.3
    (2) 14.2, 15.2
    (3) 31.6, 31.12, 51.3
231 .... 6.9, 31.38
232 (1) 7.25
    (3) 7.25
    (6) 7.25
233 (1) 7.25
    (2) 7.25
234 .... 27.4
    (1)–(3) 31.36
235 .... 6.5
    (1) 30.18, 30.19, 52.3
240 .... 32.5
Sch 1
    para 3 .... 32.4
        56 .... 50.17
Sch 2
    para 16 .... 34.2
Employment Rights (Dispute Resolution)
    Act 1998 .... 18.1, 18.2, 19.33, 22.2
s 2 .... 18.10
4 .... 18.8
7 .... 2.10, 19.37
9 .... 13.18
11 .... 2.4
15 .... 52.9
Sch 1
    para 2, 3, 9 .... 19.34
        11 .... 19.34
        22 .... 52.9
        24 .... 19.34
Employment Tribunals Act 1996 .... 1.6, 18.6
s 3 .... 55.38
4 .... 31.12, 34.6
    (2), (5) 18.9
    (6A) 18.10
6 .... 19.55
7 (3A) 18.10
    (4) 19.4
10 .... 34.6
11 .... 13.7
    (1) (a) 19.19
    (2) 19.18
    (6) 13.7, 19.18
12 .... 19.18
    (1)–(2) 9.34
    (3) 9.34, 19.18
    (7) 9.34
15 .... 19.66
18 .... 2.4, 6.6, 19.33
    (1)–(3) 2.4, 13.6
    (4)–(5) 2.4
    (7) 2.4, 13.6, 19.29
21 .... 20.1
28 .... 34.6

PARA

Employment Tribunals Act 1996–*contd*
s 28 (3), (4) 20.2
29 (1) 20.14
    (2) 20.21
30 (3) 20.1
32 .... 9.34, 19.18
33 .... 19.76, 28.7
35 .... 20.21
    (1) 20.11
37 (1), (2) 20.26
Enterprise and New Towns (Scotland) Act
    1990
s 2 (3) 12.30
Equal Pay Act 1970 .... 1.6, 4.8, 4.9, 7.13,
                            7.17, 11.10, 11.12, 12.8,
                            12.10, 13.10, 18.19, 18.22,
                            19.29, 19.33, 22.1, 22.2,
                            22.10, 22.14, 22.17, 22.19,
                            22.24, 23.2, 23.7, 39.12
s 1 .... 22.25, 24.11
    (1) 22.4, 22.5
    (2) (a) 22.5
        (b) 22.5
        (c) 22.5, 22.8
    (3) 22.5, 22.10, 22.11, 22.12,
                                                    22.23
        (a), (b) 22.11
    (4) 22.6
    (5) 22.7
    (6) 22.9
        (a) 22.4
        (c) 22.9, 22.22
    (8) 22.4
    (11), (13) 22.4
2 .... 13.14, 13.18, 18.11, 22.17
    (1) 22.20
    (1A), (2) 22.20
    (3) 22.20
    (4) 18.28, 22.13, 22.19, 22.20
    (5) 22.9, 22.19, 22.20, 22.22
2A 18.11, 22.17, 22.23
    (1) 22.23
    (2) 22.8, 22.23
    (2A) 22.23
2ZA 22.20
    (2)–(7) 18.28
2ZB 22.20
3 .... 22.25
5 .... 22.21
7A 34.2
7B 19.8, 22.23
    (4) 19.9
11 (2A) 18.28
Equal Pay Act (Northern Ireland) 1970 .. 22.4
European Communities Act 1972 .... 23.1
s 2 (1) 23.2
    (4) 22.22
European Communities (Amendment)
    Act 1986 .... 22.22, 23.1

PARA

European Communities (Amendment) Act
  1993 .... 23.1
Factories Act 1961 .... 3.5
  s 1–7 .... 26.27
    18 .... 26.27
    28 .... 26.27
    29 .... 26.27
    57–60 .... 26.27
    69 .... 26.27
    175 (5) 26.27
Fair Employment (Northern Ireland) Act
  1976 .... 11.8
Family Law Reform Act 1969
  s 1 .... 3.1
Finance Act 1988
  s 74 .... 45.10
Finance Act 2000 .... 43.28
  s 47 .... 43.31
    58 .... 43.33
    62 .... 43.32
  Sch 8 .... 43.31
  Sch 12 .... 43.35
  Sch 14 .... 43.32
Finance Act 2001
  s 62 .... 43.32
  Sch 14 .... 43.32
Finance Act 2003
  s 136 .... 43.35
  Sch 21 .... 43.29, 43.31
    para 16 .... 43.30
  Sch 22 .... 43.29, 43.31
Finance Act 2004
  s 78, 79 .... 43.22
  Pt 4(ss 149–284) 39.6
  Sch 13 .... 43.22
Financial Services Act 1986
  s 189 .... 17.4
  Sch 14 .... 17.4
Financial Services and Markets Act 2000
  Pt IV (ss 40–55) 8.23
  Pt VI (ss 72–103) 8.22
Fire Precautions Act 1971 .... 25.38, 26.13
  s 23 .... 26.13
Gender Recognition Act 2004 .... 22.13
  s 9 .... 12.5
Health and Safety at Work etc Act
  1974 .... 4.10, 16.1, 18.4, 25.1,
             25.3, 25.16, 25.25, 26.13,
             30.23, 53.1, 54.20, 54.21
  Pt I (ss 1–54) 25.17, 25.29
  s 1 (1) 25.17
    2 .... 25.28, 25.37, 25.43, 26.3,
                            26.26
    (1) 25.18
    (2) 25.18
      (a) 25.5
      (c) 10.7, 25.5
      (e) 26.23
    (3) 10.7, 25.18

PARA

Health and Safety at Work etc Act
  1974–contd
  s 2 (4), (6) 26.21
    3 .... 25.28, 25.37, 25.43
    (1) 25.19, 25.37
    (2) 25.19
    (3) 25.19
    4 .... 25.20, 25.28, 25.37, 25.43
    5 .... 25.28, 25.37, 25.43
    6 .... 25.28, 25.37, 25.43
    (8), (8A) 25.21
    7 .... 25.22, 25.28, 25.37, 25.43
    8 .... 25.23, 25.37, 25.43
    9 .... 25.24, 25.37, 26.12
    10 .... 25.26
    14 (1) 25.26
    (2) 25.26
      (a), (b) 25.40
    16 .... 4.10, 25.28
    17 .... 4.11
    (2) 25.37
    20 .... 25.37
    (2) (a)–(l) 25.30
    (4) 25.30
    (7), (8) 25.30
    21 .... 25.31
    22 .... 25.32
    (4) 25.32
    23 (2) (a) 25.32
    (5) 25.33
    24 (2) 25.34
    (3) (a), (b) 25.35
    (4) 25.34
    25 .... 25.37
    (1) 25.30
    27 .... 25.27
    (1), (4) 25.37
    28 .... 25.37
    33 .... 25.1, 25.37
    (1) 10.7
      (a) 25.37
      (b) 25.23, 25.37, 25.39
      (c) 25.37
      (d) 25.37
      (e) 25.37
      (f) 25.37
      (g) 25.37, 25.41
      (h) 25.37
      (i)–(o) 25.37
    (1A) 10.7, 25.37
    (2) 25.37
    (2A) 25.37, 25.39
    (3) 10.7, 25.37
      (b) 25.23
    (4) (a)–(c) 25.37
    (7) 25.37
    34 (1)– (3) 25.40
    37 .... 25.38
    40 .... 25.41

Table of statutes

PARA

Health and Safety at Work etc Act 1974–*contd*
s 42 (1), (2) 25.39
   (4) 25.37
47 (1) (a) 25.43
   (2) 25.43
   (5) 25.43
53 (1) 25.29
Sch 1 .... 25.17, 25.29, 25.37, 25.38

Highways Act 1980
s 137 (1) 42.12

Housing Act 1980 .... 40.5
s 52 .... 40.5
55 .... 40.6

Housing Act 1985
Sch 1
  para 2 (1)–(3) 40.7
    5 (1) 40.7

Housing Act 1988 .... 40.1, 40.5
s 1 .... 40.5
7 .... 40.6
9 .... 40.6
13, 14 .... 40.8
19A 40.5
20 .... 40.5
20A 40.5
21 .... 40.6
22 .... 40.8
24, 25 .... 40.9
27 .... 40.3
29 .... 40.3
32 .... 40.4
Sch 2
  Ground 16 .... 40.6
Sch 2A 40.5

Housing Act 1996 .... 40.5
s 96 .... 40.5
97 .... 40.5
98, 99 .... 40.6
100 .... 40.8
103 .... 40.9

Human Rights Act 1998 .... 1.7, 2.10, 10.14, 11.10, 18.7, 19.16, 19.37, 25.37, 26.4, 28.1, 28.5, 28.7, 42.1
s 1, 2 .... 28.6
3 .... 28.6, 28.7
4 .... 20.1, 28.6
   (5) 28.7
6 .... 18.13, 19.51, 28.6
   (3) 28.6
7 .... 18.13, 28.6
8 .... 28.6
10 .... 28.6
19 .... 28.6

Immigration and Asylum Act 1999
s 22 .... 24.9

PARA

Income and Corporation Taxes Act 1988 .... 15.1, 43.1
s 148 .... 45.10, 55.32
150 .... 41.6
186 .... 43.28
187 .... 43.28
188 .... 55.32
   (4) 45.10
198 .... 43.27
588, 589 .... 14.1
590C 39.6
Sch 9, 10 .... 43.28

Income Tax (Earnings and Pensions) Act 2003 .... 43.1
s 7 .... 43.2
44–47 .... 43.2
48–61 .... 43.2, 43.35
62 .... 43.2, 43.22
63 .... 43.2, 43.3
64 .... 43.2
65 .... 43.2
66 .... 43.2
67 .... 43.2, 43.3
68 .... 43.2, 43.3
69 .... 43.2
70 .... 43.2, 43.20
71 .... 43.2, 43.20
72 .... 43.2, 43.20
73 .... 43.2, 43.20
74 .... 43.2, 43.20
75 .... 43.2, 43.20
76–83 .... 43.2, 43.20
84 .... 43.2, 43.20
   (2A) 43.22
85–96 .... 43.2, 43.20
97, 98 .... 43.2, 43.20
99, 100 .... 43.2, 43.20, 43.22
101–113 .... 43.2, 43.20
114–148 .... 43.2, 43.20, 43.24
149–153 .... 43.2, 43.20, 43.25
154 .... 43.2, 43.20
155–170 .... 43.2, 43.20, 43.26
171–200 .... 43.2, 43.20
201–202 .... 43.2
203–204 .... 43.2, 43.2, 43.20
205 .... 43.2, 43.20
206–215 .... 43.2
216–220 .... 43.2, 43.3
221–223 .... 43.2
225, 226 .... 43.2
229–232 .... 43.20
235, 236 .... 43.20
237 .... 43.22
242–244 .... 43.22
245–248 .... 43.22
248A 43.26
250–260 .... 43.22
261–263 .... 43.22

PARA

Income Tax (Earnings and Pensions) Act 2003-*contd*
s 264 .... 43.22
270A 43.22
271–289 .... 43.20, 43.22
313 .... 43.22
316 .... 43.22
317 .... 43.22
318–318D 43.22
319 .... 43.22
320 .... 43.22
325 .... 43.20, 43.22
333–336 .... 43.27
386–400 .... 43.2
401–403 .... 43.2, 43.8
404–417 .... 43.2
418 .... 43.2, 43.31
419–487 .... 43.2
488–515 .... 43.2, 43.31
516–520 .... 43.2, 43.29
521–526 .... 43.2, 43.30
527–541 .... 43.2, 43.32
542–554 .... 43.2
684 .... 43.4
686 .... 43.4
708 .... 43.4
713–715 .... 43.33
Sch 2 .... 43.31
Sch 3 .... 43.29
Sch 4 .... 43.30
Sch 5 .... 43.32
Industrial Courts Act 1919 .... 47.6
Industrial Relations Act 1971 .... 4.1, 4.2,
48.3, 50.1
s 134 .... 42.10
Industrial Training Act 1964
s 5 (1), (2) 14.4
(4) (d) 14.4
6 (1) 14.4
11 .... 14.4
Industrial Training Act 1982 .... 14.4
Infants Relief Act 1874 .... 3.10
Insolvency Act 1986 .... 28.1
s 19 .... 8.28, 29.10
29 (2) 29.10
37 .... 29.10
44 .... 8.28, 29.10
(2), (2C) 29.10
s 386 .... 29.2
Sch 6 .... 29.2
para 9–15 .... 29.2
Insolvency Act 1994 .... 8.28, 29.10
s 1 .... 29.10
Judgments Act 1838 .... 19.67
Law of Property Act 1925
s 146 .... 40.5
Law Reform (Contributory Negligence) Act 1945
s 1 (1) 25.44

PARA

Law Reform (Frustrated Contracts) Act 1943
s 1 (3) 45.3
Law Reform (Personal Injuries) Act 1948
s 1 (3) 25.7
Learning and Skills Act 2000 .... 14.5, 14.9
Limitation Act 1980 .... 29.10
s 5 .... 55.40
33 .... 18.30
(3) 13.3
Local Government Act 1972
s 112 .... 34.2
116 .... 34.2
Local Government Act 1988 .... 34.2
s 17 .... 13.17
Pt III (ss 24–26) 48.20
Local Government Act 1992 .... 34.2
Local Government and Housing Act 1989
s 1–3 .... 34.2
7 .... 9.24, 34.2
10 .... 46.5
12 .... 34.2
Local Government, Planning and Land Act 1990 .... 34.2
Magistrates' Courts Act 1980
s 32 (2) 10.7
Merchant Shipping Act 1979
s 39 .... 32.2
Merchant Shipping Act 1995 .... 54.3
s 85 .... 54.33
314 (2) 32.2
Sch 13
para 46 .... 32.2
Minors' Contracts Act 1987
s 1 .... 3.10
Misuse of Drugs Act 1971
s 8 .... 26.3
National Health Service and Community Care Act 1990
s 6 (1) 7.13
National Minimum Wage Act 1998 .... 6.13,
14.2, 18.11, 24.3, 51.11,
54.5, 54.22
s 2, 3 .... 31.10
5–8 .... 31.10
9 .... 31.11
10 .... 31.11
11 (2) 31.11
12 .... 31.11
13 (1) (b) 31.13
14 .... 31.13
15 .... 31.13
18 .... 31.12
19 (4)–(9) 31.13
20 .... 31.13
21 (3), (5)–(7) 31.13
22 .... 31.13
23, 24 .... 31.12
25 .... 31.12, 51.3
27 .... 31.12

Table of statutes

PARA

National Minimum Wage Act 1998–*contd*
s 28 .... 31.12
31 .... 51.3
(1)–(5), (9) 31.13
32 .... 31.13
33 (1) 31.13
34 .... 31.10, 44.6
35–43 .... 31.10
44, 44A 31.10
45 .... 31.10
49 (3), (4) 19.33
54 .... 31.9
(3) 31.10, 31.12, 44.6
Sch 1 .... 31.10
National Minimum Wage (Enforcement Notices) Act 2003 .... 31.13
Nationality, Immigration and Asylum Act 2002
s 147 .... 24.9
Naval Discipline Act 1957 .... 34.2
Occupiers' Liability Act 1957 ..... 25.1, 25.12
s 2 (2), (3) 25.14
(4) (b) 25.15
Occupiers' Liability Act 1984 ..... 25.1, 25.12
Offices, Shops and Railway Premises Act 1963 .... 3.5
s 4–16 .... 26.27
Offshore Safety Act 1992
s 4 .... 25.37, 25.39
Offshore Safety (Protection against Victimisation) Act 1992 .... 51.3
Osteopaths Act 1993
s 39 (2), (4) 17.4
Payment of Wages Act 1960
s 1 .... 31.4
11 .... 31.3
Pension Schemes Act 1993 .... 18.11, 39.6
s 124 (1), (2) 29.6
(3), (3A) 29.6
(4), (5) 29.6
126 .... 29.7
127 (1) 29.6
145–151 .... 39.12
190 .... 32.2
Sch 8
para 4 .... 32.2
Pensions Act 1995 .... 12.31, 22.2, 22.16,
22.17, 22.18, 22.19, 29.6,
39.1, 39.6, 46.12
s 1 .... 39.12
10 .... 39.7
16–21 .... 39.10
46 (5) 51.3
50 .... 39.12
62 .... 12.10, 18.11, 39.12
(1)–(3) 22.17
(4) 22.17
(6) 22.17
63 .... 18.11

PARA

Pensions Act 1995–*contd*
s 63 (1), (2) 22.17
(4), (6) 22.17
64 .... 12.10, 18.11
(2), (3) 22.17
65 .... 18.11
124 (1) 13.8
126 .... 22.17
157 .... 39.12
Police Act 1996 .... 34.2, 40.7
s 15 .... 34.2
64 (4A), (4b) 34.2
88 .... 53.1, 53.2
91 .... 34.2
Police Act 1997
Pt V (ss 112–127) 17.7
s 112 .... 17.7
113 (2)–(5) 17.7
114 .... 17.7
115 (2)–(4) 17.7
(5) (a)–(g) 17.7
(7)–(9) 17.7
116–121 .... 17.7
122 (1), (2) 17.7
123–127 .... 17.7
Police and Criminal Evidence Act 1984
s 54 (9) 12.5
Powers of Criminal Courts Act 1973
s 30 .... 1.10
Private International Law (Miscellaneous Provisions) Act 1995
s 11 (1) 24.10
12 (1) 24.10
Protection from Eviction Act 1977
s 1 (2) 40.3
(3) 40.3
(3A), (3B) 40.3
2 .... 40.3
3 (1) 40.3
5 .... 40.5
(1A) 40.4
8 (2) 40.3
Protection from Harassment Act 1997 .... 11.12, 26.26
Public Interest Disclosure Act 1998 .... 10.1,
16.10, 18.11, 19.7
s 1 .... 10.18, 26.9, 51.3
2 .... 10.17, 10.18,
26.9
3 .... 26.10
5 .... 10.17, 10.18, 51.3
7 .... 10.17
8 (4) 10.18
11, 13 .... 10.17
Public Order Act 1986
s 4A 26.26
Pt II (ss 11–16) 42.12
Race Relations Act 1965 .... 11.2
Race Relations Act 1968 .... 11.2

PARA

Race Relations Act 1976 .... 1.6, 9.9,
9.10, 9.12, 9.16, 9.17,
11.2, 11.5, 11.6, 11.8,
12.4, 12.6, 12.19, 13.1,
19.9, 19.29, 21.1, 21.2,
23.7, 24.9, 33.1, 37.4,
52.15

s 1 (1) (a) 11.4, 11.6
(b) 11.7
(ii) 12.8
(1A) 11.7
(c) 12.8
(2) 11.5
2 (1), (2) 11.10
3 (1) 11.6
(4) 11.5, 11.10
3A (2) 11.11
4 .... 12.15, 23.4, 24.11
(1) 11.12, 12.34
(2) 18.29
(b) 11.12, 12.17
(c) 11.12, 11.13
(3) 9.24, 12.11
(4) 12.17
(4A) 11.12
4A (2) (a) 12.4
5 .... 12.4
(2) (d) 12.5
(3)–(4) 12.5
6 .... 12.11
(7) 11.12
7 (1) 12.21
(2) (a) 12.22
(3), (3A) 12.21
(5) 12.21
8 .... 24.11
(1) 11.12, 12.15, 23.4
(1A) 11.12, 12.15
(3) 11.12, 12.15
(4) 11.12
(5) 11.12, 12.15
9 (1), (3) 12.11
(5) 12.11
10 (1), (1A), (1B) 12.25
(2)–(6) 12.25
Pt II (ss 11–16) 11.13, 15.1, 18.22
s 11 (1)–(4) 12.26
12 (1), (1A) 12.27
(2) 12.27
13 (1)–(3) 12.28
14 (1) 12.29
(2) 12.30
(3) 12.29
(4)–(6) 12.29
15 (1), (1A) 12.30
(2) 12.30
16 .... 11.13, 34.2
(1) 11.12
20 .... 12.17

PARA

Race Relations Act 1976–*contd*

s 26A (1), (2) 12.24
(3), (3A) 12.24
(4) 12.24
26B 12.24
27A 11.12
(1) 12.33
(2) 11.12, 12.33
(3) 12.33
28 .... 11.13, 13.12, 13.14
(3) 12.40
29 .... 11.12, 13.12, 13.15
(1) 11.12, 12.34
(2) 12.34
(3) 11.12, 12.34
(4) 11.12, 12.34
(5) 11.12, 12.34
30 .... 11.13, 12.40, 13.12, 13.15
31 .... 11.13, 13.12, 13.15
(1), (2) 11.13, 12.40
32 .... 11.13, 13.2
(1) 11.13, 12.23, 12.35, 53.1
(2) 11.13, 12.38
(3) 11.13, 12.35, 12.38
33 .... 13.2
(1) 11.13, 12.36
(2) 12.37
(3) 11.13, 12.36
(4) 12.36
37 .... 11.5, 12.9
38 (1) 11.5, 12.9
(2) 11.5, 12.9
(3) 11.5, 12.9
(4) 11.5, 12.9
(5) 12.9
40 (1) 11.12
41 (1), (1A) 12.18
(2) 12.18
43 (1) 13.11
47 .... 4.6
(1) 13.11
(10) 4.7, 13.11
48 .... 13.12
49 (2)–(4) 13.12
50 (2) (a), (b) 13.12
(3) (a), (b) 13.12
(5), (6) 13.12
51 .... 13.12
(1) 13.12
52 (1)–(3) 13.12
53 (1), (2) 13.1
54 .... 13.13, 18.11
(1) 13.2
(2) 12.27, 13.2
54A 13.2
56 (1) 13.15
(a)–(c) 13.8
(2) 13.8
(4) 19.66

Table of statutes

PARA

Race Relations Act 1976–*contd*
s 56 (4) (a), (b) 13.8
57 (3), (6) 13.8
58 (4), (5) 13.13
59 .... 18.11
  (1)–(4) 13.13
60 .... 13.12, 13.13
61 (4) 13.13
62 (1) 13.14, 13.15
63 .... 11.12, 12.34, 12.40, 18.11
  (1)–(5) 13.15
64 (1) 13.15
65 .... 19.8
  (2) (a) 13.5
  (b) 13.5, 19.9
66 .... 13.16
68 (1) 13.3, 18.29
  (4), (5) 13.15
  (6) 13.3, 13.15, 18.30
  (7) 18.29
  (b) 13.3
72 .... 7.17, 7.18
  (1) 13.17
  (3) 13.17
  (4) 13.18
    (a) 2.4
    (aa) 19.33
  (4A) 19.33
  (5) 13.17
72A 7.18, 13.17
75 .... 34.2
  (2)–(7) 12.32
  (8)–(9B) 12.32
75A, 75B 12.32
76 .... 12.22
  (2)–(9) 12.22
76ZA (1)–(6) 12.22
  (7) (b) 12.22
  (8) (c) 12.22
  (9) (a), (b) 12.22
76A (2) 12.23
  (3) (b) 12.23
  (4)–(6) 12.23
76B (3) 12.23
78 .... 11.12
  (1) 11.12, 12.34, 14.2
  (4) 13.13
Race Relations (Amendment) Act
2000 .... 11.13
Race Relations (Remedies) Act 1994 .... 13.8
Railways and Transport Safety Act
2003 .... 26.25
Redundancy Payments Act 1965 .... 35.1
Rehabilitation of Offenders Act 1974 .... 17.5,
17.7
s 1 (1) 17.1
4 (1) 17.2
  (2) 17.2, 17.4
  (a), (b) 17.7

PARA

Rehabilitation of Offenders Act 1974–*contd*
s 4 (3) 17.4
  (a) 17.2
  (b) 17.3
  (6) 17.2
5 .... 17.6
  (1) 17.1
8 (3), (5) 17.2
Rent Act 1977 .... 15.8, 40.1, 40.5
s 44 .... 40.8
Pt IV (ss 62–75) 40.8
s 98 (2) 40.6
100 .... 40.6
Sch 15
Pt I
  Case 8 .... 40.6
  Case 19 .... 40.6
Pt II 40.6
Rent (Agriculture) Act 1976 .... 40.9
Reserve Forces (Safeguard of Employment)
Act 1985
s 1 (2) 46.20
3–5 .... 46.20
7–10 .... 46.20
School Teachers' Pay and Conditions Act
1991 .... 34.2
Sex Discrimination Act 1975 .... 1.6, 9.9,
9.10, 9.12, 9.16, 9.17,
9.27, 11.7, 11.8, 11.11,
12.3, 12.4, 12.7, 12.8,
13.1, 15.1, 19.29, 21.1,
21.2, 22.2, 22.10, 22.17,
23.6, 23.7, 30.21, 33.1,
37.4, 52.15
s 1 (1) 11.6
  (a) 11.5, 11.6
  (b) (ii) 12.8
  (2) 23.6
    (a) 11.4
    (b) 11.7
    (iii) 12.8
2 .... 11.2
  (2) 11.5, 12.9
  (3) 11.12
2A 11.2, 11.4, 12.25, 22.2,
22.13
  (1) 11.6
  (3) 11.5
3 .... 12.9
  (1) (a) 11.4, 11.6
  (b) 11.7
4 .... 22.2
  (1) 11.10
  (2) 11.10
  (4) 11.12, 22.2
  (5)–(6) 22.2
  (8) 22.2
5 (3) 11.5, 11.6
Pt II (ss 6–20A) 18.22

PARA

Sex Discrimination Act 1975–*contd*
s 6 .... 11.12, 12.33, 24.11
  (1) 11.12, 12.15, 22.13
  (2) (a) 11.5, 12.17
      (b) 11.12, 11.13, 12.5
  (4) 12.10, 22.17, 39.1
  (4A) 22.17, 22.25
  (5), (6) 12.10
  (7) 12.17
  (8) 12.10
7 (2) 12.3
  (3) 12.3
  (4) 12.3, 12.5
7A (1) (b) 12.5
  (3) 12.5
7B (1) (a) 12.5
  (3) 12.5
9 (2), (3) 12.21
  (3A), (3B) 12.21
  (4) 12.21
10 .... 24.11
  (1) 11.12, 12.15, 22.13
  (2) 11.12
      (a), (b) 12.15
  (4) 11.12
  (5) 11.12
11 (1)–(3) 12.25
  (3A), (3B) 12.25
  (4)–(6) 12.25
12 (1)–(4) 12.26
13 (1)–(3) 12.27
14 (1), (2) 12.28
15 (1) 12.29
  (2) 12.30
  (3)–(6) 12.29
16 (1), (1A) 12.30
  (2) 12.30
17 .... 34.2
  (1) 12.23
  (1A) (b) 12.23
  (2), (3) 12.10
  (4) 12.23
  (5), (5A) 12.23
  (6), (7) 12.23
  (9) 12.23
18 (1), (2) 12.10
19 (1), (3), (4) 12.10
29 .... 12.17
35A (1)–(4) 12.24
35B 12.24
37 .... 13.12, 13.14
  (3) 12.40
38 .... 11.12, 13.12, 13.13, 13.15
  (1) 11.12, 12.34
  (2) 12.34
  (3) 11.12, 12.34
  (4) 11.12, 12.34
  (5) 11.12, 12.34
39 .... 11.13, 12.40, 13.12, 13.15

PARA

Sex Discrimination Act 1975–*contd*
s 40 .... 11.13, 12.40, 13.12, 13.15
  (1) 12.40
  (2) 11.13, 12.40
41 .... 13.2
  (1) 11.13, 12.35, 53.1
  (2) 11.13, 12.38
  (3) 11.13, 12.35, 12.38
42 .... 13.2
  (1) 11.13
  (2) 12.36, 12.37
  (3) 11.13, 12.36
  (4) 12.36
46 (3)–(6) 12.10
47 .... 12.9
48 (1)–(3) 12.9
49 (1), (2) 12.9
50 (1) 11.12
51 .... 12.18
  (1) (c) (ii) 12.18
52 (1), (2) 12.19
53 .... 13.10
55 .... 13.10
56 .... 13.10
56A 4.8, 4.9, 13.10
  (10) 13.10
57 (1) 13.12
58 (2), (3) 13.12
  (3A) 13.12
59 (2) (a), (b) 13.12
  (3) (a), (b) 13.12
  (4) 13.12
  (6) 13.12
60 .... 13.12
  (1) 13.12
61 (1)–(3) 13.12
62 (1), (2) 13.1
63 .... 13.13, 13.14, 18.11
  (1) 13.2
  (2) 12.27, 13.2
63A 11.5, 13.2, 23.6
65 (1) (a) 13.8, 13.15
  (b) 13.8
  (c) 13.8, 13.15
  (1B) 13.8
  (3) 19.66
  (a), (b) 13.8
66 (4) 13.8
67 (2), (4), (5) 13.13
68 .... 18.11
  (1)–(4) 13.13
69 .... 13.12, 13.13
70 (4) 13.13
71 (1) 13.14, 13.15
72 .... 11.12, 12.34, 12.40, 18.11
  (1)–(5) 13.15
73 (1) 13.15
74 .... 19.8
  (2) (a) 13.5

Table of statutes

PARA

Sex Discrimination Act 1975–*contd*
s 74 (2) (b) 13.5, 19.9
75 .... 13.16
76 (1) 13.3, 18.29, 22.13
(3) 13.15
(4) 13.15
(5) 13.3, 13.15, 18.30, 22.13
(6) 18.29
(c) 13.3
77 .... 7.17, 7.18, 22.25
(1) 13.17
(3) 13.17, 22.24
(4) 22.24
(a) 2.4
(aa) 19.33, 22.24
(4A) .... 19.33 , 22.24
(5) 13.17
82 .... 11.6
(1) 11.12, 12.34, 14.2, 22.13
(4) 13.13
85 .... 12.32, 34.2
(2) 12.32
(4) 12.10, 12.32
(5) 12.10
(7)–(9) 12.32
(9A)–(9E) 12.32
85A, 85B 12.32
86 (1), (2) 12.22
Sch 3 .... 13.10
Sex Discrimination Act 1986 ...... 22.2, 22.25
s 1 (2) 12.3
2 .... 39.1
(1) 22.17
6 .... 5.6, 7.18, 13.17, 22.25
9 .... 22.25
Shops Act 1950 .... 3.5, 54.1
Social Security Act 1975 .... 32.10
Social Security Act 1985
s 18 (2) (d) 41.4
21 .... 32.2
Sch 4
para 1 .... 32.2
Social Security Act 1986
Sch 10
para 102 .... 32.2
Social Security Act 1989 .... 22.2, 30.10
Sch 5 .... 22.18, 39.8
para 2 .... 30.1
5, 6 .... 22.17, 30.1
Social Security Administration Act 1992
s 14 (3) 41.8
15 .... 30.13
(2) 30.15
113 .... 41.13
Social Security Contributions and Benefits
Act 1992 .... 6.10, 30.1, 30.10
s 4 (1) 41.6
10 .... 43.17
10ZA 43.17

PARA

Social Security Contributions and Benefits
Act 1992–*contd*
s 151 (2) 41.3
152 .... 41.3, 41.5
153 (2) 41.5
(12) 41.5
155 (1), (2) 41.5
156 .... 41.3
157 (1) 41.6
164 (1), (2) 30.11
(4) 30.13
(6) 30.11
166 .... 30.14
167 .... 30.16
171 (1) 30.11
Sch 11 .... 41.3
para 2 (c) 41.6
Sch 12 .... 41.5
para 2 .... 41.9
Sch 13
para 3 .... 30.14
Social Security (Incapacity for Work) Act
1994 .... 41.5
s 8 (1) 41.6
Social Security Pensions Act 1975
s 65 .... 32.2
State Immunity Act 1978 .... 28.4
s 16 (1) (a) 12.20
Statutory Sick Pay Act 1994 .... 41.6
s 1 .... 41.4
Sunday Trading Act 1994 .... 7.5, 51.3
s 4 .... 7.25
Sch 4 .... 7.25
Superannuation Act 1972 .... 34.2, 39.6
Supreme Court Act 1981
s 35A 55.31
42 (1A) 19.76
Tax Credits Act 1999 .... 6.13, 50.11, 51.3
Tax Credits Act 2002 .... 50.11, 51.11
Teaching and Higher Education Act 1998
s 32 .... 3.7
Trade Descriptions Act 1968 .... 25.38
Trade Disputes Act 1906
s 3 .... 42.1
Trade Union and Labour Relations Act
1974 .... 4.2, 48.3
Trade Union and Labour Relations
(Consolidation) Act 1992 .... 1.6, 2.1,
4.2, 10.1, 13.18, 16.12,
18.11, 18.22, 35.7, 42.1,
42.13, 48.3
s 1 .... 47.1, 48.22
2 .... 47.21
5 .... 47.22, 51.3
6 .... 47.26
(1), (3) 47.21
(4) 47.23
7 (1) 47.24
9 .... 47.24

PARA

Trade Union and Labour Relations
 (Consolidation) Act 1992–*contd*
s 10 (1) 47.2
 12 (1) 47.2
 (2) 47.17
 14 .... 48.11
 15 .... 42.16, 47.18
 (2), (3), (5) 47.18
 16 ....48.2
 20 .... 42.17
 (1) 47.16
 (2) 42.14, 47.16, 50.18
 (3) 47.16
 (6) 42.16
 21 .... 50.18
 (1)–(6) 47.16
 22 (2), (3) 47.17
 23 (1), (2) 47.17
 24 .... 47.12
 (3) 47.13
 25 (5A) 47.13
 26 (4) 47.13
 27 .... 47.12
 28 .... 47.12
 30 ....48.2
 32 .... 47.12
 32A 47.12
 33 .... 47.12
 37A– 37E 47.3
 40 .... 47.12
 45 .... 47.3, 47.14
 45A 47.3
 45B 47.14
 45C (5A) 47.14
 45D 47.13, 47.14
 46 .... 47.12
 (1), (3) 47.14
 (4) 47.14
 47 .... 47.14
 48 .... 47.14
 49 .... 47.14
 50 .... 47.14
 51 (6) 47.14
 52 .... 47.14
 54 .... 47.14
 55 (2), (3) 47.14
 (5A) 47.14
 56 (3), (4) 47.14
 56A 47.14
 62 .... 42.18, 48.2
 (2), (3) 42.17
 (5), (6) 42.17
 (8) 42.17
 63 (1)–(4) 48.15
 64 (1) 48.16
 (2) 48.16
 (4), (5) 48.16
 65 (2) 48.9, 48.16
 (3)–(5) 48.16

PARA

Trade Union and Labour Relations
 (Consolidation) Act 1992–*contd*
s 65 (6) 48.16
 66 .... 48.14, 48.16
 (1)–(3) 48.16
 67 (1)–(9) 48.16
 68 .... 19.29, 48.21, 51.3
 (1)–(4) 48.21
 68A 18.9, 48.21
 (1)–(3) 48.21
 69 ....48.2
 70A 47.11
 70B 2.4, 16.13, 47.38, 48.1
 71 .... 47.12, 47.15
 72 .... 47.15
 72A 47.15
 73 .... 47.15
 74–81 .... 47.15
 82 (2), (3) 47.15
 84 (1), (2) 47.15
 86 .... 47.15, 51.3
 87 .... 47.15
 97–105 .... 47.39
 108A–108C 47.3
 109 .... 48.17
 117 ....47.2
 119 .... 47.14, 47.19, 48.22
 137 (1) (b) 48.4
 (3)–(6) 48.4
 (7) (a), (b) 48.4
 138 .... 48.4
 138A 50.11, 50.17
 139 (1) 48.4
 140 (1) 48.4
 (b) 48.4
 (2) 48.4
 (3) 48.4
 141 .... 48.4
 142 .... 48.4
 143 (2) 48.4
 (3), (4) 48.4
 144 .... 42.7, 48.20
 145 ....42.7
 (1)–(5) 48.20
 146 .... 48.18, 51.3
 (1) (a) 28.4
 (c) 48.8
 (3) 48.8, 48.18
 (5) 48.8, 48.19
 147 .... 48.19
 148 .... 48.18
 (1), (2) 48.19
 (3) 48.18
 149 .... 48.19
 150 .... 48.19
 152 .... 51.3, 51.11, 52.8, 52.16,
 52.19
 (1) (c) 48.5
 (2) 51.3

Table of statutes

PARA

Trade Union and Labour Relations
  (Consolidation) Act 1992–*contd*
s 152 (3) 48.6
    (4) 48.5
  153 .... 48.5, 52.9, 52.16, 52.19
  154 .... 6.13, 48.5, 50.11, 51.3
  155 .... 48.7, 52.8, 52.19
  156 ....48.7
    (1) 48.16, 52.8, 52.9
    (2) 52.9
  157 .... 52.16
  158 (1) 52.14, 52.17
    (2), (3) 52.17
    (4), (5) 52.18
    (6) 52.17
  160 .... 48.7, 51.16
    (1), (2) 19.23, 52.20
    (3) 52.20
  161 .... 18.9, 18.18
    (1)–(3) 52.21
  162 .... 18.18
    (1)–(4) 52.21
  163 .... 18.18, 52.21
  164 .... 52.21
  165 .... 18.9, 52.21
  166 .... 18.9, 52.21
  168 .... 19.29, 51.3
    (1), (2) 46.2
    (3) 46.2
    (4) 46.2, 46.6
  168A 46.2, 51.3
  169 .... 19.29, 22.3, 29.2, 51.3
    (4) 46.2
    (5) 46.2, 46.6
  170 .... 19.29, 49.17, 51.3
    (1)–(3) 46.3
    (4) 46.3, 46.6
  171 ....46.6
  172 (1)–(3) 46.6
  174 .... 48.11, 48.13
    (1)–(3) 48.13
    (4) 48.13, 48.14
  175 .... 48.13, 48.14
  176 .... 48.13
    (1)–(3) 48.14
    (5) 48.14
  177 (2), (5) 48.13
Pt IV (ss 178–218)..................... 47.19
Pt IV Ch I (ss 178–187) 10.2
s 178 ....5.1, 47.27
    (1) 36.4, 47.20
    (2) 36.4, 46.2, 47.20, 54.4
    (3) 36.4, 47.20
  179 (1), (2) 5.2
  180 ....5.5
  181 .... 10.3, 47.6, 47.8, 47.19
  182 (1), (2) 10.3
  183 ....47.6, 47.8
    (1) 10.5

PARA

Trade Union and Labour Relations
  (Consolidation) Act 1992–*contd*
s 183 (2) 2.5, 10.5, 47.8
    (3) 10.5, 47.8
    (4) 10.5, 47.8
    (5) 10.5, 47.8
  184 .... 10.5, 47.8
    (2) , (4) 47.8
  185 ....47.9
    (1) 10.5
    (2) 10.5, 47.8
    (3) 10.5
    (4), (5) 10.5, 47.8
  186 .... 42.7, 48.20
  187 ....42.7
    (3) 48.20
Pt IV Ch II (ss 188–198) 36.3, 46.14,
                      51.3, 52.16, 52.21
s 188 .... 18.33, 23.8, 36.3,
              36.6, 46.2, 49.15, 49.18,
                      51.3, 51.11
    (1), (1A), (1B) 36.4
    (2) 36.4
    (4) 36.4, 36.6
    (7), (7A) 36.6
    (7B) 36.4
  188A 36.4, 36.5, 36.6
    (1), (2) 36.5
  189 .... 23.8, 29.2, 36.6
    (1A) 36.6
    (2), (4) 36.6
    (5) 18.33, 36.6
  190 ....23.8
    (1)–(3) 36.6
    (5) 36.6
  191 ....23.8
    (1)–(7) 36.6
  192 .... 18.9, 19.29, 23.8
    (1)–(3) 36.6
  193 ....23.8, 36.2
    (1), (2) 36.7
    (4) 36.7
    (7) 36.7
  194 ....23.8
    (1) 36.7
  195 ....23.8
    (1), (2) 36.3
  196 ....23.8
    (2) 36.4
  197 ....23.8
  198 ....23.8
  199 .... 2.9, 4.14
    (4) 36.4
  200 ....4.2
  201 .... 4.2, 4.14
  202 ....4.14
  203 .... 4.4, 4.14, 42.14, 47.14,
                      47.32
  204 ....42.14, 47.14, 47.32

PARA

Trade Union and Labour Relations
(Consolidation) Act 1992–*contd*
s 204 (2) 4.4
205 .... 4.14
206 .... 4.14
207 (1) 4.3, 4.5
(2) 4.3
(3) 4.5
208 (2) 4.4
209 .... 2.1
210 .... 2.3
212 (1) 2.6
(b) 47.7
(2) 2.6
(3) 2.6
(4) (b) 2.6
(5) 2.6
212A 2.10, 19.37
213 .... 2.7
214 (1), (2) 2.8
219 .... 42.3, 42.4, 42.6, 42.8,
42.16, 42.20, 47.16, 50.17
(3) 42.9
220 .... 42.9, 42.10, 42.12, 42.16
(1) (b) 42.6, 42.9
221 (1) 42.16
(2) 42.16
222 (1), (3) 42.7
223 .... 42.8
224 (1) 42.6, 42.9
(2) 42.6
(3) 42.9
(4–6) 42.6
225 .... 42.7
226 (1) 42.14
(2) (b) 42.14
(3) 42.14
226A 42.14
226B 42.14, 42.17
226C 42.14, 42.17
227 .... 42.17
(1) 42.14
228 .... 42.17
(4) 42.14
228A 42.14, 42.17
229 .... 42.17
(1A) 42.14
(2), (4) 42.14
230 .... 42.17
(1) 42.14
(2) 42.14
(4) (a) 42.14
231 .... 42.14, 42.17
231A, 231B 42.14, 42.17
232 .... 42.14, 42.17
232A (C) 42.14
232B 42.14
233 .... 42.14, 42.17
(3) (a) 42.15

PARA

Trade Union and Labour Relations
(Consolidation) Act 1992–*contd*
s 234 (1) 42.15, 42.17
(2)–(6) 42.15
234A 42.15
235A (1)–(5) 42.18
236 .... 5.5, 7.24, 42.16
237 .... 42.8, 42.16, 50.18
(2)–(6) 50.18
238 .... 42.16, 50.17, 50.18
(2) 51.3
238A 6.13, 42.16, 50.17, 51.3
(7) 50.17
239 (1) 50.17
240 (1), (3) 42.20
241 (1) (d) 42.12
(2) 42.12
244 (1) 42.4
(2) 34.2
(3) 42.4
(5) 42.4
245 .... 34.3, 42.2
247 .... 2.1
248 .... 2.2
251A 2.1
254 .... 47.3
258 .... 47.3
259 .... 47.4
260 .... 47.5, 47.25
282 .... 6.13
285 (1) 48.4
288 .... 7.17, 47.9, 48.4
(2A), (2B) 19.33
291 (2) 48.4
296 (1) 47.26
Sch A1 .... 47.11, 47.19, 47.20, 47.23,
48.1
para 1–4 .... 47.27
5, 6 .... 47.29
7 .... 47.29
(1) 47.26
8 .... 47.28, 47.29
9 .... 47.29
10 .... 47.28
11, 12 .... 47.29
15 .... 47.29
18 .... 47.29
19 .... 47.29, 47.30
20 .... 47.30, 47.31
21–24 .... 47.31
25–29 .... 47.32
33–42 .... 47.29
52 .... 47.34
55 .... 47.34
56 .... 47.34
58–63 .... 47.34
64–89 .... 47.35
99–153 .... 47.36
156 .... 2.4, 47.37

Table of statutes

PARA

Trade Union and Labour Relations
(Consolidation) Act 1992–*contd*
Sch A1
  para 157–159 .... 47.37
      161 .... 6.13, 47.37, 51.3
      162 .... 6.13, 47.37, 50.11,
                                    51.11
      163–165 .... 47.37
      171 .... 47.25
Sch 3
  para 5 .... 5.2
      7 .... 47.6
Trade Union Reform and Employment
Rights Act 1993 .... 1.6, 2.1,
         14.5, 18.1, 19.18, 19.33,
         23.2, 23.9, 30.1, 36.2,
                           49.18
s 28 ....51.3
  29 ....51.3
  32 ....5.6, 22.25
  33 ....10.6
    (2) 49.3
    (3) 49.4
    (4) 49.9, 49.12
    (5) 49.15
    (6) 49.18
  34 ....51.11
    (2) (a) 36.4
       (c) 36.6
    (3) 36.6
    (4) 36.7
    (5) 36.3
  40 ....13.7
  43 (1) 2.1
    (2) 2.7
  44 ....2.1
Sch 5 ....51.3

PARA

Trade Union and Labour Relations
(Consolidation) Act 1992–*contd*
Sch 6
  para 1 ....13.18
      2 (4A) 13.18
Sch 7
  para 15 ....4.9
Sch 8
  para 77 ....50.17
Transport and Works Act 1992 ....26.3
Truck Act 1831
  s 1 ....31.3
    3 ....31.4
    9 ....31.4
    20 ....31.5
    23 ....31.5
Truck Amendment Act 1887
  s 4 ....31.5
Unfair Contract Terms Act 1977 .... 55.17,
                                     55.37
  s 2 (1) 7.21
    (2) 7.21, 37.5
    3 ....7.21
    10 ....7.21
    11 ....7.21
      (3) 37.5
Sch 1
  para 4 ....7.21
Wages Act 1986 .... 7.23, 15.1, 18.11, 31.2
  s 11 ....31.3
Water Act 1989 ....34.7
Water Industry Act 1991 ....34.7
Welfare Reform and Pensions Act 1999
  Pt I(ss 1–8) 39.6, 39.7
  s 3 ....39.7
    75 ....43.35
Young Persons (Employment) Act 1938 . 3.5

Table of EU Legislation

PARA

Treaties and Conventions
Convention for the Protection of Human
Rights and Fundamental Freedoms
(Rome, 4 November 1950) 1.7,
11.6, 19.2, 26.4, 28.1,
28.2, 28.5, 29.7, 34.2
art 3 .... 28.4
6 .... 18.7, 18.13, 19.16,
19.42, 19.76, 28.6, 28.7
(1) 12.20, 28.4, 28.7
8 .... 11.6, 19.51, 28.4, 28.6,
28.7
(1) 28.7
(2) 28.4, 28.7
9 (1) 11.6
10 .... 28.4, 28.6, 28.7
11 .... 28.6, 47.19, 48.18
(1), (2) 28.4
12 .... 28.4
13 .... 28.4
14 .... 28.4, 28.6
First Protocol
art 1 .... 28.7, 31.9, 31.21
Convention on Jurisdiction and the
Enforcement of Judgments in Civil and
Commercial Matters (Brussels, 27
September 1968)
art 5 (1), (3) 24.11
17 .... 24.11
18 (2) 24.11
21 .... 24.11
Convention on Jurisdiction and the
Enforcement of Judgments in Civil and
Commercial Matters (Lugano, 16
September 1988) 24.11
European Social Charter 28.8
Maastricht Treaty 1991 ..... 23.1, 23.3, 25.25
Social Chapter 28.8
Rome Convention on the Law Applicable to
Contractual Obligations of 1980
art 3 (1), (3) 24.10
6 (1), (2) 24.10
7 (1) 24.10
17 .... 24.10
Single European Act 1986 .... 23.1
Treaty establishing the European Community
1957 (Treaty of Rome) 23.3
art 2 .... 23.6
3 (2) 23.6
10 (5) 23.5
11 (1), (2) 42.4

PARA

Treaty establishing the European Community
1957 (Treaty of Rome)–*contd*
art 13 .... 23.1, 23.6
(1) 11.2
39 .... 23.4
(4) 24.2, 34.7
40 .... 23.4
41 .... 23.4
42 .... 23.4
48 .... 11.12, 12.15, 24.2, 34.7
87 .... 43.35
94 .... 23.1
95 .... 23.1
136 .... 23.1
137 .... 23.1, 25.25, 54.1
138 .... 23.1
139 .... 23.1
140 .... 23.1
141 .... 6.1, 11.2, 18.12, 22.1,
22.3, 22.4, 22.5, 22.6,
22.9, 22.10, 22.11, 22.13,
22.14, 22.16, 22.17, 22.18,
22.19, 22.22, 23.1, 23.2,
23.6, 28.5, 39.1, 39.2,
39.6, 39.8, 46.4, 50.11,
50.14
(1), (4) 12.9
226 .... 23.2
227 .... 23.2
234 .... 20.27, 23.2
251 .... 23.1, 23.6
302 .... 23.1
Treaty of Amsterdam 1997 .... 11.2, 23.1,
23.3, 25.25
Treaty of Nice 2001 .... 25.25

Decisions
Council Decision 88/591 (establishing a
Court of First Instance of the Euro-
pean Comunities) 34.8

Directives
Council Directive 68/360/EEC (on the
abolition of restrictions on movement
and residence within the Community
for workers of member states and
their families) 24.2
Council Directive 75/117/EEC (Equal Pay
Directive) 22.1, 22.3,
39.8
art 1 .... 23.6

Table of EU legislative material

PARA

Council Directive 75/129/EEC (on the approximation of the laws of the member states relating to collective redundancy 23.8, 36.2
Council Directive 76/207/EEC (Equal Treatment Directive) 6.1, 11.2, 11.5, 11.6, 11.12, 12.16, 12.33, 13.1, 18.12, 22.3, 23.2, 23.3, 23.5, 23.6, 39.6, 39.8
  art 2 (2) 12.8, 12.10
    (4) 11.5, 12.9
    (8) 12.9
  5 (1) 11.5, 22.3
  6 .... 12.19, 19.18
Council Directive 77/187/EEC (Acquired Rights Directive) 16.12, 23.9, 39.3, 49.1, 49.3, 49.8
  art 1-5 ....49.1
  6 ....49.1, 49.18
  7 ....49.1
Council Directive 79/7/EEC (Social Security Directive) 11.5, 23.5
Council Directive 80/987/EEC (Insolvency Protection Directive) 23.7, 29.1, 29.3
Council Directive 83/189/EEC (laying down a procedure for the provision of information in the field of technical standards and regulations) 23.2
Council Directive 86/188/EEC (on the protection of workers from the risks related to exposure to noise at work) 26.19
Council Directive 86/378/EEC (on the implementation of the principle of equal treatment for men and women in occupational social security schemes) 22.3, 22.18, 23.5, 23.6, 30.1
Council Directive 87/164/EEC (amending 80/987 on account of the accession of Spain) 29.5
Council Directive 89/48/EEC (First Diploma Directive) 23.4
Council Directive 89/391/EEC (Health and Safety Framework Directive) 26.13, 26.17
  art 5 (4) 25.25
Council Directive 89/654/EEC (concerning the minimum safety and health requirements for the workplace) . 25.25, 26.27
  Annex II 26.14
Council Directive 89/655/EEC (Directive relating to the use of machines and equipment) 25.25, 26.12
Council Directive 89/656/EEC (on the minimum health and safety require-ments for the use by workers of personal protective equipment at the workplace) 25.25, 26.12

PARA

Council Directive 90/269/EEC (on the minimum health and safety requirements for the manual handling of loads where there is a risk particularly of back injury to workers) 25.25, 26.18
  Annex II 26.18
Council Directive 90/270/EEC (Directive relating to the use of display screen equipment) 25.25, 26.6
  art 2 (a) 26.6
Council Directive 90/364/EEC (on the right of residence) 24.2
Council Directive 90/365/EEC (on the right of residence for employees and self-employed persons who have ceased their occupational activity) 24.2
Council Directive 90/394/EEC (on the protection of workers from the risks related to exposure to carcinogens at work) 25.25
Council Directive 90/679/EEC (on the protection of workers from risks related to exposure to biological agents at work) 25.25
Council Directive 91/353/EEC (Proof of Employment Directive) 23.7
Council Directive 91/383/EEC (Temporary Workers' Directive) 26.17
Council Directive 92/51/EEC (Second Diploma Directive) 23.4
Council Directive 92/56/EEC (amending 75/129) 23.8
Council Directive 92/57/EEC (on the implementation of minimum safety and health requirements at temporary or mobile work sites)............ 25.25, 26.5
Council Directive 92/58/EEC (concerning the minimum requirements for the provision of safety and/or health signs at work) 25.25, 26.28
Council Directive 92/85/EEC (Pregnant Workers Directive) 23.6, 25.25, 26.17, 30.10
  art 10 .... 11.5
  11(2) (b) 22.14
Council Directive 93/13/EEC (Unfair Terms in Consumer Contracts Directive) ..7.21
Council Directive 93/104/EC (Working Time Directive) 3.6, 23.11, 25.25, 26.15, 54.1, 54.2, 54.31
  art 7 ....27.2, 54.1
  13 .... 54.18
Council Directive 94/33/EC (Young Workers Directive on the Protection of Young People at Work) 3.2, 3.5, 3.6, 25.25, 26.15, 26.17, 54.2, 54.3
  Annex 3.5

PARA

Council Directive 94/45/EC (European Works Council Directive) 16.1, 16.4, 16.5, 16.6, 23.3, 23.12

Council Directive 95/46/EC (Data Protection Directive) 10.12, 10.13

Council Directive 95/63/EC (amending 89/655) 23.10, 26.12

Council Directive 96/34/EC (Directive on Parental Leave) 16.4, 23.3, 23.6, 30.26, 46.19

Council Directive 96/71/EC (Directive on the Posting of Workers) 23.7, 24.3
art 1 .... 24.3
3 .... 24.3
6 .... 24.3

Council Directive 96/96/EC (amending 77/388) 22.3, 22.18, 23.6

Council Directive 97/42/EC (amending 90/394) 25.25

Council Directive 97/74/EC (extending to the UK and Northern Ireland, 94/45) 16.5
art 4 (2) 16.6

Council Directive 97/80/EC(Burden of Proof Directive) 23.3, 23.6

Council Directive 97/81/EC (Part-time Work Directive) 23.6

Council Directive 98/59/EC (on the approximation of the laws of the Member States relating to collective redundancies) 23.8

Council Directive 99/63/EC (on the hearings provided for in 17/62) 23.11, 54.3, 54.31

Council Directive 99/70/EC (Directive on Fixed-term Contracts) 23.3, 23.7

Council Directive 2000/34/EC (amending 93/104) 23.11, 54.1

Council Directive 2000/43/EC (Race Discrimination Framework Directive) 11.7, 23.3, 23.6
art 2 (2) (b) 12.8
3 (2) 11.2
5 ....12.9, 23.6
6 .... 23.6
7 (1) 11.2

Council Directive 2000/78/EC (Equal Treatment in Employment and Occupation Directive) 9.1, 11.2, 12.4, 12.7, 12.13, 13.1, 23.3, 23.6, 39.2

PARA

Council Directive 2000/78/EC (Equal Treatment in Employment and Occupation Directive)–contd
recital 2 .... 12.13
art 2 (2) (b) 12.8
7 .... 12.9

Council Directive 2000/79/EC(Mobile Workers in Civil Aviation and its domestic implementation) ... 54.1, 54.3, 54.32, 54.33

Council Directive 2001/23/EC (Transfers Directive) 16.12, 23.9
art 1 (1) (b) 49.1
(c) 34.2, 49.3

Council Directive 2001/45/EC (amending 89/655) 23.10, 26.12

Council Directive 2001/86/EC (Directive on worker involvement) 16.4

Council Directive 2002/14/EC (Information and Consultation Directive) .... 10.11, 16.4 , 23.12

Council Directive 2002/15/EC (on the organisation of the working time of persons performing mobile road transport activities) 54.3, 54.33

Council Directive 2002/73/EC (amending 76/207) 11.12, 12.9, 23.3, 23.6

Council Directive 2002/74/EC (amending 80/987) 23.7, 29.3

Council Directive 2003/88/EC (concerning certain aspects of the organisation of working time)..................... 23.11, 54.1

Regulations

Council Regulation 1612/68 (on freedom of movement for workers within the Community).....................................24.2
art 8 ....48.2

Council Regulation 1251/70 (on the right of workers to remain in the territory of a member state after having been employed in that state) 24.2

Council Regulation 574/72 (fixing the procedure for implementing 1408/71) .23.5

Council Regulation 3820/85 (Drivers' Hours Regulations)........................... 54.1, 54.33

Council Regulation 44/2001 (Brussels I Regulation) 24.11

Council Regulation 2157/2001 (Regulation establishing a European Company Statute) 16.4

Table of statutory instruments

PARA

ACAS Arbitration Scheme (Great Britain)
Order 2004, SI 2004/753 .... 2.10, 19.37
Schedule
para 17–28 .... 19.37
34–40 .... 19.37
42–59s 19.37
63, 65 .... 19.37
67 .... 19.37
73 .... 19.37
76–77 .... 19.37
81 .... 19.37
85 .... 19.37
97 .... 19.37
100 .... 19.37
106–112s 19.37
170 .... 19.37
201s–204s 19.37
206s–208s 19.37
210s 19.37
ACAS (Flexible Working) Arbitration
Scheme (England and Wales) Order
2003, SI 2003/694 .... 2.10, 19.37
ACAS (Flexible Working) Arbitration
Scheme (Great Britain) Order 2004,
SI 2004/2333 .... 19.37
Accession (Immigration and Worker
Registration) Regulations 2004, SI
20041219 .... 24.1
Act of Sederunt (Interest on Sheriff Court
Decrees or Extracts) 1975, SI 1975/948
13.8, 22.20
Armed Forces Act 1996 (Commencement
No 3 and Transitional Provisions)
Order 1997, SI 1997/2164 .... 22.4
Attachment of Earnings (Employer's
Deduction) Order 1991, SI 1999/356
32.9
Charitable Deductions (Approved Schemes)
Regulations 1986, SI 1986/2211 .. 43.33
Chemicals (Hazard Information and
Packaging for Supply) (Amendment)
(No 2) Regulations 1999, SI 1999/3165
26.25
Chemicals (Hazard Information and
Packaging for Supply) (Amendment)
Regulations 1996, SI 1996/1092 .. 26.25
Chemicals (Hazard Information and
Packaging for Supply) (Amendment)
Regulations 1997, SI 1997/1460 .. 26.25
Chemicals (Hazard Information and
Packaging for Supply) (Amendment)
Regulations 1998, SI 1998/3106 .. 26.25

PARA

Chemicals (Hazard Information and
Packaging for Supply) (Amendment)
Regulations 2000, SI 2000/2381 .. 26.25
Chemicals (Hazard Information and
Packaging for Supply) (Amendment)
Regulations 1999, SI 1999/197 .... 26.25
Chemicals (Hazard Information and
Packaging for Supply) Regulations
1994, SI 1994/3247 .... 26.25
Child Support (Collection and Enforcement)
Regulations 1992, SI 1992/1989 .. 32.11
Children (Protection at Work) (No 2)
Regulations 2000, SI 2000/2548 .... 3.2
Children (Protection at Work) Regulations
1998, SI 1998/276 .... 3.2, 3.4, 25.25
Children (Protection at Work) Regulations
2000, SI 2000/1333 .... 3.2, 3.4,
25.25
Civil Aviation (Working Time) Regulations
2004, SI 2004/756 .... 54.32
Civil Jurisdiction and Judgments Order 2001,
SI 2001/3929 .... 24.11
Civil Procedure Rules 1998, SI 1998/
3132 .... 19.1, 19.71
Pt 1
r 1.1 (2) (e) 38.21
Pt 3
r 3.9 .... 19.16
(1) 13.3
Pt 6
r 6.19 .... 24.11
6.20 .... 24.11
6.21 (2A) 24.11
Pt 24 .... 7.23, 19.15, 19.17,
55.41
Pt 25
r 25.6 .... 55.41
Pt 31 .... 19.11
Pt 36 .... 55.41
Pt 52
r 52.3 .... 20.26
Pt 53 .... 34.4
Pt 54 .... 13.13
Sch 1
Rules of the Supreme Court
Ord 14, 14A 7.23
Sch 2
County Court Rules
Ord 27
r 7 (9) 32.1
Code of Practice on Equal Pay Order 2003,
SI 2003/2865 .... 4.8

Collective Redundancies and Transfer of
Undertakings (Protection of
Employment) (Amendment)
Regulations 1995, SI 1995/2587 .... 6.13,
10.6, 16.12, 23.8, 23.9,
36.4, 36.6, 36.7, 49.1,
49.18, 51.3, 51.11
reg 8 .... 6.1
Collective Redundancies and Transfer of
Undertakings (Protection of
Employment) (Amendment)
Regulations 1999, SI 1999/1925 . 16.12,
29.9, 36.4, 36.5, 36.6,
49.1, 49.18
Community Charge and Council Tax
(Administration and Enforcement)
(Amendment) (Jobseeker's Allow-
ance) Regulations 1996, SI 1996/
2405 .... 32.10
Companies (Inspection and Copying of
Registers, Indices and Documents)
Regulations 1991, SI 1991/1998 .... 8.8
Companies Act 1985 (Accounts of Small
and Medium-sized Companies and
Minor Accounting Amendments)
Regulations 1997, SI 1997/220 .... 8.23
Companies Act 1985 (Accounts of Small
and Medium-Sized Enterprises and
Publication of Accounts in ECUs)
Regulations 1992, SI 1992/2452 ..... 8.23
Companies (Tables A to F) Regulations
1985, SI 1985/805
Schedule
Table A 8.1
art 82 .... 8.20
83 .... 8.18
84 .... 8.2, 8.3, 8.20
87 .... 8.26
Company Accounts (Disclosure of Directors'
Emoluments) Regulations 1997, SI
1997/570 .... 8.22, 8.23, 8.26, 8.28
Compromise Agreements (Description of
Person) Order 2004 (Amendment)
Order 2004, SI 2004/2515 .... 13.18
Compromise Agreements (Description of
Person) Order 2004, SI 2004/754 13.18
Conduct of Employment Agencies and
Employment Businesses Regulations
1976, SI 1976/715 .... 44.3,
44.4
Conduct of Employment Agencies and
Employment Businesses Regulations
2003, SI 2003/3319 .... 44.3, 44.4
reg 2 .... 44.5
5 .... 44.5
6 44,5
12 .... 44.5
14 .... 15.3
(2) 44.5

Conduct of Employment Agencies and
Employment Businesses Regulations
2003, SI 2003/3319–contd
reg 14 (4)–(6) 44.5
15 .... 15.3, 44.5
17 .... 44.5
19 .... 44.5
20 .... 44.5
(2)–(6) 44.5
21 (1) (a) (i) 44.5
22 .... 44.5
26 (3) 44.5
(5), (6) 44.5
28 .... 44.5
30 (1) 44.5
31 (1), (2) 44.5
32 (1) 44.5
(9) 44.5
(12) 44.5
Sch 3 .... 44.5
Construction (Design and Management)
(Amendment) Regulations 2002, SI
2002/2380 .... 26.5
Construction (Design and Management)
Regulations 1994, SI 1994/3140 ..... 26.5
Construction (Head Protection) Regulations
1989, SI 1989/2209 .... 26.5
Construction (Health, Safety and Welfare)
Regulations 1996, SI 1996/1592 . 23.10,
26.5
Control of Asbestos at Work Regulations
1987, SI 1987/2115 .... 26.25
Control of Asbestos at Work Regulations
2002, SI 2002/2675 .... 25.17
Control of Industrial Major Accident
Hazards Regulations 1984, SI 1984/
1902 .... 25.20
Control of Lead at Work Regulations 1980,
SI 1980/1248
reg 16 .... 31.29
Control of Lead at Work Regulations 1998,
SI 1998/543 .... 26.25
Control of Major Accident Hazards
Regulations 1999, SI 1999/743 ... 25.20,
26.1
Control of Substances Hazardous to Health
Regulations 1988, SI 1988/1657 .. 25.17
reg 11 .... 31.29
Control of Substances Hazardous to Health
Regulations 2002, SI 2002/2677 .. 26.25
reg 2 (1) 26.25
3 .... 26.25
4 .... 26.25
6 .... 26.25
7 (1)–(4) 26.25
8 (1), (2) 26.25
9–12 .... 26.25
14 .... 26.25
20 .... 26.25

Council Tax (Administration and
    Enforcement) Regulations 1992, SI
    1992/613 .... 32.10
  reg 32 (1) 32.10
    34 .... 32.10
    37 (1)–(3) 32.10
    38 .... 32.10
    39 (1), (2) 32.10
      (4), (6) 32.10
    40, 42 .... 32.10
    56 (2) 32.10
  Sch 4 .... 32.10
Court Funds Rules 1987, SI 1987/821
  r 27 (1) 13.8, 19.67,
                                              22.20
Criminal Justice and Public Order Act 1994
    (Commencement No 5 and Trans-
    itional Provisions) Order 1995, SI
    1995/127 .... 17.6
Dangerous Substances and Preparations
    (Safety) (Consolidation) and
    Chemicals (Hazard Information
    and Packaging for Supply)
    (Amendment) Regulations 2000,
    SI 2000/2897 .... 26.25
Dangerous Substances (Notification and
    Markings of Sites) Regulations 1990,
    SI 1990/304 .... 26.25
Deregulation (Deduction from Pay of Union
    Subscriptions) Order 1998, SI 1998/
    1529
  reg 3 (1)–(3) 48.21
Directors' Remuneration Report Regulations
    2002, SI 2002/1986 .... 8.22,
                                              8.24
Disability Discrimination Act 1995
    (Amendment) Regulations 2003, SI
    2003/1673 .... 9.1
  reg 6 .... 9.24
    16 .... 9.31
    27 .... 9.24
Disability Discrimination Act 1995
    (Pensions) Regulations 2003, SI 2003/
    2770 .... 9.14
Disability Discrimination (Blind and Partially
    Sighted Persons) Regulations 2003, SI
    2003/712 .... 9.8
Disability Discrimination (Description of
    Insurance Services) Regulations 1999,
    SI 1999/2114 .... 9.20
Disability Discrimination (Employment
    Field) (Leasehold Premises) Regu-
    lations 2004, SI 2004/153
  reg 3 .... 9.11, 9.20
    7 .... 9.13
    9 .... 9.13
Disability Discrimination (Employment)
    Regulations 1996, SI 1996/1456 .... 9.11,
                                              39.9

Disability Discrimination (Meaning of
    Disability) Regulations 1996, SI 1996/
    1455
  reg 3 (1), (2) 9.2
    4 .... 9.20
      (1) 9.2
    5 .... 9.7
Disability Discrimination (Questions and
    Replies) Order 2004, SI 2004/1168 ... 9.35
Education (Modification of Enactments
    Relating to Employment) Order 1998,
    SI 1998/218 .... 9.24, 34.2
Electricity at Work Regulations 1989, SI
    1989/635 .... 25.17, 26.7
  reg 4 .... 26.7
    6–9 .... 26.7
    12–16 .... 26.7
Employers' Health and Safety Policy
    Statements (Exception) Regulations
    1975, SI 1975/1584 .... 25.18
Employers' Liability (Compulsory Insurance)
    Regulations 1998, SI 1998/2573 .. 26.16
Employment Act 1989 (Amendments and
    Revocations) Order 1989, SI 1989/
    2311 .... 3.5
Employment Act 2002 (Dispute Resolution)
    Regulations 2004, SI 2004/752 .... 2.9,
      18.3, 18.15, 18.19, 18.25,
      18.30, 19.10, 51.3, 52.13,
                                54.22, 54.23
  reg 2 (1) 51.3
    3 (1), (2) 51.3
    4 (1) (a)–(g) 51.3
    5 (1) 51.3
      (b) 52.21
      (2), (3) 51.3
    6–8 .... 50.7
    9,10 .... 18.19, 50.7
    11 (3) (a)–(c) 18.19
      (4) 51.3
    12 (1), (3), (4) 51.3
    13 (1), (3), (4) 51.3
    15 .... 3.6, 13.3, 18.20, 18.25,
                              18.31, 18.32, 51.3
    17 .... 51.3
    18 .... 18.20
      (b) 18.16, 18.19
Employment Appeal Tribunal (Amendment)
    Rules 1996, SI 1996/3216 .... 9.34
Employment Appeal Tribunal (Amendment)
    Rules 2001, SI 2001/1128 .... 20.4
Employment Appeal Tribunal (Amendment)
    Rules 2004, SI 2004/2526 .... 19.73,
                              20.3, 20.4, 20.22
  r 15 .... 13.7
Employment Appeal Tribunal Rules 1993,
    SI 1993/2854 .... 19.18, 20.4
  r 3 (1), (3) 20.5
    (7) 20.8, 20.9

PARA

Employment Appeal Tribunal Rules 1993,
SI 1993/2854–*contd*
r 3 (8)–(10) 20.8
  6 (12) 20.6
  (14)–(16) 20.6
  19–20 .... 20.8
  21 .... 20.6, 20.8
  23 .... 19.18, 20.13
   (2), (3) 13.7, 20.13
   (5), (5A) 13.7, 20.13
   (5B), (5C) 20.13
  23A 19.18
  24 .... 20.9
  25 .... 20.9
  30 .... 34.6
  33 .... 20.25
  34 (4)–(6) 20.22
  34A 20.23
   (1)–(3) 20.22
  34B 20.23
   (1), (2) 20.22
  34C 20.4, 20.22, 20.24
  34D 20.22
   (2)–(5) 20.23
   (7) 20.23
  37 (1A) 20.5
  39 .... 20.9
Schedule
  Form 1 .... 20.5
Employment Code of Practice (Access to
Workers during Recognition and
Derecognition Ballots) Order 2000,
SI 2000/1443 .... 42.14, 47.32
Employment Code of Practice (Industrial
Action Ballots and Notice to
Employers) Order 1995, SI 1995/
2729 ....4.4, 42.14
Employment Code of Practice (Picketing)
Order 1992, SI 1992/476 ....4.4, 42.11
Employment Codes of Practice (Revocation)
Order 1991, SI 1991/1264 .... 4.2, 4.4
Employment Equality (Religion or Belief)
Regulations 2003 (Amendment)
(No 2) Regulations 2004, SI 2004/
2520 .... 13.18
Employment Equality (Religion or Belief)
(Amendment) Regulations 2003, SI
2003/2828 .... 12.31, 13.8
Employment Equality (Religion or Belief)
Regulations 2003, SI 2003/1660 . 11.13,
        12.34, 13.1, 19.29, 21.1,
        21.2, 23.6, 34.2, 37.4
reg 1 (2) 11.2
  2 (1) 11.6
   (3) 11.12
  3 (1) (a) 11.4
   (b) 11.7
   (2) 11.6
   (3) 11.5, 11.7

PARA

Employment Equality (Religion or Belief)
Regulations 2003, SI 2003/1660–*contd*
reg 4 (1) 11.10
   (2) 11.10
  5 (1), (2) 11.11
  6 (1) 11.12
   (2) (b) 12.17
   (d) 11.12
   (4) 11.12, 12.17
   (5) 11.12
  7 (2) (b), (c) 12.6
   (3) (b), (c) 12.6
  8 (1)–(4) 12.21
  9 .... 11.12, 24.11
   (1) 12.15
   (2) 11.12, 12.15
   (3) (a) 11.12, 12.15
   (b) 12.15
   (4), (5) 12.15
  9A (1), (2) 12.31
   (4) 13.8
  10 (1)–(4) 12.22
   (6), (7) 12.22
   (8) (a), (b) 12.22
   (9) 12.22
   (10) (a)–(d) 12.22
  11 .... 12.32, 34.2
   (1)–(8) 12.23
  12 (1)–(5) 12.24
  13 .... 12.24
  14 (1)–(6) 12.25
   (8) 12.25
  15 (1)–(3) 12.26
   (4) 12.26
  16 (1)–(3) 12.27
  17 (1)–(4) 12.28
  18 (1) 12.29
   (3)–(6) 12.29
  19 (1)–(3) 12.30
  21 .... 13.8
   (1) 12.33
   (2) 11.12, 12.33
   (3) 12.33
  22 .... 13.2
   (1) 11.13, 12.35
   (2) 11.13, 12.38
   (3) 11.13, 12.35, 12.38
  23 .... 13.2
   (1) 11.13, 12.36
   (2) 1.27
   (3), (4) 11.13, 12.36
  24 .... 12.19
  25 (1)–(3) 11.5, 12.9
  26 (1)–(4) 11.5, 12.12
  27 (2) 13.1, 13.8
  28 .... 18.11
   (1) 13.2
   (2) 12.27

PARA

Employment Equality (Religion or Belief)
Regulations 2003, SI 2003/1660–contd
reg 28 (2) (a) 13.2
29 .... 13.2
30 (1) (a)–(c) 13.8
(3) 13.8, 19.66
33 .... 19.9
(2) (b) 19.9
(3), (4) 13.5
34 (1) 13.3, 18.29
(3) 13.3, 18.30
(4) 13.3, 18.29
35 .... 13.17, 13.18
36 .... 12.10, 12.32, 13.2
(2), (4) 12.32
(7)–(10) 12.32
37–38 .... 12.32
Sch 1A
para 1–5 .... 12.31
6 .... 13.8
7 (1) (b) 13.8
Sch 2 .... 13.5
Sch 3 .... 13.5
Sch 4
Pt 1 .... 7.18
para 1 (1) 13.17
(3) 7.17, 13.17
2 .... 13.18, 19.33
3 (1) 13.17
Pt 2 .... 7.18, 13.177
para 5 .... 18.11
Employment Equality (Sexual Orientation)
(Amendment) Regulations 2003, SI
2003/2827 .... 11.2, 12.31, 13.8
Employment Equality (Sexual Orientation)
Regulations 2003 (Amendment)
Regulations 2004, SI 2004/2519 . 13.18
Employment Equality (Sexual Orientation)
Regulations 2003, SI 2003/1661 .... 11.2,
11.13, 12.34, 13.1, 19.29,
21.1, 21.2, 23.6, 34.2,
37.4
reg 2 .... 11.6
(3) 11.12
3 (1) 11.6
(a) 11.4
(b) 11.7
(2) 11.5
4 (1), (2) 11.10
5 (1) 11.11
6 (1) 11.12
(2) 11.12
(b) 12.17
(d) 11.12
(4) 11.12, 12.17
(5) 11.12
7 (2) 12.7
(3) (a)–(c) 12.7
8 (1)–(4) 12.21

PARA

Employment Equality (Sexual Orientation)
Regulations 2003, SI 2003/1661–contd
reg 9 .... 24.11
(1) 12.15
(2) 11.12, 12.15
(3) 11.12
(a), (b) 12.15
(4), (5) 11.12, 12.15
9A 39.6
(1), (2) 12.31
(4) 13.8
10 (1)–(4) 12.22
(6), (7) 12.22
(8) (a), (b) 12.22
(9) 12.22
(10) (a)–(d) 12.22
11 .... 12.32, 34.2
(1)–(8) 12.23
12 (1)–(5) 12.24
13 .... 12.24
14 (1)–(6) 12.25
(8) 12.25
15 (1)–(3) 12.26
(4) 12.26
16 (1)–(4) 12.27
17 (1)–(4) 12.28
18 (1) 12.29
(3)–(6) 12.29
19 (1)–(3) 12.30
21 .... 13.8
(1) 12.33
(2) 11.12, 12.33
(3) 12.33
22 .... 13.2
(1) 11.13, 12.35
(2) 11.13, 12.38
(3) 11.13, 12.35, 12.38
23 .... 13.2
(1) 11.13, 12.36
(2) 12.37
(3), (4) 11.13, 12.36
24 .... 12.19
25 .... 11.9, 12.13
26 (1) 11.5, 12.9
(2) 12.9
(3) 12.9
27 (2) 13.1, 13.8
28 .... 18.11
(1) 13.2
(2) 12.27
(a) 13.2
29 .... 13.2
30 (1) (a)–(c) 13.8
(3) 13.8, 19.66
33 .... 19.9
(2) 13.5
(b) 19.9
(4) 13.5
34 (1) 13.3, 18.29

Employment Equality (Sexual Orientation)
Regulations 2003, SI 2003/1661–*contd*
reg 34 (3) 13.3, 18.30
    (4) 13.3, 18.29
  35 .... 7.17, 7.18, 13.17,
                                        13.18
  36 .... 12.10, 12.32, 13.2
    (4) 12.32
    (7)–(10) 12.32
  37–38 .... 12.32
  Sch 1A 39.6
    para 1–5 .... 12.31
      6 .... 13.8
      7 (1) (b) 13.8
  Sch 2 .... 13.5
  Sch 3 .... 13.5
  Sch 4 .... 7.18
    para 1 (1) 7.17, 13.17
      (3) 13.17
      2 .... 13.18, 19.33
      3 (1) 13.17
  Pt 2 .... 7.18, 13.17
    para 5 .... 18.11
Employment Protection Code of Practice
  (Disclosure of Information) Order
  1998, SI 1998/45 .... 4.2, 10.4
Employment Protection Code of Practice
  (Time Off) Order 1998, SI 1998/46 ... 4.2
Employment Protection Code of Practice
  (Time Off) Order 2003, SI 2003/
  1191 .... 2.9, 4.2, 46.2
Employment Protection (Continuity of
  Employment) Regulations 1996, SI
  1996/3147 .... 6.6, 6.12
Employment Protection (Offshore
  Employment) Order 1976, SI 1976/
  766 .... 50.15
Employment Protection (Part-time
  Employees) Regulations 1995, SI
  1995/31 .... 6.1, 35.4
Employment Protection (Recoupment of
  Jobseeker's Allowance and Income
  Support) Regulations 1996, SI 1996/
  2349 .... 19.68, 52.6
Employment Relations Act 1999
  (Commencement No 2 and Transitional
  and Saving Provisions) Order 1999, SI
  1999/2830
  Sch 3
    para 2 .... 50.15
Employment Relations Act 1999
  (Commencement No 5 and Tran-
  sitional Provision) Order 2000, SI
  2000/875 .... 6.13, 50.11
  art 3 .... 50.17
Employment Relations Act 1999
  (Commencement No 6 and Transitional Provision) Order 2000, SI
  2000/1338 .... 50.11

Employment Relations Act 1999
  (Commencement No 7 and Trans-
  itional Provision) Order 2000, SI
  2000/2242 .... 50.11
Employment Rights (Increase of Limits)
  Order 1998, SI 1998/924 .. 52.14, 52.17
Employment Rights (Increase of Limits)
  Order 2003, SI 2003/3038 .... 29.5,
    31.27, 31.39, 35.13, 48.4,
        52.8, 52.10, 52.15
Employment Tribunals Act 1996
  (Application of Conciliation Pro-
  visions) Order 2000, SI 2000/1337 ... 2.4
Employment Tribunals (Constitution and
  Rules of Procedure) (Amendment)
  Regulations 1996, SI 1996/1757 .... 9.34,
                                        20.29
Employment Tribunals (Constitution and
  Rules of Procedure) (Amendment)
  Regulations 2004, SI 2004/2351 .... 18.2,
                                   18.4, 22.23
Employment Tribunals (Constitution and
  Rules of Procedure) Regulations 1993,
  SI 1993/2687 .... 13.13, 19.18
  Sch 1
    r 14 (1A), (1B) 9.34
Employment Tribunals (Constitution and
  Rules of Procedure) Regulations 2001,
  SI 2001/1171 .... 8.2, 18.3,
      19.1, 19.17, 19.69, 19.70,
                                        22.23
  Sch 1
    r 8 .... 34.6
      14 (5) 52.4
      15 (1) 19.18
      19 (3) 19.24
  Sch 3 .... 22.8, 22.23
  Sch 5 .... 25.31
    r 2 (1), (2) 25.34
Employment Tribunals (Constitution and
  Rules of Procedure) Regulations 2004,
  SI 2004/1861 .... 18.3, 18.5, 19.7,
                           19.17, 20.3, 22.23
  reg 2 (2) 19.71
    3 .... 18.14, 19.1, 22.23
    4 .... 18.6
    6, 7 .... 18.6
    8 (5) 18.7
    9 (3) 18.8
    10, 11 .... 18.7
    14 .... 18.15
      (1) (c) 18.16
    15 (5) 19.38
      (6) 19.15, 20.5
    17 .... 19.65
    19 .... 24.11
    20 .... 19.62, 22.23
      (2)–(5) 19.69
    37 (1) 19.64

Employment Tribunals (Constitution and
  Rules of Procedure) Regulations 2004,
  SI 2004/1861–contd
  r 38 (1) (b) 19.71
    (2) 19.70
    (5) 19.70
    (7)–(10) 19.71
  39 .... 19.71
  40 (1)– (3) 19.71
  41 (1) 19.71
    (3) 19.71
  42–44 .... 19.72
  45 (2)–(4) 19.72
  46 (1), (2) 19.70
  47 .... 19.71
  48 .... 20.24
    (1)–(6) 19.73
    (9) 19.73
  49 .... 13.7, 19.19, 19.65, 20.13
  50 .... 19.18, 20.13
    (1) 13.7
    (b) 19.18
    (2) 13.7, 19.18
    (3)–(5) 13.7, 19.18
    (6) 13.7, 19.18
    (7) 19.18
    (8) (a)–(c) 19.18
    (9), (11) 13.7
  51 .... 19.18
  54 (1) (a) 19.51
  55 .... 19.22
  60 (1) 19.18, 19.20, 19.52
  Sch 2 .... 18.4, 19.77
  Sch 3 .... 18.4
  Sch 4 .... 18.4
  Sch 5 .... 13.13, 18.4
  Sch 6 .... 18.2, 18.4, 19.77
  r 3 .... 22.23
  4 (4) 22.23
  5 .... 22.23
  6 (2) 22.23
  7 (3)–(6) 22.23
  9 (1)–(3) 22.23
  10 (1), (3)–(6) 22.23
  11 (1)–(6) 22.23
  12 (4), (5) 22.23
  13 (2) 22.23
  14 .... 22.23
Employment Tribunals (Constitution and
  Rules of Procedure) (Scotland)
  Regulations 2001, SI 2001/1170 ..... 18.2
Employment Tribunals Extension of
  Jurisdiction (England and Wales) Order
  1994, SI 1994/1623 .... 18.9, 18.11,
                                        39.12
  art 3 .... 24.11
    (c) 7.23
  4 .... 7.23, 55.38
  5 .... 7.23

Employment Tribunals Extension of
  Jurisdiction (England and Wales) Order
  1994, SI 1994/1623–contd
  art 7 .... 7.23, 18.32, 55.40
  8 .... 7.23, 18.32
Employment Tribunals Extension of
  Jurisdiction (Scotland) Order 1994,
  SI 1994/1624 .... 55.38
  art 7 .... 55.40
Employment Tribunals (Interest on Awards
  in Discrimination Cases) Regulations
  1996, SI 1996/2803 .... 13.8,
                              19.67, 22.13, 22.20
  reg 2 (1) (b) 19.67
    3 (1) 13.8, 22.20
      (2) 13.8, 19.67, 22.20
      (3) 13.8, 19.67
    4 .... 13.8, 22.20
    6 .... 19.67
      (1) (a) 13.8, 22.20
        (b) 13.8, 22.20
      (2) 13.8, 22.20
      (3) 22.20
    7 .... 19.63
    8 .... 19.67
Employment Tribunals (Interest) Order
  1990, SI 1990/479 .... 19.67
Equal Opportunities (Employment
  Legislation) (Territorial Limits)
  Regulations 1999, SI 1999/3163 ....22.4,
  23.7
Equal Pay Act 1970 (Amendment)
  Regulations 2003, SI 2003/1656 . 18.28,
  22.2, 22.20
Equal Pay Act 1970 (Amendment)
  Regulations 2004, SI 2004/2352 .. 22.23
Equal Pay (Amendment) Regulations 1983,
  SI 1983/1794 .... 22.2, 22.22
Equal Pay (Complaints to Employment
  Tribunals) (Armed Forces) Regulations
  1997, SI 1997/2162 .... 22.4, 34.2
Equal Pay (Questions and Replies) Order
  2003, SI 2003/722 .... 22.2, 22.10,
                                        22.23
European Communities (Employment in
  the Civil Service) Order 1991, SI
  1991/1221 .... 34.7
Fire Precautions (Workplace) (Amendment)
  Regulations 1999, SI 1999/1877 .. 26.13
Fire Precautions (Workplace) Regulations
  1997, SI 1997/1840 .... 26.13
Fishing Vessels (Working Time : Sea-
  fishermen) Regulations 2004, SI 2004/
  1713 .... 54.31
Fixed-term Employees (Prevention of Less
  Favourable Treatment) Regulations
  2002, SI 2002/2034 .... 6.13, 18.33,
                              23.7, 50.11, 51.14
  reg 1 .... 50.6

Fixed-term Employees (Prevention of Less Favourable Treatment) Regulations 2002, SI 2002/2034–contd
reg 5 .... 19.9
6 .... 51.3
(3) 51.11
7 .... 18.11, 18.22
8 .... 19.33
9 .... 18.33
(5) 18.11
(6) 18.33
11 .... 50.15
Sch 2
Pt 1
para 3 (1) 50.15
(15) 50.15
Sch 2
Pt 2
para 5 .... 50.15
Flexible Working (Eligibility, Complaints and Remedies) Regulations 2002, SI 2002/ 3236 .... 46.19
Flexible Working (Procedural Requirements) Regulations 2002, SI 2002/3207 .. 46.19
Health and Safety at Work etc Act 1974 (Application outside Great Britain) Order 2001, SI 2001/2127 .... 12.12, 25.41
art 8 (1) (a) 11.5
Health and Safety (Consultation with Employees) Regulations 1996, SI 1996/1513 .... 10.8, 16.12, 26.9, 26.20, 26.21, 46.9, 51.3
reg 4–8 .... 26.22
Sch 2
para 2–5 .... 46.10
Health and Safety (Display Screen Equipment) Regulations 1992, SI 1992/ 2792 .... 26.6, 26.17
reg 1 (2) 26.6
3 .... 26.6
Health and Safety (Enforcing Authority) Regulations 1989, SI 1989/1903 .. 25.29
Health and Safety (Enforcing Authority) Regulations 1998, SI 1998/494
Sch 1 .... 25.29
Health and Safety (First-Aid) Regulations 1981, SI 1981/917 .... 25.17, 26.14, 26.17
reg 3, 4 .... 26.14
Health and Safety Information for Employees (Modifications and Repeals) Regulations 1995, SI 1995/2923 .. 25.18
Health and Safety Information for Employees Regulations 1989, SI 1989/ 682 .... 25.18
Health and Safety Inquiries (Procedure) (Amendment) Regulations 1976, SI 1976/246 .... 25.26
Health and Safety Inquiries (Procedure) Regulations 1975, SI 1975/335 .... 25.26

Health and Safety (Miscellaneous Amendments) Regulations 2002, SI 2002/ 2174 .... 26.17, 26.18
reg 2 .... 26.14
3 .... 26.6
4 .... 26.18
6 .... 26.27
Health and Safety (Safety Signs and Signals) Regulations 1996, SI 1996/341 .... 26.28
Health and Safety (Training for Employment) Regulations 1990, SI 1990/1380 .... 14.7, 25.17
Health and Safety (Young Persons) Regulations 1997, SI 1997/135 .... 3.5
Immigration (Restrictions on Employment) Order 1996, SI 1996/3225 .... 11.12, 24.8
Immigration (Restrictions on Employment) Order 2004, SI 2004/755
Schedule
para 4 .... 24.9
Income Tax (Benefits in Kind) (Exemption for Welfare Counselling) Regulations 2000, SI 2000/2080 .... 43.22
Income Tax (Employments) Regulations 1993, SI 1993/744 .... 43.4
Income Tax (Exemption of Minor Benefits) Regulations 2002, SI 2002/205 .... 43.22
Income Tax (Pay As You Earn) Regulations 2003, SI 2003/2682 .... 43.4
reg 41, 42 .... 43.14
47–53 .... 43.14
70 .... 43.14
80 .... 43.14
82, 83 .... 43.14
Industrial Training Levy (Construction Board) Order 2004, SI 2004/368 ..... 14.4
Industrial Training Levy (Engineering Construction Board) Order 2004, SI 2004/369 .... 14.4
Insolvency Proceedings (Monetary Limits) Order 1986, SI 1986/1996
art 4 .... 29.2
Insolvency Rules 1986, SI 1986/1925 ..... 29.2
Insurance Companies (Third Insurance Directives) Regulations 1994, SI 1994/ 1696 .... 17.4
Ionising Radiations Regulations 1985, SI 1985/1333
reg 16 .... 31.29
Jobseeker's Allowance Regulations 1996, SI 1996/207 .... 11.5
Lifting Operations and Lifting Equipment Regulations 1998, SI 1998/2307 . 26.12, 26.17
Local Authorities (Contracting Outof Tax Billing, Collection and Enforcement Functions) Order 1996, SI 1996/ 1880 .... 32.10

Local Authorities (Goods and Services) (Public Bodies) Order 1992, SI 1992/ 2830 .... 52.10
Local Government Changes for England (Community Charge and Council Tax, Administration and Enforcement) Regulations 1995, SI 1995/247 .... 32.9
Local Government (Discretionary Payments) Regulations 1996, SI 1996/ 1680 .... 34.2
Local Government Officers (Political Restrictions) Regulations 1990, SI 1990/851 .... 34.2
Local Government Pension Scheme Regulations 1997, SI 1997/578 .... 39.6
Management of Health and Safety at Work (Amendment) Regulations 1994, SI 1994/2865 .... 30.23
Management of Health and Safety at Work Regulations 1992, SI 1992/2051 ...... 3.5, 4.10, 26.3, 26.17, 26.21, 26.24, 26.26, 30.23, 46.9
  reg 13A (3) 30.23
    13B 30.23
Management of Health and Safety at Work Regulations 1999, SI 1999/3242 ...... 3.1, 3.5, 11.5, 25.18, 26.5, 26.17, 54.11, 54.13
  reg 3 .... 26.17
    (5) 3.5
    4 .... 26.17
    5 .... 26.17
    6 .... 26.17
    7 .... 26.17
    8 .... 26.17
    9 .... 26.17, 54.13
    10 .... 26.17
      (2) 3.4
    11–16 .... 26.17
    17 .... 26.17, 54.13
    19 .... 26.17
      (1)–(3) 3.5
  reg 21 .... 26.17
  Sch 1 .... 26.17
Manual Handling Operations Regulations 1992, SI 1992/2793 .... 26.17, 26.18
  reg 4 (3) 26.18
  Sch 1 .... 26.18
Maternity and Parental Leave (Amendment) Regulations 2001, SI 2001/ 4010 .... 12.33, 30.26
Maternity and Parental Leave (Amendment) Regulations 2002, SI 2002/2789 ....30.1, 30.26
Maternity and Parental Leave Regulations 1999, SI 1999/3312 .... 23.3, 23.6, 30.1, 30.26
  reg 4 .... 46.19
    5 .... 46.19

Maternity and Parental Leave Regulations 1999, SI 1999/3312–contd
  reg 8 .... 46.19
    9 .... 12.33
    (3) 39.8
    10 .... 30.6
    13 .... 30.26
    14 (1) 30.26, 46.19
    15 (1) (a) 30.26
      (2) 30.46
    16 .... 46.19
    17 .... 6.6, 11.12, 12.33, 30.26, 46.19, 50.4
    18 (3), (5) 46.19
    19 .... 30.8, 46.19
      (2) (e) 46.19
        (ii) 30.26
    20 .... 46.19, 51.3
      (1) (b) 30.6
      (2) 46.19
        (e) (ii) 30.26
      (3) 46.19
      (6)–(8) 30.6
    21 .... 46.19
  Sch 1 .... 46.19
  Sch 2 .... 30.26, 46.19
    para 6 .... 46.19
    8 .... 46.19
Merchant Shipping and Fishing Vessels (Health and Safety at Work) (Employment of Young Persons) Regulations 1998, SI 1998/2411 .. 25.25
Merchant Shipping and Fishing Vessels (Manual Handling Operations) Regulations 1998, SI 1998/2857 .. 26.18
Merchant Shipping and Fishing Vessels (Personal Protective Equipment) Regulations 1999, SI 1999/2205 .. 26.12
Merchant Shipping (Hours of Work) Regulations 2002, SI 2002/2125 .. 54.31
  reg 3 (1) 54.31
    18 (1) 54.31
Merchant Shipping (Working Time: Inland Waterways) Regulations 2003, SI 2003/ 3049 .... 51.3, 51.11, 54.3, 54.33
National Health Service Pension Scheme Regulations 1995, SI 1995/300 .... 22.18
National Minimum Wage Act 1998 (Commencement No 1 and Transitional Provisions) Order 1998, SI 1998/2574 .... 51.3
National Minimum Wage (Offshore Employment) Order 1999, SI 1999/ 1128 .... 31.10
National Minimum Wage Regulations 1999 (Amendment) Regulations 2000, SI 2000/1989
  reg 31 .... 31.12

PARA

National Minimum Wage Regulations 1999
(Amendment) Regulations 2001, SI
2001/1108 .... 31.9
National Minimum Wage Regulations 1999
(Amendment) Regulations 2004, SI
2004/1161 .... 31.9
National Minimum Wage Regulations 1999
(Amendment) (No 2) Regulations 2004,
SI 2004/1930 .... 31.9
National Minimum Wage Regulations 1999,
SI 1999/584
   reg 3–6 .... 31.9
     9 .... 31.9
     10 .... 31.9
     11 .... 31.9
     12 .... 31.10
      (2) 14.2, 31.9
     13 (1) 31.9
     28 .... 31.12
     30–37 .... 31.9
     38 (2) 31.11
Noise at Work Regulations 1989, SI 1989/
1790 .... 26.19
   reg 2 (1), (2) 26.19
     4 .... 26.19
     6 .... 26.19
     7 .... 26.19
     8 (1), (2) 26.19
     9 .... 26.19
     10 (1), (2) 26.19
     11 .... 26.19
     13 .... 26.19
   Schedule 26.19
Notices to Quit, etc (Prescribed Information)
Regulations 1988, SI 1988/2201 .... 40.4,
                                40.5
Notification of New Substances Regulations
1993, SI 1993/3050 .... 26.25
Occupational Pension Schemes (Disclosure of
Information) Regulations 1986, SI
1986/1046 .... 10.1
Occupational Pension Schemes (Disclosure
of Information) Regulations 1996, SI
1996/1655
   reg 3–6 .... 10.10
   Sch 1–Sch 3 .... 10.10
Occupational Pension Schemes (Equal Access
to Membership) Amendment Regulations
1995, SI 1995/1215 .... 22.16, 22.17
Occupational Pension Schemes (Equal Treat-
ment) Regulations 1995, SI 1995/3183
   reg 3–7 .... 22.17
     9–12 .... 22.17
Occupational Pension Schemes (Internal
Dispute Resolution Procedures)
Regulations 1996, SI 1996/1270 .. 39.12
Occupational Pension Schemes (Member-
nominated Trustees and Directors)
Regulations 1996, SI 1996/1216 .. 39.10

PARA

Offshore Electricity and Noise Regulations
1997, SI 1997/1993 .... 26.7
Part-time Workers (Prevention of Less
Favourable Treatment) Regulations
2000, SI 2000/1551 .... 6.13,
               18.33, 22.2, 22.15, 23.6,
                                 50.11
   reg 2 (1), (2) 22.15
     (3) (d) 22.15
     (4) (a) (ii) 22.15
     (b) 22.15
     3 .... 22.15
     4 .... 22.15
     5 (1) 22.15
     (2) 22.15
     (b) 22.15
     (3) 22.15
     (4) 22.15
     6 .... 19.9
     7 .... 51.3
     (3) 51.11
     8 .... 18.11, 18.22
     9 .... 19.33
Part-time Workers (Prevention of Less
Favourable Treatment) Regulations
2000 (Amendment) Regulations 2002,
SI 2002/2035 .... 22.15
Paternity and Adoption Leave Regulations
2002, SI 2002/2788 .... 30.27
   reg 4–11 .... 46.19
     12 .... 6.6, 39.8, 46.19
     13 .... 30.27, 46.19
     14 .... 46.19
     15–17 .... 46.19
     18 .... 30.27, 46.19
     19 .... 6.6, 39.8, 46.19
     20 .... 46.19
     21 .... 6.6, 39.8,
                                   46.19
     22–27 .... 46.19
     28 .... 30.27, 46.19
     29 .... 30.27, 46.19,
                                  51.3
Pensions Act 1995 (Commencement No 2)
Order 1995, SI 1995/3104 .... 22.17
Personal Protective Equipment at Work
Regulations 1992, SI 1992/2966 .. 26.17
   reg 4 .... 26.12
     7 (1) 26.12
Police Act 1997 (Commencement No 9)
Order 2002, SI 2002/413 .... 17.7
Police Act 1997 (Criminal Records)
(Registration) (Amendment) Regu-
lations 2001, SI 2001/2498 .... 17.7
Police Act 1997 (Criminal Records)
(Registration) Regulatioins 2001, SI
2001/1194 .... 17.7
Police Act 1997 (Criminal Records)
Regulations 2002, SI 2002/233 .... 17.7

Police Act 1997 (Enhanced Criminal
Record Certificates) (Protection of
Vulnerable Adults) Regulations 2002,
SI 2002/446 .... 17.7
Police (Health and Safety) Regulations
1999, SI 1999/860 .... 26.12, 26.21
Protection from Harassment Act 1997
(Commencement No 1) Order 1997,
SI 1997/1418 .... 11.12
Provision and Use of Work Equipment
Regulations 1992, SI 1992/2932 . 25.38,
26.12
Provision and Use of Work Equipment
Regulations 1998, SI 1998/2306 .. 26.12
reg 4 .... 26.12
5 (1) 26.12
6–10 .... 26.12
11–24 .... 26.12
Public Interest Disclosure (Compensation)
Regulations 1999, SI 1999/1548 .. 10.18
Public Interest Disclosure (Prescribed Persons)
Order 1999, SI 1999/1549 .... 10.18
Quarries Regulations 1999, SI 1999/
2024 .... 26.17
Race Relations Act 1976 (Amendment)
Regulations 2003, SI 2003/1626 .... 11.2,
11.7, 11.13, 12.4,
12.11, 12.18, 12.33,
13.5, 23.6
Race Relations (Complaints to Employment
Tribunals) (Armed Forces) Regulations
1997, SI 1997/2161 ... 12.10, 13.2, 34.2
Race Relations (Formal Investigations)
Regulations 1977, SI 1977/841 .... 13.12
Race Relations (Offshore Employment)
Order 1987, SI 1987/929 .... 11.12
Race Relations (Questions and Replies) Order
1977, SI 1977/842
art 5 .... 13.5
Recognition and Derecognition Ballots
(Qualified Persons) Order 2000, SI
2000/1306 .... 47.32
Redundancy Payments Pensions Regulations
1965, SI 1965/1932 .... 35.10, 35.13
Rehabilitation of Offenders Act 1974
(Exceptions) (Amendment No 2)
Order 1986, SI 1986/2268 .... 17.4
Rehabilitation of Offenders Act 1974
(Exceptions) (Amendment) Order
1986, SI 1986/1249 .... 17.4
Rehabilitation of Offenders Act 1974
(Exceptions) (Amendment) Order
2002, SI 2002/441 .... 17.4
Rehabilitation of Offenders Act 1974
(Exceptions) Order 1975, SI 1975/
1023 .... 17.4
Reinstatement in Civil Employment
(Procedure) Regulations 1944, SR & O
1944/880 .... 46.20

Reporting of Injuries, Diseases and Dangerous
Occurrences Regulations 1985, SI 1985/
2023 .... 26.1
Reporting of Injuries, Diseases and Dangerous
Occurrences Regulations 1995, SI 1995/
3163 .... 25.17, 26.1
reg 3–7 .... 26.1
10 .... 26.1
Sch 1 .... 26.1
Sch 2 .... 26.1
Sch 3 .... 26.1
Sch 4 .... 26.1
Right to Time Off for Study or Training
Regulations 1999, SI 1999/986 .... 3.7
Right to Time Off for Study or Training
Regulations 2001, SI 2001/2801
Schedule 3.7
Safety Representatives and Safety
Committees Regulations 1977, SI
1977/500 .... 4.10, 16.12,
26.20, 26.21, 46.9
reg 3 (1), (4) 26.21
4 (1), (2) 26.21
4A 26.21
7 (1)–(3) 10.8
8 (2) 26.21
9 .... 26.21
11 (1)–(4) 46.10
Sex Discrimination Act 1975 (Application
to Armed Forces, etc) Regulations
1994, SI 1994/3276 .... 12.10, 23.6
Sex Discrimination (Amendment) Order
1988, SI 1988/249 .... 12.19
Sex Discrimination and Equal Pay
(Miscellaneous Amendments)
Regulations 1996, SI 1996/438 .... 13.8
Sex Discrimination and Equal Pay (Offshore
Employment) Order 1987, SI 1987/
930 .... 11.12
Sex Discrimination and Equal Pay (Remedies)
Regulations 1993, SI 1993/2798 .... 13.8,
22.2, 22.20
Sex Discrimination (Complaints to
Employment Tribunals) (Armed
Forces) Regulations 1997, SI 1997/
2163 .... 12.10, 13.2,
34.2
Sex Discrimination (Formal Investigations)
Regulations 1975, SI 1975/1993 .. 13.12
Sex Discrimination (Gender Reassignment)
Regulations 1999, SI 1999/1102 .... 11.2,
12.5, 22.2
Sex Discrimination (Indirect Discrimination
and Burden of Proof) Regulations 2001,
SI 2001/2660 .... 23.3, 23.6
Sex Discrimination (Questions and Replies)
Order 1975, SI 1975/2048
art 5 .... 13.5
Sch 1 .... 13.5

PARA

Social Security Act 1989 (Commencement
No 5) Order 1994, SI 1994/1661 .... 30.1
Social Security (Claims and Payments)
Regulations 1979, SI 1979/628
reg 25 .... 26.1
Social Security Contributions (Intermediaries)
Regulations 2000, SI 2000/727 .... 43.35
Social Security Contributions, Statutory
Maternity Pay and Statutory Sick Pay
(Miscellaneous Amendments)
Regulations 1996, SI 1996/777 .... 41.3
reg 2 .... 41.7
3 .... 41.3
4 .... 30.11
Social Security Maternity Benefits and
Statutory Sick Pay (Amendment)
Regulations 1994, SI 1994/1367
reg 3 .... 30.11, 30.14
Social Security (Refunds) (Repayment of
Contractual Maternity Pay) Regu-
lations 1990, SI 1990/536 .... 30.10
Statutory Maternity Pay (Compensation of
Employers) Amendment Regulations
2003, SI 2003/672 .... 30.16
Statutory Maternity Pay (Compensation
of Employers) and Miscellaneous
Amendment Regulations 1994, SI 1994/
1882 .... 30.16
reg 5 .... 30.16
Statutory Maternity Pay (General)
Amendment Regulations 1990, SI
1990/622 .... 30.15
Statutory Maternity Pay (General)
Amendment Regulations 1996, SI
1996/1335
reg 2 .... 30.14
Statutory Maternity Pay (General)
Regulations 1986, SI 1986/1960
reg 3 .... 30.11
4 .... 30.11, 30.18
(3) 30.14
5 .... 30.21
6 .... 30.18
(3) 30.21
7 .... 29.8, 30.15, 30.18
(4) 30.21
(6), (7) 30.18, 30.21
8 .... 30.20
9 .... 30.11, 30.18
10 .... 30.19
11 (1), (5) 30.18
12 .... 30.21
18A 30.18, 30.21
21 .... 30.18, 30.21
25A 30.15
27, 29 .... 30.14
30 .... 29.8, 30.15
Statutory Maternity Pay (Medical Evidence)
Regulations 1987, SI 1987/235 .... 30.13

Statutory Maternity Pay (Persons Abroad
and Mariners) Regulations 1987, SI
1987/418 .... 30.11
Statutory Paternity Pay and Statutory
Adoption Pay (Administration)
Regulations 2002, SI 2002/2820 .. 46.19
Statutory Paternity Pay and Statutory
Adoption Pay (Weekly Rates)
Regulations 2002, SI 2002/2818 . 30.28,
46.19
Statutory Paternity Pay and Statutory
Adoption Pay (General) Regulations
2002, SI 2002/2822 .... 30.28, 46.19
reg 43 .... 29.8
Statutory Sick Pay and Statutory Maternity
Pay (Decisions) Regulations 1999, SI
1999/776 .... 30.15, 41.8
Statutory Sick Pay (General) Amendment
(No 2) Regulations 1987, SI 1987/
868 .... 41.3
Statutory Sick Pay (General) Amendment
Regulations 1986, SI 1986/477 ...... 41.3,
41.4, 41.5, 41.13
reg 5 .... 41.7
Statutory Sick Pay (General) Amendment
Regulations 1996, SI 1996/3042
reg 2 .... 41.7
Statutory Sick Pay (General) Regulations
1982, SI 1982/894 .... 41.3, 41.5,
41.13
reg 3 (3) 41.5
7 .... 41.3
9B 29.8
13 .... 41.7
15 .... 41.4, 41.5
15A 41.12
Statutory Sick Pay (Medical Evidence)
Regulations 1985, SI 1985/1604 ..... 41.8
Suspension from Work (on Maternity
Grounds) Order 1994, SI 1994/
2930 .... 26.17,
30.23
Teachers (Compensation for Redundancy and
Premature Retirement) Regulations
1997, SI 1997/311 .... 34.2
Teaching and Higher Education Act 1998
(Commencement No 5) Order 1999, SI
1999/987 .... 3.7
Trade Union Ballots and Elections
(Independent Scrutineer Qualifications)
Order 1993, SI 1993/1909 .... 42.14,
47.14
Trade Union Recognition (Method of
Collective Bargaining) Order 2000, SI
2000/1300 .... 47.33,
47.34
Trade Unions and Employers' Association
(Amalgamations, etc) Regulations
1975, SI 1975/536 .... 47.39

Transfer of Undertakings (Protection of
Employment) (Amendment)
Regulations 1987, SI 1987/442 ......29.9,
49.1, 49.8
Transfer of Undertakings (Protection of
Employment) Regulations 1981, SI
1981/1784 .... 5.4, 6.12, 8.33,
10.1, 16.12, 19.6, 22.19,
23.2, 23.9, 36.6, 38.22,
39.6, 45.1, 46.2, 47.19,
49.1, 50.20, 52.7
reg 2 (1) 49.3, 49.9
(2) 49.3
3 (1), (3), (4) 49.4
4 .... 29.9
(1) 49.8
5 .... 7.22, 49.11
(1) 49.9, 49.10
(2) 49.9, 49.14
(a) 35.5
(3) 49.9, 49.10
(4) 49.15
(4A), (4B) 49.12
(5) 49.12, 49.20
6 (a) 5.6, 49.16
(b) 49.16
7 .... 49.15
8 (1) 6.1, 6.13, 49.20, 51.3
(2) 49.20, 51.3
(b) 51.14
9 .... 10.6, 49.17
10 .... 10.6, 18.11, 46.14,
49.18, 51.3, 52.16, 52.21
(2A) 49.18
(3) 19.23
(4) 49.18
(5) 49.18
(7) 49.18
(8A) 49.18
10A (1) 49.18
11 .... 10.6, 18.11, 19.33,
46.14, 51.3, 52.16, 52.21
(1) 49.18
(2A), (2B) 49.18
(3) 19.23, 49.18
(4) 49.18
(5) 18.9, 19.29, 49.18
(8) 18.33, 49.18
(11) 49.18
11A 49.18
12 .... 19.33, 49.23
13 (1) 49.4
Transnational Information and Consultation
of Employees Regulations 1999, SI
1999/3323 .... 6.13, 16.1, 23.3, 23.12
reg 5 (1) 16.7
6 (1) (b) 16.6
(2), (3) 16.6
7 .... 16.6, 16.11

Transnational Information and Consultation
of Employees Regulations 1999, SI
1999/3323–contd
reg 8 .... 16.6
9 (1)–(3) 16.7
10 .... 16.7
12–16 .... 16.8
17 (4), (5) 16.9
18, 19 .... 16.9
20, 21 .... 16.9
22 (2) 16.9
23, 24 .... 16.10
25–27 .... 16.11, 46.16
28 .... 16.11, 50.11, 51.3
(6) 51.3
31 (1)–(4) 16.11
(5), (6) 16.11
32 .... 16.11
38 (8) 16.9
39 (1) 16.9
41 .... 16.11
44, 45 .... 16.5
Schedule
para 7 (3) 16.9
Unfair Dismissal and Statement of Reasons
for Dismissal (Variation of Qualifying
Period) Order 1999, SI 1999/1436 .. 6.1,
45.14, 50.11
Unfair Terms in Consumer Contracts
Regulations 1999, SI 1999/2083 ..... 7.21
Wages Act 1986 (Commencement) Order
1986, SI 1986/1998 .... 31.3
Welfare Reform and Pensions Act 1999
(Commencement No 2) Order 1999,
SI 1999/3420 .... 43.35
Working Time (Amendment) Regulations
2001, SI 2001/3256 .... 27.2, 54.2
Working Time (Amendment) Regulations
2002, SI 2002/3128 .... 3.6, 23.11,
54.2, 54.3
Working Time (Amendment) Regulations
2003, SI 2003/1584 .... 54.2, 54.26
Working Time Regulations 1998, SI 1998/
1833 .... 3.6, 7.17, 7.24,
15.1, 15.6, 23.11, 24.3,
25.25, 26.15, 27.1, 27.8,
31.6, 51.3, 51.11, 52.8,
54.2, 54.28
reg 2 .... 54.3
(1) 27.2, 54.3,
54.4, 54.5, 54.9, 54.33
(a) 54.5
4 (1) 54.6, 54.7, 54.21
(2) 54.6, 54.7, 54.21
(3) 54.6
(4) 54.6
(5) 54.6, 54.29
(6) 54.6
(7) 54.6

Transnational Information and Consultation of Employees Regulations 1999, SI 1999/3323–contd

reg 5 (2), (3) 54.7
5A 3.6, 54.3, 54.6
(2) 54.6
(4) 54.21
6 (1) 54.10
(2) 54.10, 54.21
(3) 54.10
(4) 54.10
(5) 54.10
(7) 54.11, 54.21
(8) 54.11
6A 3.6, 54.3, 54.10
7 (1) 54.12, 54.21
(2) 3.6, 54.12, 54.21
(4), (5) 54.12
(6) 54.13, 54.21
8 .... 54.18, 54.21
9 .... 54.7, 54.8, 54.13, 54.21
10 (1) 54.15, 54.22
(2) 3.6, 54.15, 54.22
(3) 54.15
11 (1)–(3) 54.16, 54.22
(4) 54.16
(6)–(8) 54.16
(3) 3.6
12 .... 54.29
(1)–(3) 54.17
(4) 3.6, 54.17
(5) 54.6, 54.17
13 .... 3.2, 27.3, 54.19
(1) 27.2, 27.3, 54.22
(3) 27.3
(7) 27.2
(8) 27.2
(9) 27.3
14 (2) 54.22
(3) 27.4
15 (1)–(5) 27.5
15A 27.3
16 .... 27.4
(1) 54.22
(4), (5) 27.4
18 .... 54.3, 54.33
(2) (b) 54.32
19 .... 3.6, 54.30
20 .... 54.15, 54.28
(1), (2) 54.28
21 .... 54.15, 54.29, 54.33

Transnational Information and Consultation of Employees Regulations 1999, SI 1999/3323–contd

reg 22 (1) 54.16
(a) 54.15
(c) 54.15
23 .... 54.10, 54.11, 54.15
(b) 54.6
24 .... 54.4, 54.15, 54.16, 54.21, 54.22
24A 54.33
25 .... 54.22
(2), (3) 3.6
25A (1) 54.6
27 .... 54.15, 54.17, 54.22
(2) 3.6
27A 54.3, 54.10
(1)–(3) 3.6
(4) (a) 54.21
(4) (b) 3.6
28 .... 54.20, 54.21
29 .... 54.21
29A–29E 54.20, 54.21
30 .... 3.6, 18.11
(1) 27.6, 54.22
(a), (b) 54.22
(2) 27.6
(4) 27.4
(5) 27.4, 27.6
31 .... 18.11, 54.23
32 .... 18.11, 51.3
(1), (2) 54.24
35 .... 54.25
(1) (a) 27.4
(2) (b) 19.33
(3) 19.33
35A 54.1, 54.26
36 .... 54.3
37–42 .... 54.3
43 .... 54.19
Sch 1 .... 51.3, 52.16, 52.21
para 3 .... 54.4
Sch 2 .... 27.7, 54.19
Sch 3 .... 54.20, 54.21

Working Time Regulations 1999, SI 1999/3372 .... 54.2
reg 4 .... 54.28

Workplace (Health, Safety and Welfare) Regulations 1992, SI 1992/3004 .... 26.17, 26.27
reg 4–25 .... 26.27

Table of Cases

PARA

A

A v B [2003] IRLR 405, [2003] All ER (D) 184 (May), EAT 51.9
A v B, ex p News Group Newspapers Ltd [1998] ICR 55, sub nom Chessington World of
   Adventures Ltd v Reed [1997] IRLR 556, EAT 20.1
A v Chief Constable of West Yorkshire Police [2002] EWCA Civ 1584, [2003] 1 All ER
   255, [2003] 1 CMLR 782, [2003] ICR 161, [2003] IRLR 32, [2002] 3 FCR 751,
   [2003] 1 FLR 223, [2003] Fam Law 98, [2003] 01 LS Gaz R 24, (2002) Times, 14
   November, 146 Sol Jo LB 254, [2002] All ER (D) 50 (Nov); affd [2004] UKHL 21,
   [2004] 3 All ER 145, [2004] 2 WLR 1209, [2004] 2 CMLR 884, [2004] ICR 806,
   [2004] IRLR 573, [2004] 2 FCR 160, [2004] 20 LS Gaz R 34, [2004] NLJR 734,
   (2004) Times, 7 May, 148 Sol Jo LB 572, [2004] All ER (D) 47 (May) 11.6, 12.5,
                                                                                                      19.18, 28.4
A v Company B Ltd [1997] IRLR 405, 577 IRLB 8 .... 7.23
AB v CD [2001] IRLR 808, [2001] All ER (D) 354 (May) 47.14
AB v South West Water Services Ltd [1993] QB 507, [1993] 1 All ER 609, [1993] 2 WLR
   507, [1993] NLJR 235, [1993] PIQR P167, CA 34.5
ADI (UK) Ltd v Willer [2001] EWCA Civ 971, [2001] 3 CMLR 139, [2001] IRLR 542,
   [2001] All ER (D) 237 (Jun) 49.5
AGCO Ltd v Massey Ferguson Works Pension Trust Ltd [2003] EWCA Civ 1044, [2004]
   ICR 15, [2003] IRLR 783, [2003] 35 LS Gaz R 37, (2003) Times, 24 July, 147 Sol
   Jo LB 1085, [2003] OPLR 199, [2003] All ER (D) 292 (Jul) 39.1
AGR Regeling v Bestuur van der Bedrijfsvereniging voor de Metaallnijverheid: C-125/97
   [1998] ECR I-4493, [1999] 1 CMLR 1410, [1999] ICR 605, [1999] IRLR 379,
   [1998] All ER (D) 336, ECJ 29.5
ALM Medical Services Ltd v Bladon [2002] EWCA Civ 1085, [2002] ICR 1444, [2002]
   IRLR 807, (2002) Times, 29 August, [2002] All ER (D) 400 (Jul) 19.7
AM v WC [1999] ICR 1218, [1999] IRLR 410, EAT 12.36
Abbey Life Assurance Co Ltd v Tansell. See MHC Consulting Services Ltd v Tansell
Abbey National plc v Formoso [1999] IRLR 222, EAT 11.5, 13.8
Abdoulaye v Régie nationale des usines Renault SA: C-218/98 [1999] ECR I-5723, [2001]
   2 CMLR 372, [2001] ICR 527, [1999] IRLR 811, [1999] All ER (D) 1014, ECJ 22.14
Abels v Administrative Board of the Bedrijfsvereniging voor de Metaalindustrie en de
   Electrotechnische Industrie: 135/83 [1985] ECR 469, [1987] 2 CMLR 406, ECJ 49.7
Aberdeen Steak Houses Group plc v Ibrahim [1988] ICR 550, [1988] IRLR 420, [1988]
   NLJR 151, EAT 19.52
Abernethy v Mott, Hay and Anderson [1974] ICR 323, [1974] IRLR 213, 118 Sol Jo 294,
   CA 51.1
Abler v Sodexho MM Catering Betriebsgesellschaft mbH: C-340/01 [2004] IRLR 168, [2003]
   All ER (D) 277 (Nov), ECJ 49.5
Abrahams v Performing Right Society [1995] ICR 1028, [1995] IRLR 486, CA 38.20,
                                                                                                      45.9, 55.21
Abrahamsson v Fogelqvist: C-407/98 [2000] ECR I-5539, [2002] ICR 932, [2000] IRLR 732,
   ECJ 11.12, 12.9
Adams v British Airways plc [1996] IRLR 574, CA 5.3
Adams v Hackney Borough Council [2003] IRLR 402, [2003] All ER (D) 54 (Feb), EAT 47.37,
                                                                                                      48.14, 48.19
Adams v Lancashire County Council [1997] ICR 834, sub nom Adams v Lancashire County
   Council and Bet Catering Services Ltd [1997] IRLR 436, CA 49.15
Adams v West Sussex County Council [1990] ICR 546, [1990] IRLR 215, [1990] 17 LS
   Gaz R 32, EAT 20.19
Adamson v B & L Cleaning Services Ltd [1995] IRLR 193, EAT 7.13
Addey and Stanhope School Governing Body v Vakante [2003] ICR 290, [2002] All ER
   (D) 79 (Oct), EAT 12.16

Table of cases

PARA

Addis v Gramophone Co Ltd [1909] AC 488, 78 LJKB 1122, [1908-10] All ER Rep 1,
101 LT 466, HL 52.12, 55.29
Addison v Babcock FATA Ltd [1988] QB 280, [1987] 2 All ER 784, [1987] 3 WLR 122,
[1987] ICR 805, 131 Sol Jo 538, [1987] LS Gaz R 1409, sub nom Babcock FATA
Ltd v Addison [1987] IRLR 173, [1987] 1 FTLR 505, CA 52.13
Addison v Denholm Ship Management (UK) Ltd [1997] ICR 770, [1997] IRLR 389,
EAT 50.15
Adekeye v Post Office [1993] ICR 464, [1993] IRLR 324, EAT 13.3
Adekeye v Post Office (No 2). See Post Office v Adekeye
Adin v Sedco Forex International Resources Ltd [1997] IRLR 280, Ct of Sess 7.13
Adlington v British Bakeries (Northern) Ltd. See British Bakeries (Northern) Ltd v Adlington
Affleck v Newcastle Mind [1999] ICR 852, [1999] IRLR 405, EAT...............................19.24
Afolabi v Southwark London Borough Council [2003] EWCA Civ 15, [2003] ICR 800,
[2003] IRLR 220, [2003] 11 LS Gaz R 32, (2003) Times, 30 January, 147 Sol Jo LB
115, [2003] All ER (D) 217 (Jan) 13.3, 18.30
Ahmed v United Kingdom (Application 22954/93) (1998) 29 EHRR 1, [1999] IRLR 188,
5 BHRC 111, ECtHR 34.2
Ainsworth v Glass Tubes and Components Ltd [1977] ICR 347, [1977] IRLR 74, EAT 22.9
Air Canada v Secretary of State for Trade [1983] 2 AC 394, [1983] 2 WLR 494, 126 Sol
Jo 709, sub nom Air Canada v Secretary of State for Trade (No 2) [1983] 1 All ER
161, CA; affd [1983] 2 AC 394, [1983] 1 All ER 910, sub nom Air Canada v Secretary
of State for Trade [1983] 2 WLR 494, 127 Sol Jo 205, HL 34.6
Airlie v Edinburgh District Council [1996] IRLR 516, EAT 7.22
Ako v Rothschild Asset Management Ltd [2002] EWCA Civ 236, [2002] 2 All ER 693,
[2002] ICR 899, [2002] IRLR 348, [2002] 17 LS Gaz R 36, [2002] All ER (D) 07
(Mar) 7.23, 19.26
Alabaster v Woolwich plc and Secretary of State for Social Security [2000] ICR 1037, [2000]
IRLR 754, EAT; on appeal [2002] EWCA Civ 211, [2002] IRLR 420; refd C-147/02
[2004] 2 CMLR 186, [2004] IRLR 486, [2004] All ER (D) 558 (Mar), ECJ 22.9,
22.14, 22.22, 30.14
Alamo Group (Europe) Ltd v Tucker [2003] ICR 829, [2003] IRLR 266, [2003] All ER (D)
367 (Apr), EAT 36.6, 49.18
Albion Hotel (Freshwater) Ltd v Maia E Silva [2002] IRLR 200, [2001] All ER (D) 265
(Nov), EAT 19.52
Alboni v Ind Coope Retail Ltd [1998] IRLR 131, CA 51.4, 51.14
Alcan Extrusions v Yates [1996] IRLR 327, EAT.............................. 7.22, 45.1, 50.5
Alcock v Chief Constable of South Yorkshire Police [1992] 1 AC 310, [1991] 4 All ER
907, [1991] 3 WLR 1057, 8 BMLR 37, [1992] 3 LS Gaz R 34, 136 Sol Jo LB 9,
HL 25.8
Alderson v Secretary of State for Trade and Industry [2003] EWCA Civ 1767, [2004] 1
All ER 1148, [2004] 1 CMLR 1180, [2004] LGR 389, [2004] ICR 512, [2004] 03
LS Gaz R 33, (2003) Times, 12 December, 147 Sol Jo LB 784, [2003] All ER (D) 137
(Dec) 49.3
Aldred v Nacanco [1987] IRLR 292, CA 53.2
Alexander v Home Office [1988] 2 All ER 118, [1988] 1 WLR 968, [1988] ICR 685, [1988]
IRLR 190, 132 Sol Jo 1147, CA 13.8
Alexander v Midland Bank plc [1999] IRLR 723 ....26.29
Alexander v Standard Telephones and Cables plc [1990] ICR 291, [1990] IRLR 55 ..... 5.3, 7.23
Alexander v Standard Telephones and Cables Ltd (No 2) [1991] IRLR 286 .... 5.3, 7.22,
55.19, 55.25
Alexanders Holdings Ltd v Methven EAT/782/93 ....18.25
Ali v Christian Salvesen Food Services Ltd [1997] 1 All ER 721, [1997] ICR 25, [1997]
IRLR 17, 140 Sol Jo LB 231, sub nom Christian Salvesen Food Services Ltd v Ali
[1996] 41 LS Gaz R 29, CA 5.3
Ali v Southwark London Borough Council [1988] ICR 567, [1988] IRLR 100 .... 7.23
Allen v Amalgamated Construction Co Ltd: C-234/98 [2000] All ER (EC) 97, [1999] ECR
I-8643, [2000] 1 CMLR 1, [2000] IRLR 119, 632 IRLB 2, ECJ 49.4
Allen (Jack) (Sales and Service) Ltd v Smith [1999] IRLR 19, 1999 SLT 820, OH 38.21
Alliance Paper Group plc v Prestwich [1996] IRLR 25 .... 38.7

1

Table of cases

PARA

Allied Dunbar (Frank Weisinger) Ltd v Weisinger [1988] IRLR 60 .... 38.2
Allonby v Accrington and Rossendale College [2001] EWCA Civ 529, [2001] 2 CMLR 559,
    [2001] ICR 1189, [2001] IRLR 364, [2001] All ER (D) 285 (Mar); refd C-256/01:
    [2004] 1 CMLR 1141, [2004] ICR 1328, [2004] IRLR 224, ECJ 11.8, 12.8, 12.21,
    22.9, 22.10, 22.17, 22.19
Allsop v North Tyneside Metropolitan Borough Council (1992) 90 LGR 462, [1992] ICR
    639, [1992] RVR 104, CA 34.2
Allué and Coonan v Università degli Studi di Venezia: 33/88 [1989] ECR 1591, [1991] 1
    CMLR 283, ECJ 34.7
American Cyanamid Co v Ethicon Ltd [1975] AC 396, [1975] 1 All ER 504, [1975] 2
    WLR 316, [1975] FSR 101, [1975] RPC 513, 119 Sol Jo 136, HL 7.23, 38.21
Anandarajah v Lord Chancellor's Department [1984] IRLR 131, EAT 33.2
Anderson v Dalkeith Engineering Ltd [1985] ICR 66, [1984] IRLR 429, EAT 49.20
Anderson v Newham College of Further Education [2002] EWCA Civ 505, [2003] ICR
    212, [2002] All ER (D) 381 (Mar) 25.44
Anderson v Pringle of Scotland Ltd [1998] IRLR 64, 1998 SLT 754, OH 7.23
Andreou v Lord Chancellor's Department [2002] EWCA Civ 1192, [2002] IRLR 728,
    [2002] All ER (D) 309 (Jul) 19.54, 28.7
Andrews v King (Inspector of Taxes) [1991] STC 481, [1991] ICR 846, 135 Sol Jo LB 84. 7.1,
    15.3
Angel (Morris) & Son Ltd v Hollande [1993] 3 All ER 569, [1993] ICR 71, [1993] IRLR
    169, CA 49.9, 49.13
Angestelltenbetriebsrat der Wiener Gebietskrankenkasse v Wiener Gebietskrankenkasse:
    C-309/97 [1999] ECR I-2865, [1999] 2 CMLR 1173, [1999] IRLR 804, [1999] All
    ER (D) 483, ECJ 22.6
Anglian Home Improvements Ltd v Kelly [2004] IRLR 763, CA 19.62
Angus Council v Edgley EAT/289/99 .... 26.3
Aniagwu v Hackney London Borough [1999] IRLR 303, EAT 18.30
Annandale Engineering v Samson [1994] IRLR 59, EAT 7.15
Anya v University of Oxford [2001] EWCA Civ 405 , [2001] ICR 847, [2001] IRLR 377,
    [2001] All ER (D) 266 (Mar) 19.63
Anyanwu and Ebuzoeme v South Bank Students' Union and South Bank University
    (Commission for Racial Equality interveners) [2000] 1 All ER 1, [2000] ICR 221,
    [2000] IRLR 36, [1999] 43 LS Gaz R 34, 143 Sol Jo LB 271, CA; revsd sub nom
    Anyanwu v South Bank Student Union (Commission for Racial Equality, interveners)
    [2001] UKHL 14, [2001] 2 All ER 353, [2001] 1 WLR 638, [2001] ICR 391, [2001]
    IRLR 305, [2001] 21 LS Gaz R 39, 151 NLJ 501, [2001] All ER (D) 272 (Mar) 11.13,
    12.36, 19.17
Aparau v Iceland Frozen Foods plc [1996] IRLR 119, EAT; revsd [2000] 1 All ER 228,
    [2000] IRLR 196, [1999] 45 LS Gaz R 31, CA 7.13, 7.22, 20.19, 39.4
Apelogun-Gabriels v Lambeth London Borough Council [2001] EWCA Civ 1853, [2002]
    ICR 713, [2002] IRLR 116, [2001] All ER (D) 350 (Nov) 13.3, 18.30
Appleyard v F M Smith (Hull) Ltd [1972] IRLR 19, IT 51.7
Arafa v Potter. See Potter v Arafa
Arbeiterwohlfahrt der Stadt Berlin e V v Bötel: C-360/90 [1992] ECR I-3589, [1992] 3
    CMLR 446, [1992] IRLR 423, [1993] 21 LS Gaz R 45, ECJ 22.3, 22.10
Archibald v Fife Council [2004] UKHL 32, [2004] 4 All ER 303, [2004] ICR 954, [2004]
    IRLR 651, [2004] 31 LS Gaz R 25, 148 Sol Jo LB 826, [2004] All ER (D) 32 (Jul) ... 9.12,
    9.14, 9.24
Argyll Training Ltd v Sinclair [2000] IRLR 630, EAT 49.5
Armitage v Weir Valves and Controls (UK) Ltd [2004] ICR 371, [2003] All ER (D) 80 (Dec),
    EAT 19.16
Armour v Skeen [1977] IRLR 310, 1977 JC 15, 1977 SLT 71, JC 25.38
Armstrong (W A) & Sons v Borril [2000] ICR 367, EAT 31.39
Arnold v Barnfield College [2004] All ER (D) 63 (Jul), EAT 12.9
Arnold v Beecham Group Ltd [1982] ICR 744, [1982] IRLR 307, EAT 22.7
Arthur v A-G [1999] ICR 631, EAT 12.27
Artisan Press Ltd v Srawley [1986] ICR 328, [1986] IRLR 126, EAT 52.4
Asda Stores Ltd v Thompson [2002] IRLR 245, [2002] All ER (D) 32 (Feb), EAT 19.12

Table of cases

PARA

Asda Stores Ltd v Thompson [2004] IRLR 598, [2003] All ER (D) 434 (Nov), EAT 19.12, 51.10

Ashburn Anstalt v Arnold [1989] Ch 1, [1988] 2 All ER 147, [1988] 2 WLR 706, 55 P & CR 137, [1987] 2 EGLR 71, 284 Estates Gazette 1375, [1988] 16 LS Gaz R 43, 132 Sol Jo 416, CA 40.2

Ashby v Addison (t/a Brayton News) [2003] ICR 667, [2003] IRLR 211, [2003] NLJR 145, (2003) Times, 24 January, [2003] All ER (D) 98 (Jan), EAT................................. 3.2, 54.3

Ashley v Ministry of Defence [1984] ICR 298, [1984] IRLR 57, EAT 46.2

Ashmore v British Coal Corpn [1990] 2 QB 338, [1990] 2 All ER 981, [1990] 2 WLR 1437, [1990] ICR 485, [1990] IRLR 283, CA 19.24

Ashton v Chief Constable of West Mercia Constabulary [2001] ICR 67 .... 11.6

Askew v Governing Body of Clifton Middle School. See Clifton Middle School Governing Body v Askew

Aslan v Murphy [1989] 3 All ER 130, [1990] 1 WLR 766, 59 P & CR 407, 21 HLR 532, [1989] 2 EGLR 57, [1989] 38 EG 109, [1989] NLJR 936, CA 40.2

Aspden v Webbs Poultry and Meat Group (Holdings) Ltd [1996] IRLR 521 ....7.13, 39.11, 41.15, 55.19

Associated British Ports v Palmer [1995] 2 AC 454, [1995] 2 All ER 100, [1995] 2 WLR 354, [1995] ICR 406, [1995] IRLR 258, [1995] 17 LS Gaz R 48, [1995] NLJR 417, HL 48.18

Associated British Ports v Transport and General Workers' Union [1989] 3 All ER 796, [1989] 1 WLR 939, [1989] ICR 557, [1989] IRLR 305, CA; revsd [1989] 3 All ER 822, [1989] 1 WLR 939, [1989] ICR 557, [1989] IRLR 399, HL 42.2, 42.3, 42.4, 42.5, 42.14, 42.16, 42.20

Associated Newspapers Ltd v Wilson [1995] 2 AC 454, [1995] 2 All ER 100, [1995] 2 WLR 354, [1995] ICR 406, [1995] IRLR 258, [1995] 17 LS Gaz R 48, [1995] NLJR 417, HL 48.18

Astles v AG Stanley Ltd IDS Brief No 588 .... 19.54

Astley v Celtec Ltd [2002] EWCA Civ 1035, [2002] 3 CMLR 366, [2002] ICR 1289, [2002] IRLR 629, [2002] 37 LS Gaz R 38, (2002) Times, 9 August, [2002] All ER (D) 287 (Jul) 6.9, 49.8

Atkinson (Octavius) & Sons Ltd v Morris [1989] ICR 431, [1989] IRLR 158, CA 45.13, 50.13

A-G v Blake (Jonathan Cape Ltd third party) [2001] 1 AC 268, [2000] 4 All ER 385, [2000] 2 All ER (Comm) 487, [2000] 3 WLR 625, [2001] IRLR 36, [2000] NLJR 1230, [2000] 32 LS Gaz R 37, 144 Sol Jo LB 242, [2001] 1 LRC 260, [2000] EMLR 949, [2000] IP & T 1261, [2000] All ER (D) 1074, HL 7.24, 38.9

A-G v Wheen [2000] IRLR 461, [2000] All ER (D) 767, EAT; affd [2001] IRLR 91, [2000] All ER (D) 2186, CA 19.76, 28.7

A-G's Reference (No 2 of 1999) [2000] QB 796, [2000] 3 All ER 182, [2000] 3 WLR 195, [2000] IRLR 417, [2000] 2 BCLC 257, [2000] 2 Cr App Rep 207, [2000] Crim LR 475, [2000] 09 LS Gaz R 39, CA 25.42

Austin Rover Group Ltd v HM Inspector of Factories [1990] 1 AC 619, [1989] 3 WLR 520, [1990] ICR 133, [1989] IRLR 404, sub nom Mailer v Austin Rover Group plc [1989] 2 All ER 1087, HL 25.20

Australian Commercial Research and Development Ltd v ANZ McCaughan Merchant Bank Ltd [1989] 3 All ER 65 .... 7.23

Automatic Switching Ltd v Brunet [1986] ICR 542, EAT 19.22

Avon County Council v Foxall [1989] ICR 407, [1989] IRLR 435, EAT 22.8, 22.23

Avon County Council v Howlett [1983] 1 All ER 1073, [1983] 1 WLR 605, 81 LGR 555, [1983] IRLR 171, 127 Sol Jo 173, 133 NLJ 377, CA 31.15

Avonmouth Construction Co Ltd v Shipway [1979] IRLR 14, EAT 51.11

Aziz v Bethnal Green City Challenge Co Ltd [2000] IRLR 111, CA 20.6

Aziz v Trinity Street Taxis Ltd [1989] QB 463, [1988] 2 All ER 860, [1988] 3 WLR 79, [1988] ICR 534, [1988] IRLR 204, 132 Sol Jo 898, [1988] 26 LS Gaz R 42, CA 11.10

B

BCCI SA (in liquidation) v Ali (No 3) [2002] EWCA Civ 82, [2002] 3 All ER 750, [2002] ICR 1258, [2002] IRLR 460 .... 7.23

PARA

BG plc v O'Brien [2001] IRLR 496, [2001] All ER (D) 169 (May), EAT; affd sub nom
 O'Brien v Transco plc (formerly BG plc) [2002] EWCA Civ 379, [2002] ICR 721,
 [2002] IRLR 444, [2002] All ER (D) 80 (Mar) 50.7
BL Cars Ltd v Brown [1983] ICR 143, [1983] IRLR 193, 80 LS Gaz R 94, EAT 11.12
BMK Ltd v Logue [1993] ICR 601, [1993] IRLR 477, EAT 55.7
BNP Paribas v Mezzotero [2004] IRLR 508, 148 Sol Jo LB 666, [2004] All ER (D) 226
 (Apr), EAT 13.5, 19.13
BP Chemicals Ltd v Gillick [1995] IRLR 128, EAT 12.21
BSC Sports and Social Club v Morgan [1987] IRLR 391, EAT 45.5, 55.1
BSG Property Services v Tuck [1996] IRLR 134, EAT 49.5, 49.20
Babcock FATA Ltd v Addison. See Addison v Babcock FATA Ltd
Bache v Essex County Council [2000] 2 All ER 847, [2000] IRLR 251, [2000] 05 LS Gaz
 R 33, [2000] NLJR 99, CA 19.40, 19.55, 20.12, 28.7
Bahl v Law Society [2003] IRLR 640, 147 Sol Jo LB 994, [2003] All ER (D) 570 (Jul),
 EAT; affd [2004] EWCA Civ 1070, [2004] IRLR 799, [2004] NLJR 1292, 148 Sol
 Jo LB 976, [2003] All ER (D) 570 (Jul) 11.5, 11.6, 19.63
Bailey v BP Oil (Kent Refinery) Ltd [1980] ICR 642, [1980] IRLR 287, CA 51.10
Bainbridge v Circuit Foil UK Ltd [1997] ICR 541, [1997] IRLR 305, CA 41.14
Bakers' Union v Clarks of Hove Ltd. See Clarks of Hove Ltd v Bakers' Union
Balamoody v UK Central Council for Nursing, Midwifery and Health Visiting [2001] EWCA
 Civ 2097, [2002] ICR 646, [2002] IRLR 288, [2001] All ER (D) 80 (Dec) 11.5, 19.17
Balfour v Foreign and Commonwealth Office [1994] 2 All ER 588, [1994] 1 WLR 681,
 [1994] ICR 277, [1994] 2 LRC 48, CA 19.13, 34.6
Balfron Trustees Ltd v Peterson [2001] IRLR 758, [2002] Lloyd's Rep PN 1, [2001]
 NLJR 1180, [2001] All ER (D) 103 (Jul) 53.2
Balgobin v Tower Hamlets London Borough Council [1987] ICR 829, [1987] IRLR 401,
 [1987] LS Gaz R 2530, EAT 11.13, 12.35
Balston Ltd v Headline Filters Ltd [1987] FSR 330 .... 38.9
Bamsey v Albion Engineering and Manufacturing plc [2004] EWCA Civ 359, [2004] 2
 CMLR 1353, [2004] IRLR 457, [2004] 17 LS Gaz R 31, (2004) Times, 15 April, 148
 Sol Jo LB 389, [2004] All ER (D) 482 (Mar) 27.4
Bank of Credit and Commerce International SA, Re [1994] IRLR 282 .... 7.24, 31.14,
 31.22
Bank of Credit and Commerce International SA (in liquidation) v Ali [1999] 4 All ER 83,
 [1999] IRLR 508, [1999] 30 LS Gaz R 28; affd [2002] EWCA Civ 82, [2002] 3 All
 ER 750, [2002] ICR 1258, [2002] IRLR 460, (2002) Times, 15 February, [2002] All
 ER (D) 308 (Jan) 55.29
Banking Insurance and Finance Union v Barclays Bank plc [1987] ICR 495, [1987] LS Gaz
 R 901, EAT 49.18
Banks v Lavin IDS Brief No 410, EAT 45.15
Banks v Tesco Stores Ltd [2000] 1 CMLR 400, [1999] ICR 1141, EAT 22.14
Barber v Guardian Royal Exchange Assurance Group: C-262/88 [1991] 1 QB 344, [1990] 2
All ER 660, [1991] 2 WLR 72, [1990] ECR I-1889, [1990] 2 CMLR 513, [1990] ICR 616,
 [1990] IRLR 240, [1990] NLJR 925, ECJ 22.3, 22.5, 22.16, 23.2, 39.1, 39.4
Barber v RJB Mining (UK) Ltd [1999] 2 CMLR 833, [1999] ICR 679, [1999] IRLR 308,
 143 Sol Jo LB 141, [1999] All ER (D) 244 .... 54.21, 54.22
Barber v Staffordshire County Council [1996] 2 All ER 748, [1996] IRLR 209, [1996] 06
 LS Gaz R 26, sub nom Staffordshire County Council v Barber [1996] ICR 379, CA 7.23,
 18.12, 19.17, 19.26, 22.22
Barber v Thames Television plc [1992] ICR 661, [1992] IRLR 410, CA 20.15, 50.14
Barclay v City of Glasgow District Council [1983] IRLR 313, EAT 45.5, 50.10
Barclays Bank plc v Kapur [1991] 2 AC 355, [1991] 1 All ER 646, [1991] 2 WLR 401,
 [1991] ICR 208, [1991] IRLR 136, HL 11.12, 13.3, 18.29
Barclays Bank plc v O'Brien. See O'Brien v Barclays Bank plc
Barker v Service Children's Schools: C-374/95 (unreported), ECJ 11.12
Barking and Dagenham London Borough v Oguoko [2000] IRLR 179, EAT 19.58, 22.14
Barnsley Metropolitan Borough Council v Prest [1996] ICR 85, EAT 52.9
Barralet v A-G [1980] 3 All ER 918, sub nom Re South Place Ethical Society, Barralet v
 A-G [1980] 1 WLR 1565, 54 TC 446, [1980] TR 217, 124 Sol Jo 744 .... 11.6

Table of cases

PARA

Barretts & Baird (Wholesale) Ltd v Institution of Professional Civil Servants [1987] IRLR 3, [1988] NLJR 357 .... 42.2
Barros D'Sa v University Hospital and Warwickshire NHS Trust [2001] EWCA Civ 983, [2001] IRLR 691, 62 BMLR 39, [2001] All ER (D) 173 (Jun) 7.23
Barry v Midland Bank plc [1998] 1 All ER 805, [1999] ICR 319, [1998] IRLR 138, CA; affd [1999] 3 All ER 974, [1999] 1 WLR 1465, [1999] ICR 859, [1999] IRLR 581, [1999] 31 LS Gaz R 36, [1999] NLJR 1253, 143 Sol Jo LB 221, HL 22.10, 22.11
Bartholomew v London Borough of Hackney [1999] IRLR 246, CA 37.4
Bartholomew v Southwark London Borough Council [2004] ICR 358, [2003] All ER (D) 190 (Dec), EAT 19.75
Barton v Investec Henderson Crosthwaite Securities Ltd [2003] ICR 1205, [2003] IRLR 332, [2003] 22 LS Gaz R 29, (2003) Times, 16 April, [2003] All ER (D) 61 (Apr), EAT 11.6, 22.11
Bass Leisure Ltd v Thomas [1994] IRLR 104, EAT 7.13, 20.25, 35.7
Bass Taverns Ltd v Burgess [1995] IRLR 596, CA 51.3
Batchelor v British Railways Board [1987] IRLR 136, CA 50.13
Battersby v Campbell [2001] STC (SCD) 189 .... 43.35
Baxter v Harland & Wolff plc [1990] IRLR 516, NICA 25.2
Baynham v Philips Electronics (UK) Ltd (1995) IDS Brief No 551 .... 39.5
Baynton v Saurus General Engineers Ltd [2000] ICR 375, [1999] IRLR 604, EAT 9.11
Beacard Property Management and Construction Co Ltd v Day [1984] ICR 837, EAT 19.16
Beckmann v Dynamco Whicheloe MacFarlane Ltd: C-164/00 [2002] All ER (EC) 865, [2002] ECR I-4893, [2002] 2 CMLR 1152, [2003] ICR 50, [2002] IRLR 578, (2002) Times, 17 June, [2002] All ER (D) 05 (Jun), ECJ 39.3, 49.15
Beedell v West Ferry Printers Ltd [2000] IRLR 650, EAT 51.4
Bell v Department of Health and Social Security (1989) Times, 13 June 25.3
Bell v Lever Bros Ltd [1932] AC 161, 101 LJKB 129, 37 Com Cas 98, [1931] All ER Rep 1, 76 Sol Jo 50, 146 LT 258, 48 TLR 133, HL 55.42
Bennett v Southwark London Borough Council [2002] EWCA Civ 223, [2002] ICR 881, [2002] IRLR 407, (2002) Times, 28 February, 146 Sol Jo LB 59 .... 19.16, 19.17, 19.40, 19.50, 19.55
Benson v Secretary of State for Trade and Industry [2003] ICR 1082, [2003] IRLR 748, [2003] All ER (D) 113 (May), EAT 29.5
Benteler Automotive UK and ISTC, Re (2000) IDS Brief No 677 .... 47.30
Bentley Engineering Co Ltd v Mistry [1979] ICR 47, [1978] IRLR 437, EAT 51.10
Benton v Sanderson Kayser Ltd [1989] ICR 136, [1989] IRLR 19, CA 35.12
Bentwood Bros (Manchester) Ltd v Shepherd [2003] EWCA Civ 380, [2003] ICR 1000, [2003] IRLR 364, [2003] All ER (D) 398 (Feb) 13.8, 52.12
Benveniste v University of Southampton [1989] ICR 617, [1989] IRLR 122, CA 22.11
Berg and Busschers v Besselsen: 144/87 and 145/87 [1988] ECR 2559, [1989] 3 CMLR 817, [1990] ICR 396, [1989] IRLR 447, ECJ 49.4, 49.14
Bernadone v Pall Mall Services Group Ltd [2001] ICR 197 .... 49.14
Bernard v A-G of Jamaica [2004] UKPC 47, [2004] All ER (D) 96 (Oct) 53.2
Bernstein v Immigration Appeal Tribunal and Department of Employment [1988] Imm AR 449, CA 23.2
Berriman v Delabole Slate Ltd [1985] ICR 546, sub nom Delabole Slate Ltd v Berriman [1985] IRLR 305, CA 49.20
Berwick Salmon Fisheries Co Ltd v Rutherford [1991] IRLR 203, EAT 6.7
Bestuur van het Algemeen Burgerlijk Pensioenfonds v Beune: C-7/93 [1995] All ER (EC) 97, [1994] ECR I-4471, [1995] 3 CMLR 30, [1995] IRLR 103, ECJ 22.18
Betriebsrat der Bofrost Josef H Boquoi Deutschland West GmbH & Co KG v Bofrost Josef H Boquoi Deutschland West GmbH & Co KG: C-62/99 [2001] ECR I-2579, [2004] 2 CMLR 1223, [2001] IRLR 403, [2001] All ER (D) 350 (Mar), ECJ 16.6
Betriebsrat der Firma ADS Anker GmbH v ADS Anke GmbH (2004) IDS Brief No 763 .... 16.6
Betts v Brintel Helicopters Ltd (t/a British International Helicopters) [1997] 2 All ER 840, [1997] ICR 792, [1997] IRLR 361, [1997] NLJR 561, sub nom Betts v Brintel Helicopters Ltd and KLM ERA Helicopters (UK) Ltd [1998] 2 CMLR 22, CA 49.5
Beveridge v KLM UK Ltd [2000] IRLR 765, EAT 31.6

liv

PARA

Bewley v HM Prison Service [2004] ICR 422, (2004) Times, 4 February, [2004] All ER
  (D) 22 (Mar), EAT 54.4
Bhatt v Chelsea and Westminster Health Care NHS Trust [1998] ICR 576, [1997] IRLR
  660, EAT 50.15
Bhudi v IMI Refiners Ltd [1994] 2 CMLR 296, [1994] ICR 307, [1994] IRLR 204,
  EAT 22.22
Biggs v Somerset County Council [1995] ICR 811, [1995] IRLR 452, EAT; affd [1996] 2
  All ER 734, [1996] 2 CMLR 292, [1996] ICR 364, [1996] IRLR 203, [1996] 06 LS
  Gaz R 27, [1996] NLJR 174, 140 Sol Jo LB 59, CA 18.12, 18.25, 18.30, 18.33,
                                                                                                      22.9, 22.22, 23.2
Bilka-Kaufhaus GmbH v Weber von Hartz: 170/84 [1986] ECR 1607, [1986] 2 CMLR 701,
  [1987] ICR 110, [1986] IRLR 317, ECJ 11.9, 22.3, 22.10,
                                                                                                                           22.11
Bingham v Hobourn Engineering Ltd [1992] IRLR 298, EAT 20.16, 52.12
Birch v Nuneaton and Bedworth Borough Council [1995] IRLR 518, EAT 49.3
Birch v University of Liverpool [1985] ICR 470, [1985] IRLR 165, 129 Sol Jo 245, CA .. 55.2,
                                                                                                                           50.8
Birds Eye Walls Ltd v Harrison [1985] ICR 278, [1985] IRLR 47, EAT 19.11
Birds Eye Walls Ltd v Roberts: C-132/92 [1993] ECR I-5579, [1993] 3 CMLR 822, [1994]
  IRLR 29, sub nom Roberts v Birds Eye Walls Ltd [1994] ICR 338, ECJ 22.12, 22.17,
                                                                                                                          22.18
Birmingham City Council v Equal Opportunities Commission [1989] AC 1155, [1989] 2
  WLR 520, 87 LGR 557, [1989] IRLR 173, 133 Sol Jo 322, [1989] 15 LS Gaz R 36,
  [1989] NLJR 292, sub nom Equal Opportunities Commission v Birmingham City
  Council [1989] 1 All ER 769, HL 11.5
Birmingham Optical Group plc v Johnson [1995] ICR 459, EAT 18.25
Blackburn v Gridquest Ltd (t/a Select Employment) [2002] EWCA Civ 1037, [2002] ICR
  1206, [2002] IRLR 604, [2002] All ER (D) 325 (Jul) 27.4
Blackpool and Fylde College v National Association of Teachers in Further and Higher
  Education [1994] ICR 648, [1994] IRLR 227, CA 42.14, 42.15
Blaik v Post Office [1994] IRLR 280, EAT 19.17, 22.22
Bliss v South East Thames Regional Health Authority [1987] ICR 700, [1985] IRLR 308,
  CA 50.7, 52.12
Blockleys plc v Miller [1992] ICR 749, [1992] 34 LS Gaz R 39, EAT 20.25
Blue Circle Staff Association v Certification Officer [1977] 2 All ER 145, [1977] 1 WLR
  239, [1977] ICR 224, [1977] IRLR 20, 121 Sol Jo 52, EAT 47.23
Bodha v Hampshire Area Health Authority [1982] ICR 200, EAT 18.25
Bolch v Chipman [2004] IRLR 140, [2003] All ER (D) 122 (Nov), EAT 19.17
Bond v CAV Ltd [1983] IRLR 360 .... 7.13
Bonner v H Gilbert Ltd [1989] IRLR 475, EAT 35.10
Boorman v Allmakes Ltd [1995] ICR 842, [1995] IRLR 553, CA 52.9
Boote v Ministry of Defence (3 March 2004, unreported) 12.8
Booth v United States of America [1999] IRLR 16, 611 IRLB 9, EAT 6.7
Borders Regional Council v Maule [1993] IRLR 199, EAT 46.2, 46.5
Bork (P) International A/S v Foreningen af Arbejdsledere i Danmark: 101/87 [1988] ECR
  3057, [1990] 3 CMLR 701, [1989] IRLR 41, ECJ 49.4, 49.10
Bossa v Nordstress Ltd [1998] ICR 694, [1998] IRLR 284, EAT 11.12, 12.15, 23.4
Bostock v Bryant (1990) 61 P & CR 23, 22 HLR 449, [1990] 2 EGLR 101, [1990] 39
  EG 64, CA 40.2
Boston Deep Sea Fishing and Ice Co v Ansell (1888) 39 Ch D 339, [1886-90] All ER Rep
  65, 59 LT 345, CA 55.6, 55.20
Botzen v Rotterdamsche Droogdok Maatschappij BV: 186/83 [1985] ECR 519, [1986] 2
  CMLR 50, ECJ 49.11
Bouchaala v Trusthouse Forte Hotels Ltd [1980] ICR 721, [1980] IRLR 382, EAT 51.13
Bowater plc v Charlwood [1991] ICR 798, [1991] IRLR 340, EAT 19.22
Bowden v Tuffnells Parcels Express Ltd [2000] IRLR 560, EAT; refd C-133/00: [2001]
  All ER (EC) 865, [2001] ECR I-7031, [2001] 3 CMLR 1342, [2001] IRLR 838,
  [2001] All ER (D) 32 (Oct), ECJ 54.3
Bowman v Harland & Wolff plc [1992] IRLR 349 .... 25.2

Table of cases

PARA

Boxfoldia Ltd v National Graphical Association [1988] ICR 752, [1988] IRLR 383 .... 42.16,
47.17
Boyle v Equal Opportunities Commission: C-411/96 [1998] All ER (EC) 879, [1998] ECR I-
6401, [1998] 3 CMLR 1133, [1999] ICR 360, [1998] IRLR 717, [1999] 1 FCR 581,
[1999] 1 FLR 119, 608 IRLB 5, [1998] All ER (D) 500, ECJ 22.14, 39.8
Boyo v Lambeth London Borough Council [1994] ICR 727, [1995] IRLR 50, CA .. 7.23, 45.19,
50.9, 55.7, 55.18, 55.25
Boys and Girls Welfare Society v Macdonald [1997] ICR 693, EAT 51.9
Brace v Calder [1895] 2 QB 253, 59 JP 693, 64 LJQB 582, 14 R 473, [1895-9] All ER Rep
1196, 72 LT 829, 11 TLR 450, CA 55.8
Bracebridge Engineering Ltd v Darby [1990] IRLR 3, EAT 11.12, 12.35
Bradford Hospitals NHS Trust v Al-Shabib [2003] IRLR 4, [2002] All ER (D) 68 (Oct),
EAT 11.6
Bradley v National and Local Government Officers Association [1991] ICR 359, [1991]
IRLR 159, EAT 48.14
Bradley v Secretary of State for Employment [1989] ICR 69, [1989] 3 LS Gaz R 43,
EAT 29.7
Brasserie du Pecheur SA v Germany: C-46/93 [1996] QB 404, [1996] All ER (EC) 301,
[1996] 2 WLR 506, [1996] ECR I-1029, [1996] 1 CMLR 889, [1996] IRLR 267,
ECJ 23.2
Bratko v Beloit Walmsley Ltd [1996] ICR 76, [1995] IRLR 629, EAT 39.4, 50.14
Braund (Walter) (London) Ltd v Murray [1991] ICR 327, [1991] IRLR 100, EAT 52.10
Breach v Epsylon Industries Ltd [1976] ICR 316, [1976] IRLR 180, EAT 7.13, 55.21
Brennan v J H Dewhurst Ltd [1984] ICR 52, [1983] IRLR 357, EAT 11.12
Brent London Borough Council v Charles (1997) 29 HLR 876, CA 40.7
Bridgen v Lancashire County Council [1987] IRLR 58, CA 50.7
Brigden v American Express Bank Ltd [2000] IRLR 94, 631 IRLB 13, [1999] All ER (D)
1130 .... 7.21, 55.37
Briggs v North Eastern Education and Library Board [1990] IRLR 181, NICA 11.8
Briggs v Oates [1991] 1 All ER 407, [1990] ICR 473, [1990] IRLR 472, [1990] NLJR
208 .... 38.20, 45.1, 55.8
Brind v Secretary of State for the Home Department. See R v Secretary of State for the
Home Department, ex p Brind
Briscoe v Lubrizol Ltd [2002] EWCA Civ 508, [2002] IRLR 607, [2002] All ER (D) 190
(Apr) 41.14, 41.15, 55.17
British Aerospace plc v Green [1995] ICR 1006, [1995] IRLR 433, CA 19.12, 51.11
British Aircraft Corpn v Austin [1978] IRLR 332, EAT 25.1, 25.18, 26.11
British Airways Engine Overhaul Ltd v Francis [1981] ICR 278, [1981] IRLR 9, EAT 51.3
British Airways (European Operations at Gatwick) Ltd v Moore [2000] ICR 678, [2000]
IRLR 296, EAT 22.4, 30.24
British Association of Advisers and Lecturers in Physical Education v National Union of
Teachers [1986] IRLR 497, CA 47.1
British Bakeries (Northern) Ltd v Adlington [1989] ICR 438, sub nom Adlington v British
Bakeries (Northern) Ltd [1989] IRLR 218, CA 46.2
BBC v Hearn [1978] 1 All ER 111, [1977] 1 WLR 1004, [1977] ICR 685, [1977] IRLR
273, 121 Sol Jo 374, CA 42.4
BBC v Kelly-Phillips [1998] 2 All ER 845, [1998] ICR 587, [1998] IRLR 294, [1998]
NLJR 658, 592 IRLB 6, CA 50.15
BBC Scotland v Souster [2001] IRLR 150, Ct of Sess 11.6
British Coal Corpn v British Coal Staff Superannuation Scheme Trustees Ltd [1995] 1 All
ER 912, [1994] ICR 537 .... 39.11
British Coal Corpn v Cheesbrough [1990] 2 AC 256, [1990] 1 All ER 641, [1990] 2 WLR
407, [1990] ICR 317, [1990] IRLR 148, 134 Sol Jo 661, [1990] 11 LS Gaz R 39,
HL 31.36, 31.39
British Coal Corpn v Keeble [1997] IRLR 336, EAT 13.3, 18.30
British Coal Corpn v Smith [1996] 3 All ER 97, [1996] ICR 515, [1996] IRLR 404, [1996]
NLJR 843, HL 22.9
British Gas plc v McCarrick [1991] IRLR 305, CA 20.17
British Gas plc v Sharma [1991] ICR 19, [1991] IRLR 101, EAT 13.8, 19.59

PARA

British Gas Services Ltd v McCaull [2001] IRLR 60 ....9.15, 9.34, 18.29, 51.8
British Home Stores Ltd v Burchell [1980] ICR 303n, [1978] IRLR 379, 13 ITR 560,
　　EAT 37.4, 51.9, 51.10
British Judo Association v Petty [1981] ICR 660, [1981] IRLR 484, EAT 12.27
British Leyland (UK) Ltd v Swift [1981] IRLR 91, CA 51.4
British Nursing Association v Inland Revenue (National Minimum Wage Compliance Team)
　　[2002] EWCA Civ 494, [2002] IRLR 480, [2003] ICR 19 ....31.12, 31.13
British Publishing Co Ltd v Fraser [1987] ICR 517, EAT 20.20
British Railways Board v National Union of Railwaymen [1989] ICR 678, [1989] IRLR 349,
　　CA 42.14
British Road Services Ltd v Loughran [1997] IRLR 92, CA 22.10, 22.11
British Sugar plc v Kirker [1998] IRLR 624, EAT 9.22, 9.34
British Telecommunications plc v Burwell [1986] ICR 35, EAT 35.13
British Telecommunications plc v Communication Workers Union [2003] EWHC 937 (QB),
　　[2004] IRLR 58 ....42.4, 42.14
British Telecommunications plc v Grant (1994) IDS Brief No 518, EAT 11.10
British Telecommunications plc v Reid [2003] EWCA Civ 1675, [2004] IRLR 327, [2003]
　　41 LS Gaz R 33, (2003) Times, 9 October, [2003] All ER (D) 91 (Oct) 13.8
British Telecommunications plc v Roberts [1996] ICR 625, [1996] IRLR 601, EAT 11.9,
　　30.21
British Telecommunications plc v Sheridan [1990] IRLR 27, CA 20.17
British Telecommunications plc v Ticehurst [1992] ICR 383, [1992] 15 LS Gaz R 32, 136
　　Sol Jo LB 96, sub nom Ticehurst and Thompson v British Telecommunications plc
　　[1992] IRLR 219, CA.. 7.13, 7.24, 31.14, 42.16
British Telecommunications plc v Williams [1997] IRLR 668, EAT 11.5
Bromley v H & J Quick Ltd [1988] 2 CMLR 468, [1988] ICR 623, [1988] IRLR 249,
　　CA 22.7
Bromley v Smith [1909] 2 KB 235, 78 LJKB 745, [1908-10] All ER Rep 384, 100 LT
　　731 ....3.10
Brompton v AOC Internaional Ltd [1997] IRLR 639, CA 7.13, 39.11, 55.7
Brook v Haringey London Borough Council [1992] IRLR 478, EAT 11.5
Brook Lane Finance Co Ltd v Bradley [1988] ICR 423, [1988] IRLR 283, [1988] 15 LS
　　Gaz R 35, EAT 49.8
Brooker v Charrington Fuel Oils Ltd [1981] IRLR 147, Cty Ct.................................... 31.4
Brookes v Borough Care Services and CLS Care Services Ltd [1998] ICR 1198, [1998]
　　IRLR 636, EAT 49.6
Brooks v British Telecommunications plc [1992] ICR 414, [1992] IRLR 66, CA 50.14
Brooks v Olyslager OMS (UK) Ltd [1998] IRLR 590, 601 IRLB 6, CA 38.9
Broome v DPP [1974] AC 587, [1974] 1 All ER 314, [1974] 2 WLR 58, [1974] ICR 84,
　　[1974] IRLR 26, [1974] Crim LR 311, 118 Sol Jo 50, HL 42.10
Brown v Chief Adjudication Officer [1997] ICR 266, [1997] IRLR 110, [1996] 42 LS Gaz
　　R 28, 140 Sol Jo LB 221, CA 41.5
Brown v JBD Engineering Ltd [1993] IRLR 568, EAT 50.7, 55.22
Brown v Knowsley Borough Council [1986] IRLR 102, EAT 50.10
Brown v Merchant Ferries Ltd [1998] IRLR 682, NICA 50.7
Brown v Rentokil Ltd: C-394/96 [1998] All ER (EC) 791, [1998] ECR I-4185, [1998] 2
　　CMLR 1049, [1998] ICR 790, [1998] IRLR 445, [1999] 1 FCR 49, [1998] 2 FLR 649,
　　[1998] Fam Law 597, 48 BMLR 126, [1998] 34 LS Gaz R 34, [1998] All ER (D) 313,
　　ECJ 11.5
Brown v Southall and Knight [1980] ICR 617, [1980] IRLR 130, EAT 50.13, 55.5
Brown (John) Engineering Ltd v Brown [1997] IRLR 90, EAT................................... 51.11
Bruce v Wiggins Teape (Stationery) Ltd [1994] IRLR 536, EAT 31.6, 55.24
Brunnhofer v Bank der österreichischen Postsparkasse AG: C-381/99 [2001] ECR I-4961,
　　[2001] All ER (EC) 693, [2001] 3 CMLR 173, [2001] IRLR 571, ECJ 22.6, 22.11
Bruton v London and Quadrant Housing Trust [2000] 1 AC 406, [1999] 3 All ER 481,
　　[1999] 3 WLR 150, 31 HLR 902, [1999] 2 EGLR 59, [1999] 30 EG 91, [1999] EGCS
　　90, [1999] NLJR 1001, 78 P & CR D21, HL 40.2
Bryant v Housing Corpn. See Housing Corpn v Bryant
Buchan v Secretary of State for Employment [1997] IRLR 80, 565 IRLB 2, EAT 29.4

Table of cases

PARA

Buchanan-Smith v Schleicher & Co International Ltd [1996] ICR 613, [1996] IRLR 547, EAT 49.11
Budd v Scotts Co (UK) Ltd [2004] ICR 299, [2003] IRLR 145, EAT 45.12, 55.27
Budgen & Co v Thomas [1976] ICR 344, [1976] IRLR 174, EAT 51.10
Bullivant (Roger) Ltd v Ellis [1987] FSR 172, [1987] ICR 464, [1987] IRLR 491, CA 38.24
Bullock v Alice Ottley School (1993) 91 LGR 32, [1993] ICR 138, [1992] IRLR 564, CA 11.5, 22.17
Bulwick v Mills & Allen Ltd (8 June 2000, unreported), EAT 36.4
Burgoine v Waltham Forest London Borough Council (1996) 95 LGR 520, [1997] 2 BCLC 612, [1997] BCC 347 .... 34.2
Burns v Royal Mail Group plc (formerly Consignia plc) [2004] ICR 1103, sub nom Burns v Consignia plc (No 2) [2004] IRLR 425, (2004) Times, 24 June, [2004] All ER (D) 453 (Mar), EAT 19.63, 20.11
Burrett v West Birmingham Health Authority [1994] IRLR 7, EAT 11.5
Burton v De Vere Hotels Ltd [1997] ICR 1, [1996] IRLR 596, EAT 11.12, 11.13
Burton Group Ltd v Smith [1977] IRLR 351, EAT 45.5, 55.5
Busch v Klinikum Neustadt GmbH & Co Betriebs-KG: C-320/01 [2003] All ER (EC) 985, [2003] ECR I-2041, [2003] 2 CMLR 481, [2003] IRLR 625, [2004] 1 FCR 54, [2003] All ER (D) 394 (Feb), ECJ 11.5
Business Seating (Renovations) Ltd v Broad [1989] ICR 729 .... 38.15
Bux v Slough Metals Ltd [1974] 1 All ER 262, [1973] 1 WLR 1358, [1974] 1 Lloyd's Rep 155, 117 Sol Jo 615, CA 25.5, 25.44
Buxton v Equinox Design Ltd [1999] ICR 269, [1999] IRLR 158, EAT 9.34
Byrne v BOC Ltd [1992] IRLR 505, EAT 51.10
Byrne v Birmingham City District Council (1987) 85 LGR 729, [1987] ICR 519, [1987] IRLR 191, CA 6.7
Byrne v Financial Times Ltd [1991] IRLR 417, EAT 19.8
Byrne Bros (Formwork) Ltd v Baird [2002] ICR 667, [2002] IRLR 96, [2001] All ER (D) 321 (Nov), EAT 54.3

C

CIA Security International SA v Signalson: C-194/94 [1996] All ER (EC) 557, [1996] ECR I-2201, [1996] 2 CMLR 781, ECJ 23.2
CPL Distribution Ltd v Evans [2002] EWCA Civ 1481, [2003] IRLR 28, [2002] All ER (D) 100 (Oct) 49.11
CPS Recruitment Ltd v Bowen [1982] IRLR 54, EAT 35.6
Cadman v Health and Safety Executive [2004] EWCA Civ 1317, [2004] All ER (D) 191 (Oct) 22.11
Cadoux v Central Regional Council [1986] IRLR 131, 1986 SLT 117, Ct of Sess 5.4
Cain v Leeds Western Health Authority [1990] ICR 585, [1990] IRLR 168, EAT 51.9
Caisse Nationale d'Assurance Vieillesse des Travailleurs Salaries v Thibault: C-136/95 [1998] All ER (EC) 385, [1998] ECR I-2011, [1998] 2 CMLR 516, [1998] IRLR 399, [1998] All ER (D) 167, sub nom Thibault v Caisse Nationale d'Assurance Viellesse des Travailleurs Salaries (CNAVTS) [1999] ICR 160, ECJ 11.5
Calder v James Finlay Corpn Ltd [1989] ICR 157n, [1989] IRLR 55, EAT 13.8
Calder v Rowntree Mackintosh Confectionery Ltd [1993] ICR 811, [1993] IRLR 212, CA 22.11
Caledonia Bureau Investment and Property v Caffrey [1998] ICR 603, [1998] IRLR 110, 591 IRLB 6, EAT 11.5, 30.6
Caledonian Mining Co Ltd v Bassett [1987] ICR 425, [1987] IRLR 165, EAT 45.2
Callagan v Glasgow City Council [2001] IRLR 724, [2001] All ER (D) 101 (Aug), EAT 9.24
Cambridge and District Co-operative Society Ltd v Ruse [1993] IRLR 156, EAT 35.12
Camelot Group plc v Centaur Communications Ltd [1999] QB 124, [1998] 1 All ER 251, [1998] 2 WLR 379, [1998] IRLR 80, [1997] 43 LS Gaz R 30, [1997] NLJR 1618, 142 Sol Jo LB 19, [1998] EMLR 1, CA 28.5
Campbell v Dunoon and Cowal Housing Association Ltd [1992] IRLR 528, 1992 SLT 1136n, Ct of Sess 20.26
Campbell v Dunoon and Cowal Housing Association [1993] IRLR 496, Ct of Sess 51.11

PARA

Campbell v Frisbee [2002] EWCA Civ 1374, [2003] ICR 141, 146 Sol Jo LB 233, [2003]
EMLR 76, [2002] All ER (D) 178 (Oct), [2003] IP & T 86 .... 38.20
Campbell & Smith Construction Group Ltd v Greenwood [2001] IRLR 588, [2001] All ER
(D) 240 (May), EAT 31.6
Campion v Hamworthy Engineering Ltd [1987] ICR 966, CA 20.26
Canada Life Ltd v Gray [2004] ICR 673, sub nom Gray v Canada Life Ltd [2004] All ER
(D) 36 (Jan), EAT 27.6
Canniffe v East Riding of Yorkshire Council [2000] IRLR 555, EAT 11.13, 12.35
Cantor Fitzgerald International v Bird [2002] IRLR 867, [2002] All ER (D) 438 (Jul) 38.20
Cantor Fitzgerald International v Callaghan [1999] 2 All ER 411, [1999] ICR 639, [1999]
IRLR 234, CA 38.20
Cantor Fitzgerald (UK) Ltd v Wallace [1992] IRLR 215 .... 38.4
Capek v Lincolnshire County Council [2000] ICR 878, [2000] IRLR 590, [2000] 24 LS
Gaz R 39, CA 7.23, 18.32
Capper Pass Ltd v Lawton [1977] QB 852, [1977] 2 All ER 11, [1977] 2 WLR 26, [1977]
ICR 83, [1976] IRLR 366, 11 ITR 316, 120 Sol Jo 768, EAT 22.6
Cardiff Women's Aid v Hartup [1994] IRLR 390, EAT 11.12, 12.34
Care First Partnership Ltd v Roffey [2001] ICR 87, [2001] IRLR 85, CA 18.2
Carmichael v National Power plc [1999] 4 All ER 897, [1999] 1 WLR 2042, [1999] ICR
1226, [2000] IRLR 43, [1999] 46 LS Gaz R 38, 143 Sol Jo LB 281, 632 IRLB 18, HL15.3
Carrington v Harwich Dock Co Ltd [1998] ICR 1112, [1998] IRLR 567, EAT 6.6
Carrington v Helix Lighting Ltd [1990] ICR 125, [1990] IRLR 6, [1990] 1 LS Gaz R 30,
EAT 13.5, 19.12
Carter v Credit Change Ltd [1980] 1 All ER 252, [1979] ICR 908, [1979] IRLR 361, 123
Sol Jo 604, CA 19.22
Carter v Reiner Moritz Associates Ltd [1997] ICR 881, EAT 19.32, 19.66
Cartlidge v Chief Adjudication Officer [1986] QB 360, [1986] 2 All ER 1, [1986] 2 WLR
558, [1986] ICR 256, [1986] IRLR 182, 130 Sol Jo 185, CA 42.19
Cartwright v G Clancey Ltd [1983] ICR 552, [1983] IRLR 355, EAT 31.27
Caruana v Manchester Airport plc [1996] IRLR 378, EAT 11.5
Carver (née Mascarenhas) v Saudi Arabian Airlines [1999] 3 All ER 61, [1999] ICR 991,
[1999] IRLR 370, 615 IRLB 4, CA 12.15
Casella London Ltd v Banai [1990] ICR 215, [1990] 4 LS Gaz R 39, EAT 19.64
Casey v Morane Ltd [2001] ICR 316, [2001] IRLR 166, [2000] All ER (D) 615, CA 25.44
Cassell & Co Ltd v Broome [1972] AC 1027, [1972] 1 All ER 801, [1972] 2 WLR 645,
116 Sol Jo 199, HL 34.5
Cast v Croydon College [1998] ICR 500, [1998] IRLR 318, [1998] 16 LS Gaz R 26, 142
Sol Jo LB 119, CA 13.3, 18.29
Catamaran Cruisers Ltd v Williams [1994] IRLR 386, EAT 15.3, 51.14
Catherall v Michelin Tyres plc [2003] ICR 28, [2003] IRLR 61, EAT 9.21, 18.29
Caulfield v Marshalls Clay Products Ltd. See Marshalls Clay Products Ltd v Caulfield
Cerberus Software Ltd v Rowley [2000] ICR 35, [1999] IRLR 690, EAT; revsd sub nom
Rowley v Cerberus Software Ltd [2001] EWCA Civ 78, [2001] ICR 376, [2001] IRLR
160, (2001) Times, 20 February, [2001] All ER (D) 80 (Jan) 45.7, 52.13, 55.16, 55.21
Chadwick v Bayer plc [2002] All ER (D) 88 (Jun), EAT 19.10
Chamberlin Solicitors v Emokpae [2004] IRLR 592, [2004] All ER (D) 110 (Jun), EAT 11.6
Chan v Hackney London Borough Council [1997] ICR 1014, EAT 13.8
Chaplin v H J Rawlinson Ltd [1991] ICR 553, EAT 52.13
Chaplin v Leslie Frewin (Publishers) Ltd [1966] Ch 71, [1965] 3 All ER 764, [1966] 2
WLR 40, 109 Sol Jo 871, CA 3.10
Chapman v Simon [1994] IRLR 124, CA 13.4, 18.14
Chapman and Elkin v CPS Computer Group plc [1987] IRLR 462, CA 49.13
Charlton v Charlton Thermosystems (Romsey) Ltd [1995] ICR 56, [1995] IRLR 79,
EAT 49.4
Charlton v Forrest Printing Ink Co Ltd [1980] IRLR 331, CA 25.8
Cheesman v R Brewer Contracts Ltd [2001] IRLR 144, [2000] All ER (D) 2047, EAT 49.5
Chelsea Football Club and Athletic Co Ltd v Heath [1981] ICR 323, [1981] IRLR 73,
EAT 52.9

Table of cases

PARA

Chessington World of Adventures Ltd v Reed. See A v B, ex p News Group Newspapers Ltd
Chief Constable of Avon and Somerset Constabulary v Chew (2002) IDS Brief No 701 .... 11.8
Chief Constable of Bedfordshire Constabulary v Graham [2002] IRLR 239, [2001] All ER
    (D) 89 (Sep), EAT 11.6
Chief Constable of Bedfordshire Police v Liversidge [2002] EWCA Civ 894, [2002] ICR
    1135, [2002] IRLR 651, [2002] All ER (D) 395 (May) 11.13, 12.23
Chief Constable of Cumbria v McGlennon [2002] ICR 1156, [2002] All ER (D) 231 (Jul),
    EAT 12.23
Chief Constable of Greater Manchester Police v Hope [1999] ICR 338, EAT 13.8
Chief Constable of Kent Constabulary v Baskerville [2003] EWCA Civ 1354, [2003] ICR
    1463, [2003] 39 LS Gaz R 38, (2003) Times, 10 September, 147 Sol Jo LB 1028,
    [2003] All ER (D) 27 (Sep) 12.38
Chief Constable of Lincolnshire Police v Stubbs [1999] ICR 547, [1999] IRLR 81, EAT 11.13,
                                                                                                                      12.35
Chief Constable of Thames Valley Police v Kellaway [2000] IRLR 170, EAT 20.7
Chief Constable of West Yorkshire Police v A [2001] ICR 128, [2000] IRLR 465, EAT ... 13.7
Chief Constable of West Yorkshire Police v Khan [2001] UKHL 48, [2001] 1 WLR 1947,
    [2001] ICR 1065, [2001] IRLR 830, [2001] 42 LS Gaz R 37, 145 Sol Jo LB 230, [2001]
    All ER (D) 158 (Oct), sub nom Khan v Chief Constable of West Yorkshire Police
    [2001] 4 All ER 834 .... 11.10
Chief Constable of West Yorkshire Police v Vento [2002] IRLR 177, [2001] All ER (D) 20
    (Dec), EAT; revsd sub nom Vento v Chief Constable of West Yorkshire Police [2002]
    EWCA Civ 1871, [2003] ICR 318, [2003] IRLR 102, [2003] 10 LS Gaz R 28, (2002)
    Times, 27 December, 147 Sol Jo LB 181, [2002] All ER (D) 363 (Dec) 10.18, 13.8
Chohan v Derby Law Centre [2004] IRLR 685, [2004] All ER (D) 132 (Apr), EAT 13.3,
                                                                                                                      18.30
Chorion plc v Lane IDS Brief No 642 .... 19.22
Christie v John E Haith Ltd [2003] IRLR 670, [2003] All ER (D) 267 (Jul), EAT 22.11
Church v West Lancashire NHS Trust [1998] ICR 423, [1998] IRLR 4, 588 IRLB 7, EAT 35.7
City and Hackney Health Authority v Crisp [1990] ICR 95, [1990] IRLR 47, EAT 52.3
City Equitable Fire Insurance Co Ltd, Re [1925] Ch 407, 94 LJ Ch 445, [1925] B & CR
    109, [1924] All ER Rep 485, 133 LT 520, 40 TLR 853, CA 8.15
Civil Service Union v Central Arbitration Committee [1980] IRLR 274 .... 10.3
Civilian War Claimants Association Ltd v R [1932] AC 14, 101 LJKB 105, [1931] All ER
    Rep 432, 75 Sol Jo 813, 146 LT 169, 48 TLR 83, HL 23.2
Clancy v Cannock Chase Technical College [2001] IRLR 331, [2001] All ER (D) 36 (Mar),
    EAT 13.8, 52.2, 52.12
Clapson v British Airways plc [2001] IRLR 184, EAT 19.14, 19.57
Clark v BET plc [1997] IRLR 348 .... 55.25
Clark v Civil Aviation Authority [1991] IRLR 412, EAT 51.4
Clark v Fahrenheit 451 (Communications) Ltd (1999) IDS Brief No 666, EAT 45.6
Clark v Novacold Ltd [1999] 2 All ER 977, [1999] ICR 951, [1999] IRLR 318, 48 BMLR
    1, CA 9.11, 9.12, 9.15, 9.32, 22.12
Clark v Oxfordshire Health Authority [1998] IRLR 125, 41 BMLR 18, CA 15.3
Clark v Secretary of State for Employment. See Secretary of State for Employment v Clark
Clark & Tokeley Ltd (t/a Spellbrook) v Oakes [1998] 4 All ER 353, [1999] ICR 276, [1998]
    IRLR 577, 142 Sol Jo LB 253, [1998] All ER (D) 376, CA 6.9
Clarke v Arriva Kent Thameside Ltd [2001] All ER (D) 485 (Jul), EAT 18.9
Clarke v Hampshire Electro-Plating Co Ltd [1992] ICR 312, [1991] IRLR 490, EAT 13.3
Clarke v Watford Borough Council (4 May 2000, unreported), EAT 19.59
Clarke v Yorke (1882) 52 LJ Ch 32, 31 WR 62, 47 LT 381 .... 7.23
Clarke and Powell v Eley (IMI) Kynoch Ltd [1982] IRLR 131, IT; revsd sub nom Clarke
    v Eley (IMI) Kynoch Ltd [1983] ICR 165, [1982] IRLR 482, EAT 11.9
Clarks of Hove Ltd v Bakers' Union [1979] 1 All ER 152, [1978] 1 WLR 1207, [1978]
    ICR 1076, 13 ITR 356, sub nom Bakers' Union v Clarks of Hove Ltd [1978] IRLR
    366, 122 Sol Jo 643, CA 36.6
Clay Cross (Quarry Services) Ltd v Fletcher [1979] 1 All ER 474, [1978] 1 WLR 1429,
    [1979] ICR 1, 122 Sol Jo 776, sub nom Fletcher v Clay Cross (Quarry Services) Ltd
    [1978] 3 CMLR 1, [1978] IRLR 361, CA 22.11

PARA

Clayton v Vigers [1989] ICR 713, [1990] IRLR 177, EAT 30.6
Clayton (Herbert) & Jack Waller Ltd v Oliver [1930] AC 209, 99 LJKB 165, [1930] All
    ER Rep 414, 74 Sol Jo 187, 142 LT 585, 46 TLR 230, HL 55.29
Clements v London and North Western Rly Co [1894] 2 QB 482, 58 JP 818, 63 LJQB 837,
    9 R 641, 42 WR 663, 38 Sol Jo 562, 70 LT 896, 10 TLR 539, [1891-4] All ER Rep
    Ext 1461, CA 3.10
Cleveland Ambulance NHS Trust v Blane [1997] ICR 851, [1997] IRLR 332, EAT 48.19
Cleveland County Council v Springett [1985] IRLR 131, EAT 47.20
Clifford v Union of Democratic Mineworkers [1991] IRLR 518, CA 7.1
Clifton Middle School Governing Body v Askew [2000] LGR 96, [2000] ICR 286, [1999]
    ELR 425, [1999] 33 LS Gaz R 30, sub nom Askew v Governing Body of Clifton
    Middle School [1999] IRLR 708, [1999] All ER (D) 825, CA 49.9
Clymo v Wandsworth London Borough Council [1989] 2 CMLR 577, [1989] ICR 250,
    [1989] IRLR 241, [1989] 19 LS Gaz R 41, EAT 11.9
Cobb v Secretary of State for Employment [1989] ICR 506, [1989] IRLR 464, [1989]
    NLJR 868, EAT 12.8
Cobley v Forward Technology Industries plc [2003] EWCA Civ 646, [2003] ICR 1050,
    [2003] IRLR 706, [2003] 29 LS Gaz R 36, (2003) Times, 15 May, 147 Sol Jo LB 696,
    [2003] All ER (D) 175 (May) 51.14
Cocking v Sandhurst (Stationers) Ltd [1974] ICR 650, [1975] ITR 6, NIRC 19.10
Cofone v Spaghetti House Ltd [1980] ICR 155, EAT 31.16
Coker v Lord Chancellor. See Lord Chancellor v Coker and Osamor
Cold Drawn Tubes Ltd v Middleton [1992] ICR 318, [1992] IRLR 160, EAT 52.2
Coleman v Skyrail Oceanic Ltd (t/a Goodmos Tours). See Skyrail Oceanic Ltd v Coleman
Coleman and Stephenson v Magnet Joinery Ltd [1974] ICR 25, [1973] IRLR 361, 17 KIR
    11, 9 ITR 74, NIRC; affd [1975] ICR 46, [1974] IRLR 343, [1975] KILR 139, CA ... 52.2
Colen v Cebrian (UK) Ltd [2003] EWCA Civ 1676, [2004] ICR 568, [2004] IRLR 210,
    [2004] 02 LS Gaz R 27, (2003) Times, 27 November, [2003] All ER (D) 294 (Nov) 7.15,
    12.16
College of Ripon and York St John v Hobbs [2002] IRLR 185, [2001] All ER (D) 259
    (Nov), EAT 9.2
Collier v Sunday Referee Publishing Co Ltd [1940] 2 KB 647, [1940] 4 All ER 234, 109
    LJKB 974, 84 Sol Jo 538, 164 LT 10, 57 TLR 2 .... 55.21
Collino v Telecom Italia SpA: C-343/98 [2001] All ER (EC) 405, [2000] ECR I-6659,
    [2002] 3 CMLR 997, [2002] ICR 38, [2000] IRLR 788, [2000] All ER (D) 1196,
    ECJ 34.2, 49.3
Collins v John Ansell & Partners Ltd IDS Brief No 659 .... 49.20
Coloroll Pension Trustees Ltd v Russell: C-200/91 [1995] All ER (EC) 23, [1994] ECR
    I-4389, [1995] 2 CMLR 357, [1995] ICR 179, [1994] IRLR 586, [1995] 42 LS Gaz
    R 23, (1994) Times, 30 November, ECJ 22.18, 39.6
Coltman v Bibby Tankers Ltd, The Derbyshire [1988] AC 276, [1987] 3 All ER 1068,
    [1987] 3 WLR 1181, [1988] 1 Lloyd's Rep 109, [1988] ICR 67, 131 Sol Jo 1658,
    [1988] 3 LS Gaz R 36, [1987] NLJ Rep 1157, 1 S & B AvR I/165, HL 25.6
Commission for Racial Equality v Amari Plastics Ltd [1982] QB 265, [1981] 3 WLR 511,
    [1981] ICR 767, [1981] IRLR 340, 125 Sol Jo 694, EAT; affd [1982] QB 1194,
    [1982] 2 All ER 499, [1982] 2 WLR 972, [1982] ICR 304, [1982] IRLR 252, 126
    Sol Jo 227, CA 13.13
Commission for Racial Equality v Dutton [1989] QB 783, [1989] 1 All ER 306, [1989]
    2 WLR 17, [1989] IRLR 8, 133 Sol Jo 19, [1989] 1 LS Gaz R 38, CA 11.6, 11.9
Commission for Racial Equality v Imperial Society of Teachers of Dancing [1983] ICR
    473, [1983] IRLR 315, EAT 11.13, 12.40
Compton v St Regis Paper Co Ltd (23 February, unreported) 54.22
Conlin v United Distillers [1994] IRLR 169, Ct of Sess 19.63
Connolly v Sellars Arenascene Ltd [2001] EWCA Civ 184, [2001] ICR 760, [2001] IRLR
    222, 145 Sol Jo LB 37, [2001] All ER (D) 25 (Feb) 8.3, 15.3
Constantine v McGregor Cory Ltd [2000] ICR 938, EAT 52.1,
    52.13
Construction Industry Training Board v Labour Force Ltd [1970] 3 All ER 220, 114 Sol
    Jo 704, DC 15.3

Table of cases

PARA

Construction Industry Training Board v Leighton [1978] 2 All ER 723, [1978] IRLR 60,
sub nom Leighton v Construction Industry Training Board [1978] ICR 577, EAT 7.9
Conway v Rimmer [1968] AC 910, [1968] 1 All ER 874, [1968] 2 WLR 998, 112 Sol Jo
191, HL 34.6
Cook v Square D Ltd [1992] ICR 262, [1992] PIQR P33, 135 Sol Jo LB 180, sub nom
Square D Ltd v Cook [1992] IRLR 34, CA 25.3
Cook (James W) & Co (Wivenhoe) Ltd (in liquidation) v Tipper [1990] ICR 716, [1990]
IRLR 386, CA 18.25, 18.26, 51.11, 52.13
Cooke v Glenrose Fish Co [2004] ICR 1188, [2004] IRLR 866, [2004] All ER (D) 19 (Jun),
EAT 19.54
Cooper v Metropolitan Police Comr (1985) 82 Cr App Rep 238, DC 42.12
Cooper v Weatherwise (Roofing and Walling) Ltd [1993] ICR 81, EAT 19.71
Coote v Granada Hospitality Ltd: C-185/97 [1998] All ER (EC) 865, [1998] ECR I-5199,
[1998] 3 CMLR 958, [1999] ICR 100, [1998] IRLR 656, ECJ; apld Coote v Granada
Hospitality Ltd (No 2) [1999] 3 CMLR 334, [1999] ICR 942, [1999] IRLR 452,
EAT 11.12, 12.33, 37.4
Coral Leisure Group Ltd v Barnett [1981] ICR 503, [1981] IRLR 204, 125 Sol Jo 374,
EAT 7.15
Corner v Buckinghamshire County Council (1978) 77 LGR 268, [1978] ICR 836, [1978]
IRLR 320, 13 ITR 421, EAT 46.6
Cornwall County Care Ltd v Brightman [1998] ICR 529, [1998] IRLR 228, EAT 49.24
Cort (Robert) & Son Ltd v Charman [1981] ICR 816, [1981] IRLR 437, EAT 45.9, 50.13
Costain Building and Civil Engineering Ltd v Smith [2000] ICR 215, EAT 15.3, 44.2
Council of Civil Service Unions v Minister for the Civil Service [1985] AC 374, [1984]
3 All ER 935, [1984] 3 WLR 1174, [1985] ICR 14, 128 Sol Jo 837, [1985] LS Gaz
R 437, sub nom R v Secretary of State for Foreign and Commonwealth Affairs, ex p
Council of Civil Service Unions [1985] IRLR 28, HL 34.3, 34.4,
34.6
Courage Take Home Trade Ltd v Keys [1986] ICR 874, [1986] IRLR 427, EAT 52.22
Courtaulds Northern Spinning Ltd v Sibson [1988] ICR 451, [1988] IRLR 305, 132 Sol Jo
1033, CA 7.13
Cowan v Scargill [1985] Ch 270, [1984] 2 All ER 750, [1984] 3 WLR 501, [1984] ICR
646, [1984] IRLR 260, 128 Sol Jo 550 .... 39.10
Cowen v Haden Ltd [1983] ICR 1, [1982] IRLR 225, 126 Sol Jo 411, EAT; revsd [1983]
ICR 1, 126 Sol Jo 725, sub nom Haden Ltd v Cowen [1982] IRLR 314, CA 35.7
Cowley v Manson Timber Ltd [1995] ICR 367, [1995] IRLR 153, CA 52.1
Cox v Post Office, IDS Brief No 609 .... 9.14
Cox v Sun Alliance Life Ltd [2001] EWCA Civ 649, [2001] IRLR 448, [2001] All ER (D)
108 (May) 37.4
Cox Toner (W E) (International) Ltd v Crook [1981] ICR 823, [1981] IRLR 443, EAT ... 50.7
Coxall v Goodyear Great Britain Ltd [2002] EWCA Civ 1010, [2003] 1 WLR 536, [2003]
ICR 152, [2002] IRLR 742, (2002) Times, 5 August, [2002] All ER (D) 303 (Jul) 25.8
Coy v Department of Health and Social Security [1985] AC 776, [1985] 2 WLR 866,
[1985] ICR 419, [1985] IRLR 263, 129 Sol Jo 315, HL 50.14
Crawford v Secretary of State for Employment [1995] IRLR 523, EAT 18.27, 29.4
Crawford v Swinton Insurance Brokers Ltd [1990] ICR 85, [1990] IRLR 42, EAT 49.20
Credit Suisse Asset Management Ltd v Armstrong [1996] ICR 882, [1996] IRLR 450,
[1996] 23 LS Gaz R 36, 140 Sol Jo LB 140, CA 38.23, 55.21
Credit Suisse First Boston (Europe) Ltd v Lister [1999] ICR 794, [1998] IRLR 700, [1998]
44 LS Gaz R 35, 142 Sol Jo LB 269, CA 7.22, 38.22
Crédit Suisse First Boston (Europe) Ltd v Padiachy, Winram and Cracknell [1998] 2 CMLR
1322, [1999] ICR 569, [1998] IRLR 504 .... 38.22
Crees v Royal London Mutual Insurance Society Ltd [1998] ICR 848, [1998] IRLR 245,
[1998] 15 LS Gaz R 33, 142 Sol Jo LB 94, 590 IRLB 11, CA 30.21
Cresswell v Inland Revenue Board [1984] 2 All ER 713, [1984] ICR 508, [1984] IRLR
190, 128 Sol Jo 431 .... 7.13
Croft v Cathy Pacific EAT/0367/03 .... 24.11
Croft v Royal Mail Group plc [2003] EWCA Civ 1045, [2003] ICR 1425, [2003] IRLR
592, (2003) Times, 24 July, 147 Sol Jo LB 904, [2002] All ER (D) 179 (Sep) 11.5

PARA

Crofton v Yeboah [2002] EWCA Civ 794, [2002] IRLR 634, (2002) Times, 20 June,
[2002] All ER (D) 512 (May) 11.13, 12.37
Cross v Highlands and Islands Enterprise [2001] IRLR 336, Ct of Sess 25.8, 26.24
Cross v Redpath Dorman Long (Contracting) Ltd [1978] ICR 730, EAT 44.2
Crossley v Faithful & Gould Holdings Ltd [2004] EWCA Civ 293, [2004] 4 All ER 447,
[2004] IRLR 377, [2004] NLJR 653, (2004) Times, 29 March, 148 Sol Jo LB 356,
[2004] All ER (D) 295 (Mar) 7.13
Crosville Motor Services Ltd v Ashfield [1986] IRLR 475, EAT 48.5
Crosville Wales Ltd v Tracey (No 2). See Tracey v Crosville Wales Ltd
Crouch v British Rail Engineering Ltd [1988] IRLR 404, CA 25.5
Crown Estate Comrs v Dorset County Council [1990] Ch 297, [1990] 1 All ER 19, [1990]
2 WLR 89, 88 LGR 132, 60 P & CR 1 .... 19.22
Crown Suppliers (Property Services Agency) v Dawkins [1993] ICR 517, sub nom Dawkins
v Department of the Environment [1993] IRLR 284, CA 11.6
Crowther & Nicholson Ltd, Re (1981) Times, 10 June 55.27
Croydon Health Authority v Jaufurally [1986] ICR 4, EAT 18.25
Cruickshank v VAW Motorcast Ltd [2002] ICR 729, [2002] IRLR 24, [2001] All ER (D)
372 (Oct), EAT 9.2, 9.6
Curling v Securicor Ltd [1992] IRLR 549, EAT 7.13
Curr v Marks & Spencer plc [2002] EWCA Civ 1852, [2003] ICR 443, [2003] IRLR 74,
[2002] All ER (D) 205 (Dec) 6.7

D

D v M [1996] IRLR 192 .... 38.20
DJM International Ltd v Nicholas [1996] ICR 214, [1996] IRLR 76, EAT 49.14
Dabell v Nofotec Co Ltd IDS Brief No 471 .... 49.20
Dabell v Vale Industrial Services (Nottingham) Ltd [1988] IRLR 439, CA 6.9
Dacas v Brook Street Bureau (UK) Ltd [2003] IRLR 190, [2003] All ER (D) 241 (Jan),
EAT; revsd [2004] EWCA Civ 217, [2004] IRLR 358, (2004) Times, 19 March,
[2004] All ER (D) 125 (Mar) 7.3, 15.3, 44.2
Dakri (A) & Co Ltd v Tiffen [1981] ICR 256, [1981] IRLR 57, EAT 35.8
Daley v A E Dorsett (Almar Dolls) Ltd [1982] ICR 1, [1981] IRLR 385, EAT 52.12, 52.13
Daley v Allied Suppliers Ltd [1983] ICR 90, [1983] IRLR 14, EAT 11.12
Dalgleish v Lothian and Borders Police Board [1991] IRLR 422, 1992 SLT 721, Ct of
Sess 10.16
Darr v LRC Products Ltd [1993] IRLR 257, EAT 52.15
Dave v Robinska [2003] ICR 1248, [2003] NLJR 921, [2003] All ER (D) 35 (Jun),
EAT 12.25
David (Lawrence) Ltd v Ashton [1991] 1 All ER 385, [1989] ICR 123, [1989] IRLR 22,
CA 38.21
Davidson v John Calder (Publishers) Ltd [1985] ICR 143, [1985] IRLR 97, EAT 19.71
Davies v M J Wyatt (Decorators) [2000] IRLR 759, EAT 31.6
Davies v McCartneys [1989] ICR 705, [1989] IRLR 439, EAT 22.11
Davies v Neath Port Talbot County Borough Council [1999] ICR 1132, [1999] IRLR 769,
EAT 22.3
Davies v Presbyterian Church of Wales [1986] 1 All ER 705, [1986] 1 WLR 323, [1986]
ICR 280, [1986] IRLR 194, 130 Sol Jo 203, HL 15.3
Davy v Spelthorne Borough Council [1984] AC 262, [1983] 3 All ER 278, [1983] 3 WLR
742, 82 LGR 193, 47 P & CR 310, 127 Sol Jo 733, [1984] JPL 269, HL 34.4
Dawkins v Department of the Environment. See Crown Suppliers (Property Services
Agency) v Dawkins
Dawnay, Day & Co Ltd v de Braconier d'Alphen [1998] ICR 1068, [1997] IRLR 442,
[1997] 26 LS Gaz R 30, 141 Sol Jo LB 129, CA 38.7
Day v T Pickles Farms Ltd [1999] IRLR 217, EAT 26.17
Daynecourt Insurance Brokers Ltd v Iles [1978] IRLR 335, EAT 45.15
Deane v Ealing London Borough Council [1993] ICR 329, [1993] IRLR 209, EAT 11.13,
12.37, 13.8, 34.5
Deary v Mansion Hide Upholstery Ltd [1983] ICR 610, [1983] IRLR 195, 147 JP 311 .... 25.41
Deaway Trading Ltd v Calverley [1973] 3 All ER 776, [1973] ICR 546, NIRC 29.9

Table of cases

PARA

Dedman v British Building and Engineering Appliances Ltd [1974] 1 All ER 520, [1974] 1 WLR 171, [1974] ICR 53, [1973] IRLR 379, 16 KIR 1, 9 ITR 100, 117 Sol Jo 938, CA 18.23, 50.13

De Francesco v Barnum (1890) 45 Ch D 430, 60 LJ Ch 63, 39 WR 5, [1886-90] All ER Rep 414, 63 LT 438, 6 TLR 463 .... 3.10

Defrenne v Sabena: 43/75 [1981] 1 All ER 122, [1976] ECR 455, [1976] 2 CMLR 98, [1976] ICR 547, ECJ 22.9, 22.19, 22.20, 22.22, 23.2

De Grasse v Stockwell Tools Ltd [1992] IRLR 269, EAT 51.11

De Haney v Brent Mind [2003] EWCA Civ 1637, [2004] ICR 348, [2003] 45 LS Gaz R 29, (2003) Times, 11 November, 147 Sol Jo LB 1275, [2003] All ER (D) 444 (Oct) 20.2

De Keyser Ltd v Wilson [2001] IRLR 324, [2001] All ER (D) 237 (Mar), EAT 9.2, 19.14, 28.7

Dekker v Stichting Vormingscentrum voor Jong Volwassenen (VJV - Centrum) Plus: 177/88 [1990] ECR I-3941, [1992] ICR 325, [1991] IRLR 27, ECJ 11.5

Delabole Slate Ltd v Berriman. See Berriman v Delabole Slate Ltd

Delaney v Staples (t/a De Montfort Recruitment) [1991] 2 QB 47, [1991] 1 All ER 609, [1991] 2 WLR 627, [1991] ICR 331, [1991] IRLR 112, CA; affd [1992] 1 AC 687, [1992] 1 All ER 944, [1992] 2 WLR 451, [1992] ICR 483, [1992] IRLR 191, [1992] 15 LS Gaz R 32, 136 Sol Jo LB 91, HL 31.6, 43.8, 45.9, 45.10

Delauche v EC Commission: 111/86 [1987] ECR 5345, [1989] 2 CMLR 565, ECJ 34.8

Dench v Flynn & Partners [1998] IRLR 653, CA 52.12

Denham v Midland Employers' Mutual Assurance Ltd [1955] 2 QB 437, [1955] 2 All ER 561, [1955] 3 WLR 84, [1955] 1 Lloyd's Rep 467, 99 Sol Jo 417, CA 44.2

Denise v M J Wyatt (Decorators) Ltd [2000] IRLR 759, EAT 27.4

Dentmaster (UK) Ltd v Kent [1997] IRLR 636, CA 38.15

Department for Work and Pensions v Thompson [2004] IRLR 348, EAT 11.5, 18.8

Department of Education and Science v Taylor [1992] IRLR 308 ....19.17, 19.24

Department of Health v Bruce (1992) Times, 31 December, EAT 34.3

Department of Health and Social Security v Hughes. See Hughes v Department of Health and Social Security

Department of the Environment, Food and Rural Affairs v Robertson (2004) IDS Brief No 750 .... 22.9

Department of Transport v Gallacher [1994] ICR 967, [1994] IRLR 231, CA 48.18

Depledge v Pye Telecommunications Ltd [1981] ICR 82, [1980] IRLR 390, EAT 46.2

Derby Daily Telegraph Ltd v Foss, IDS Brief No 471 .... 52.21

Derby Daily Telegraph Ltd v Pensions Ombudsman [1999] ICR 1057, [1999] IRLR 476, [1999] All ER (D) 300 .... 39.3

Derby Specialist Fabrication Ltd v Burton [2001] 2 All ER 840, [2001] ICR 833, [2001] IRLR 69, [2000] All ER (D) 1348, EAT 18.29

Derbyshire, The. See Coltman v Bibby Tankers Ltd, The Derbyshire

Derbyshire County Council v Times Newspapers Ltd [1993] AC 534, [1993] 1 All ER 1011, [1993] 2 WLR 449, 91 LGR 179, [1993] 14 LS Gaz R 46, [1993] NLJR 283, 137 Sol Jo LB 52, 81, HL 28.5

Deria v General Council of British Shipping [1986] 1 WLR 1207, [1986] ICR 172, [1986] IRLR 108, 130 Sol Jo 649, [1986] LS Gaz R 2996, CA 12.15

De Souza v Automobile Association [1986] ICR 514, [1986] IRLR 103, 130 Sol Jo 110, [1986] LS Gaz R 288, CA 11.12

D'Souza v Lambeth London Borough Council [2003] UKHL 33, [2003] 4 All ER 1113, [2003] 2 CMLR 1329, [2003] ICR 867, [2003] IRLR 484, 74 BMLR 109, [2003] 30 LS Gaz R 30, (2003) Times, 23 June, 147 Sol Jo LB 782, [2003] All ER (D) 258 (Jun) 9.17, 11.12

D'Souza v Lambeth London Borough [1997] IRLR 677, EAT; revsd sub nom Lambeth London Borough v D'Souza [1999] IRLR 240, CA 13.8

D'Souza v Lambeth London Borough (2001) IDS Brief No 688 .... 11.10

D'Souza v Lambeth London Borough Council [2003] UKHL 33, [2003] 4 All ER 1113, [2003] 2 CMLR 1329, [2003] ICR 867, [2003] IRLR 484, 74 BMLR 109, [2003] 30 LS Gaz R 30, 147 Sol Jo LB 782 ....11.12, 12.33

PARA

Dethier (Jules) Equipement SA v Dassy and Sovam SPRL (in liquidation): C-319/94 [1998]
All ER (EC) 346, [1998] ECR I-1061, [1998] 2 CMLR 611, [1998] ICR 541, [1998]
IRLR 266, ECJ 49.7, 49.20
d'Urso v Ercole Marelli Elettromeccanica Generale SpA: C-362/89 [1991] ECR I-4105,
[1993] 3 CMLR 513, [1992] IRLR 136, ECJ 49.20, 49.23
Deutsche Telekom AG v Schröder: C-50/96 [2000] ECR I-743, [2002] 2 CMLR 583,
[2000] IRLR 353, ECJ 22.18
Devenney v United Kingdom (Application 24265/94) (2002) Times, 11 April, ECtHR 28.4
Devine v Designer Flowers Wholesale Florist Sundries Ltd [1993] IRLR 517, EAT 52.12
Devis (W) & Sons Ltd v Atkins [1977] AC 931, [1977] 2 All ER 321, [1977] 2 WLR 70,
[1977] ICR 377, [1976] IRLR 428, 12 ITR 12, 121 Sol Jo 52, CA; affd [1977] AC
931, [1977] 3 All ER 40, [1977] 3 WLR 214, [1977] ICR 662, [1977] IRLR 314,
13 ITR 71, 121 Sol Jo 512, 8 BLR 57, HL 4.3, 51.1, 51.10, 52.13
Devlin v United Kingdom (Application 29545/95) [2002] IRLR 155, (2001) Times, 9
November, [2001] ECHR 29545/95 , ECtHR 28.4
Devon County Council v Cook [1977] IRLR 188, EAT 55.5
Devonald v Rosser & Sons [1906] 2 KB 728, 75 LJKB 688, [1904-7] All ER Rep 988, 50
Sol Jo 616, 95 LT 232, 22 TLR 682, CA 55.21
Devonshire v Trico-Folberth Ltd [1989] ICR 747, sub nom Trico-Folberth Ltd v Devonshire
[1989] IRLR 396, CA 52.13
Dhaliwal v British Airways Board [1985] ICR 513, EAT 51.9
Dhatt v McDonalds Hamburgers Ltd [1991] 3 All ER 692, [1991] 1 WLR 527, [1991] ICR
238, [1991] IRLR 130, CA 11.5, 12.18
Dibro Ltd v Hore [1990] ICR 370, [1990] IRLR 129, [1990] 13 LS Gaz R 43, EAT 22.8
Dick v Boots the Chemist Ltd IDS Brief No 451 .... 51.11
Dick v University of Glasgow [1993] IRLR 581, Ct of Sess 51.4
Dietman v Brent London Borough Council [1987] ICR 737, [1987] IRLR 259; affd [1988]
ICR 842, [1988] IRLR 299, CA 7.23, 55.7, 55.17,
55.18
Dietrich v Westdeutscher Rundfunk: C-11/99 [2000] ECR I-5589, ECJ 26.6
Dietz v Stichting Thuiszorg Rotterdam: C-435/93 [1996] ECR I-5223, [1997] 1 CMLR
199, [1996] IRLR 692, 563 IRLB 13, ECJ 22.17, 22.18
Digital Equipment Co Ltd v Clements (No 2) [1998] ICR 258, [1998] IRLR 134, [1998]
03 LS Gaz R 24, CA 13.8, 20.25, 52.13
Dillenkofer v Germany: C-178/94, C-179/94, C-188/94, C-189/94 and C-190/94 [1997]
QB 259, [1996] All ER (EC) 917, [1997] 2 WLR 253, [1996] ECR I-4845, [1996]
3 CMLR 469, [1997] IRLR 60, ECJ 23.2
Dimbleby & Sons Ltd v National Union of Journalists [1984] 1 All ER 117, [1984] 1 WLR
67, [1984] ICR 386, [1984] IRLR 67, 128 Sol Jo 64, [1984] LS Gaz R 515, CA; affd
[1984] 1 All ER 751, [1984] 1 WLR 427, [1984] ICR 386, [1984] IRLR 161, 128
Sol Jo 189, HL 42.16
Dimskal Shipping Co SA v International Transport Workers' Federation, The Evia Luck
(No 2) [1992] 2 AC 152, [1991] 4 All ER 871, [1991] 3 WLR 875, [1992] 1 Lloyd's
Rep 115, [1992] ICR 37, [1992] IRLR 78, HL 42.16
Dimtsu v Westminster City Council [1991] IRLR 450, EAT 13.3
Dines v Initial Health Care Services [1995] ICR 11, [1994] IRLR 336, CA 49.5
DPP v Fidler [1992] 1 WLR 91, 94 Cr App Rep 286, 156 JP 257, [1992] Crim LR 62,
DC 42.12
DPP v Jones [1999] 2 AC 240, [1999] 2 All ER 257, [1999] 2 WLR 625, [1999] 2 Cr
App Rep 348, 163 JP 285, [1999] Crim LR 672, [1999] 11 LS Gaz R 71, [1999] 13
LS Gaz R 31, 6 BHRC 513, [1999] EGCS 36, 143 Sol Jo LB 98, [1999] 3 LRC 699,
HL 42.12
DPP v Marshall [1998] ICR 518, EAT 18.30
Discount Tobacco and Confectionery Ltd v Armitage [1990] IRLR 15, [1995] ICR 431n,
EAT 51.3
Discount Tobacco and Confectionery Ltd v Williamson [1993] ICR 371, [1993] IRLR 327,
EAT 31.6
Dispatch Management Services (UK) Ltd v Douglas [2002] IRLR 389, [2001] All ER (D)
26 (Dec), EAT 19.55, 28.7

Table of cases

PARA

Divine-Bortey v Brent London Borough Council [1998] ICR 886, [1998] IRLR 525, [1998] 22 LS Gaz R 29, 142 Sol Jo LB 152, CA 13.4, 19.26

Dixon v BBC [1979] QB 546, [1979] 2 All ER 112, [1979] 2 WLR 647, [1979] ICR 281, [1979] IRLR 114, 122 Sol Jo 713, CA 50.6

Dixon and Shaw v West Ella Developments Ltd [1978] ICR 856, [1978] IRLR 151, 13 ITR 235, EAT 51.3

Dixon Stores Group v Arnold EAT/772/93 .... 18.26

Dobie v Burns International Security Services (UK) Ltd [1984] 3 All ER 333, [1985] 1 WLR 43, [1984] ICR 812, [1984] IRLR 329, 128 Sol Jo 872, CA 20.19

Donaldson v Perth and Kinross Council [2004] ICR 667, [2004] IRLR 121, [2003] All ER (D) 416 (Dec) 49.7

Donnelly v Kelvin International Services [1992] IRLR 496, EAT 6.7

Doolan v United Kingdom [2002] IRLR 580, ECtHR 28.4

Doshoki v Draeger Ltd [2002] IRLR 340, [2002] All ER (D) 139 (Mar), EAT 13.8

Doughty v Rolls-Royce plc [1992] 1 CMLR 1045, [1992] IRLR 126, sub nom Rolls-Royce plc v Doughty [1992] ICR 538, CA 34.7

Doyle v White City Stadium Ltd [1935] 1 KB 110, 104 LJKB 140, [1934] All ER Rep 252, 78 Sol Jo 601, 152 LT 32, CA 3.10

Drage v Governors of Greenford High School [2000] ICR 899, [2000] IRLR 314, 144 Sol Jo LB 165, [2000] All ER (D) 343, CA 18.23

Drew v St Edmundsbury Borough Council [1980] ICR 513, [1980] IRLR 459, EAT 51.3

Drinkwater Sabey Ltd v Burnett [1995] ICR 328, [1995] IRLR 238, EAT 19.10

Driskel v Peninsula Business Services Ltd [2000] IRLR 151, EAT 11.12

Dryden v Greater Glasgow Health Board [1992] IRLR 469, EAT 26.23

Dudley Bower Building Services Ltd v Lowe [2003] ICR 843, [2003] IRLR 260, [2003] All ER (D) 243 (Feb), EAT 49.5

Duffy v Yeomans & Partners Ltd [1993] ICR 862, [1993] IRLR 368, EAT; affd [1995] ICR 1, [1994] IRLR 642, CA 19.60, 51.4, 51.11

Dugdale v Kraft Foods Ltd [1977] 1 All ER 454, [1976] 1 WLR 1288, [1977] ICR 48, [1976] IRLR 368, 11 ITR 309, 120 Sol Jo 780, EAT 22.6

Dugmore v Swansea NHS Trust [2002] EWCA Civ 1689, [2003] 1 All ER 333, [2003] ICR 574, [2003] IRLR 164, 72 BMLR 22, [2003] 05 LS Gaz R 30, (2002) Times, 9 December, 146 Sol Jo LB 271, [2002] All ER (D) 307 (Nov) 26.25

Duke v GEC Reliance Ltd (formerly Reliance Systems Ltd) [1988] AC 618, [1988] 1 All ER 626, [1988] 2 WLR 359, [1988] 1 CMLR 719, [1988] ICR 339, [1988] IRLR 118, 132 Sol Jo 226, [1988] 11 LS Gaz R 42, HL 23.2

Duncan Web Offset (Maidstone) Ltd v Cooper [1995] IRLR 633, EAT 49.11

Dundon v GPT Ltd [1995] IRLR 403, EAT 51.3, 51.11

Dunk v George Waller & Son Ltd [1970] 2 QB 163, [1970] 2 All ER 630, [1970] 2 WLR 1241, 114 Sol Jo 356, CA 14.2, 55.29

Dunlop Ltd v Farrell [1993] ICR 885, EAT 52.13

Dunlop Pneumatic Tyre Co Ltd v New Garage and Motor Co Ltd [1915] AC 79, 83 LJKB 1574, [1914-15] All ER Rep 739, 111 LT 862, 30 TLR 625, HL 55.27

Dunlop Tyres Ltd v Blows [2001] EWCA Civ 1032, [2001] IRLR 629, [2001] All ER (D) 179 (Jun) 5.3, 7.10, 31.6

Dunn v R [1896] 1 QB 116, 60 JP 117, 65 LJQB 279, 44 WR 243, [1895-9] All ER Rep 907, 40 Sol Jo 129, 73 LT 695, 12 TLR 101, CA 34.3

Dunnachie v Kingston-Upon-Hull City Council [2004] EWCA Civ 84, [2004] 2 All ER 501, [2004] ICR 481, [2004] IRLR 287, [2004] NLJR 248, (2004) Times, 26 February, 148 Sol Jo LB 233, [2004] All ER (D) 185 (Feb); revsd [2004] UKHL 36,[2004] 3 All ER 1011, [2004] 3 WLR 310, [2004] ICR 1052, [2004] IRLR 727, [2004] 33 LS Gaz R 34, [2004] NLJR 1156, 148 Sol Jo LB 909, [2004] All ER (D) 251 (Jul) 7.23, 52.12

Duport Steels Ltd v Sirs [1980] 1 All ER 529, [1980] 1 WLR 142, [1980] ICR 161, [1980] IRLR 116, 124 Sol Jo 133, HL 42.5

Durant v Clariston Clothing Co Ltd [1974] IRLR 360, IT 51.14

Duru v Granada Retail Catering Ltd EAT/281/00, IDS Brief No 697 .... 19.32

Dutton v Hawker Siddeley Aviation Ltd [1978] ICR 1057, [1978] IRLR 390, EAT 46.7

Dutton & Clark Ltd v Daly [1985] ICR 780, [1985] IRLR 363, EAT 7.13, 26.26

Dyke v Hereford and Worcester County Council [1989] ICR 800, EAT 34.1, 51.11

E
EC Commission v Belgium: C-229/89 [1991] ECR I-2205, [1993] 2 CMLR 403, [1991]
    IRLR 393, ECJ 12.8
EC Commission v Belgium: C-173/91 [1993] IRLR 404, ECJ 22.3
EC Commission v United Kingdom of Great Britain and Northern Ireland: 61/81 [1982]
    ECR 2601, [1982] 3 CMLR 284, [1982] ICR 578, [1982] IRLR 333, ECJ 23.6
EC Commission v United Kingdom: 165/82 [1984] 1 All ER 353, [1983] ECR 3431,
    [1984] 1 CMLR 44, [1984] ICR 192, [1984] IRLR 29, ECJ 23.6
EC Commission v United Kingdom: C-382/92 [1994] ECR I-2435, [1995] 1 CMLR 345,
    [1994] ICR 664, [1994] IRLR 392, ECJ 16.12, 23.2, 49.18
EC Commission v United Kingdom: C-383/92 [1994] ECR I-2479, [1995] 1 CMLR 345,
    [1994] ICR 664, [1994] IRLR 412, ECJ 23.8, 23.9
ECM (Vehicle Delivery Service) v Cox [1999] 4 All ER 669, [2000] 1 CMLR 224, [1999]
    ICR 1162, [1999] IRLR 559, [1999] All ER (D) 838, CA 49.5
EFTA Surveillance Authority v Norway: E-1/02 [2003] 1 CMLR 725, [2003] IRLR 318,
    EFTA Ct 11.12, 12.9
EMI Group Electronics Ltd v Coldicott (Inspector of Taxes) [2000] 1 WLR 540, [1999]
    STC 803, 71 TC 455, [1999] IRLR 630, [1999] 32 LS Gaz R 34, 143 Sol Jo LB 220,
    [1999] All ER (D) 803, CA 43.8, 45.10, 55.21
Eagland v British Telecommunications plc [1993] ICR 644, [1992] IRLR 323, CA 7.9
Ealing London Borough v Race Relations Board [1972] AC 342, [1972] 1 All ER 105,
    [1972] 2 WLR 71, 116 Sol Jo 60, HL 11.6
Earl v Slater & Wheeler (Airlyne) Ltd [1973] 1 All ER 145, [1973] 1 WLR 51, [1972]
    ICR 508, [1972] IRLR 115, 13 KIR 319, 8 ITR 33, 117 Sol Jo 14, NIRC 51.2
East Berkshire Health Authority v Matadeen [1992] ICR 723, [1992] IRLR 336, [1992]
    29 LS Gaz R 24, EAT 20.7, 20.17
East Lindsey District Council v Daubney [1977] ICR 566, [1977] IRLR 181, 12 ITR 359,
    EAT 51.8
Eastwood v Magnox Electric plc [2004] UKHL 35, [2004] 3 All ER 991, [2004] 3 WLR
    322, [2004] ICR 1064, [2004] IRLR 733, [2004] NLJR 1155, 148 Sol Jo LB 909,
    [2004] All ER (D) 268 (Jul) 7.13, 7.23, 50.7
Eaton v Robert Eaton Ltd [1988] ICR 302, [1988] IRLR 83, EAT 29.2
Eaton Ltd v Nuttall [1977] 3 All ER 1131, [1977] 1 WLR 549, [1977] ICR 272, [1977]
    IRLR 71, 12 ITR 197, 121 Sol Jo 353, EAT 22.6
Ebac Ltd v Wymer [1995] ICR 466, EAT 35.12
Ecclestone v National Union of Journalists [1999] IRLR 166 .... 47.14
Edge v Pensions Ombudsman [2000] Ch 602, [1999] 4 All ER 546, [2000] 3 WLR 79,
    [2000] ICR 748, [1999] PLR 215, [1999] 35 LS Gaz R 39, [1999] NLJR 1442,
    CA 39.12
Edmonds v Lawson [2000] IRLR 18, [1999] 39 LS Gaz R 38, 143 Sol Lo LB 234, [1999]
    All ER (D) 1035; revsd [2000] QB 501, [2000] 2 WLR 1091, [2000] ICR 567,
    [2000] IRLR 391, 144 Sol Jo LB 151, [2000] All ER (D) 312, CA 14.2, 31.9
Edwards v Derby City Council [1999] ICR 114, EAT 22.14
Edwards v National Coal Board [1949] 1 KB 704, [1949] 1 All ER 743, 93 Sol Jo 337, 65
    TLR 430, CA 25.5
Edwards v Society of Graphical and Allied Trades [1971] Ch 354, [1970] 3 All ER 689,
    [1970] 3 WLR 713, 114 Sol Jo 618, CA 48.12
Egg Stores (Stamford Hill) Ltd v Leibovici [1977] ICR 260, [1976] IRLR 376, 11 ITR 289,
    EAT 45.3
Eidesund v Stavanger Catering A/S: E-2/95 [1997] 2 CMLR 672, [1996] IRLR 684, EFTA,
    EFTA Ct 49.15
Ekpe v Metropolitan Police Comr [2001] ICR 1084, [2001] All ER (D) 353 (May), [2001]
    IRLR 605, EAT 9.2, 9.4
Elkouil v Coney Island Ltd [2002] IRLR 174, [2001] All ER (D) 181 (Nov), EAT 52.13
Elliott Turbomachinery Ltd v Bates [1981] ICR 218, EAT 35.7
Eltek (UK) Ltd v Thomson [2000] ICR 689, EAT 19.10
Elvidge v Coventry City Council [1994] QB 241, [1993] 4 All ER 903, [1993] 3 WLR
    976, [1994] ICR 68, 26 HLR 281, CA 40.7
Ely v YKK Fasteners (UK) Ltd [1993] IRLR 500, CA 51.1

Table of cases

PARA

Emmott v Minister for Social Welfare and A-G: C-208/90 [1991] ECR I-4269, [1991] 3 CMLR 894, [1993] ICR 8, [1991] IRLR 387, ECJ 18.33, 23.2
Employees of the Consiglio Nazionale delle Ricerche, Re, EC Commisison v Italy: 225/85 [1988] ECR 2271, [1988] 3 CMLR 635, ECJ 34.7
Employment Service v Nathan EAT/1316/95, IDS Brief No 568 .... 19.38
Enderby v Frenchay Health Authority [1991] 1 CMLR 626, [1991] ICR 382, [1991] IRLR 44, EAT; on appeal [1994] ICR 112, [1992] IRLR 15, CA; refd C-127/92: [1994] 1 All ER 495, [1993] ECR I-5535, [1994] 1 CMLR 8, [1994] ICR 112, [1993] IRLR 591, ECJ 20.27, 22.10, 22.11
Enderby v Frenchay Health Authority (No 2) [1999] IRLR 155, EAT; affd [2000] ICR 612, [2000] IRLR 257, CA 22.5, 22.9
English v Emery Reimbold & Strick Ltd [2002] EWCA Civ 605, [2002] 3 All ER 385, [2003] IRLR 710 .... 19.63, 20.11
English v UNISON (2000) IDS Brief No 668 .... 48.22
Equal Opportunities Commission v Birmingham City Council. See Birmingham City Council v Equal Opportunities Commission
Equal Opportunities Commission v Secretary of State for Employment. See R v Secretary of State for Employment, ex p Equal Opportunities Commission
Equal Opportunities Commission for Northern Ireland's Application, Re [1989] IRLR 64 ...... 22.11
Essa v Laing Ltd [2003] ICR 1110, [2003] IRLR 346, [2003] 18 LS Gaz R 34, (2003) Times, 7 April, [2003] All ER (D) 215 (Feb), EAT; affd [2004] EWCA Civ 02, [2004] ICR 746, [2004] IRLR 313, (2004) Times, 29 January, 148 Sol Jo LB 146, [2004] All ER (D) 155 (Jan) 13.8
Esso Petroleum Co Ltd v Harper's Garage (Stourport) Ltd [1968] AC 269, [1967] 1 All ER 699, [1967] 2 WLR 871, 111 Sol Jo 174, 201 Estates Gazette 1043, HL 38.1
Esso Petroleum Co Ltd v Jarvis (EAT 0831/00) 44.2
Etam plc v Rowan [1989] IRLR 150, EAT 12.3
Euro-Diam Ltd v Bathurst [1990] 1 QB 1, [1988] 2 All ER 23, [1988] 2 WLR 517, [1988] 1 Lloyd's Rep 228, 132 Sol Jo 372, [1988] 9 LS Gaz R 45, CA 7.15
Euroguard Ltd v Rycroft IDS Brief No 498 .... 51.11
Europieces SA v Saunders IDS Brief No 627, ECJ 49.7
Evans v Malley Organisation Ltd (t/a First Business Support) [2002] EWCA Civ 1834, [2003] ICR 432, [2003] IRLR 156, (2003) Times, 23 January, [2002] All ER (D) 397 (Nov) 27.4
Evening Standard Co Ltd v Henderson [1987] ICR 588, [1987] IRLR 64, CA 7.24
Everson v Secretary of State for Trade and Industry: C-198/98 [1999] ECR I-8903, [2000] All ER (EC) 29, [2000] 1 CMLR 489, [2000] IRLR 202, ECJ 29.3
Evia Luck (No 2), The. See Dimskal Shipping Co SA v International Transport Workers' Federation, The Evia Luck (No 2)
Export Credits Guarantee Department v Universal Oil Products Co [1983] 2 All ER 205, [1983] 1 WLR 399, [1983] 2 Lloyd's Rep 152, 127 Sol Jo 408, 23 BLR 106, 133 NLJ 662, HL 55.27
Express and Echo Publications Ltd v Tanton [1999] ICR 693, [1999] IRLR 367, [1999] 14 LS Gaz R 31, [1999] All ER (D) 256, CA 15.3
Express and Star Ltd v National Graphical Association [1986] ICR 589, [1986] IRLR 222, [1986] LS Gaz R 2083, CA 42.16, 47.16
Express Newspapers v Keys [1980] IRLR 247 .... 42.4
Express Newspapers Ltd v McShane [1980] AC 672, [1980] 1 All ER 65, [1980] 2 WLR 89, [1980] ICR 42, 124 Sol Jo 30, sub nom McShane and Ashton v Express Newspapers Ltd [1980] IRLR 35, HL 42.5
Expro Gulf v Birnie UKEAT/0222/04/DA 24.11

F

FS Consulting v McCaul [2002] STC (SCD) 138 .... 43.35
FSS Travel and Leisure Systems Ltd v Johnson [1999] FSR 505, [1998] IRLR 382, CA 38.9
Faccenda Chicken Ltd v Fowler [1987] Ch 117, [1986] 1 All ER 617, [1986] 3 WLR 288, [1986] FSR 291, [1986] ICR 297, [1986] IRLR 69, 130 Sol Jo 573, CA 38.9
Faccini Dori v Recreb Srl: C-91/92 [1995] All ER (EC) 1, [1994] ECR I-3325, [1995] 1 CMLR 665, ECJ 23.2

PARA

Facey v Midas Retail Security [2001] ICR 287, [2000] IRLR 812, EAT 20.12
Fairchild v Glenhaven Funeral Services Ltd [2001] EWCA Civ 1881, [2002] 1 WLR 1052,
    [2002] ICR 412, [2002] IRLR 129, [2001] All ER (D) 125 (Dec); revsd [2002] UKHL 22,
    [2003] 1 AC 32, [2002] 3 All ER 305, [2002] ICR 798, [2002] IRLR 533, 67 BMLR
    90, [2002] NLJR 998, [2003] 1 LRC 674, [2002] All ER (D) 139 (Jun) 25.14
Fairfield Ltd v Skinner [1992] ICR 836, [1993] IRLR 4, [1992] 34 LS Gaz R 39, EAT 31.6
Fairhurst Ward Abbotts Ltd v Botes Building Ltd [2004] EWCA Civ 83, [2004] ICR 919,
    [2004] IRLR 304, 148 Sol Jo LB 235, [2004] All ER (D) 225 (Feb) 49.3
Falconer v ASLEF and NUR [1986] IRLR 331, [1986] BTLC 258, Cty Ct 42.18
Falkirk Council v Whyte [1997] IRLR 560, EAT 11.8
Family Benefits for Community Civil Servants, Re, EC Commission v Belgium: 186/85
    [1987] ECR 2029, [1988] 2 CMLR 759, ECJ 34.8
Fantask A/S v Industriministeriet (Erhvervsministeriet): C-188/95 [1998] All ER (EC) 1,
    [1997] ECR I-6783, [1998] 1 CMLR 473, ECJ 23.2
Farnsworth (F W) Ltd v McCoid [1998] IRLR 362, EAT; affd [1999] ICR 1047, [1999]
    IRLR 626, [1999] 16 LS Gaz R 35, CA 48.18
Farrant v Woodroffe School [1998] ICR 184, [1998] IRLR 176, EAT 51.9
Farrow v Wilson (1869) LR 4 CP 744, 38 LJCP 326, 18 WR 43, [1861-73] All ER Rep
    846, 20 LT 810 .... 55.8
Faust v Power Packing Casemakers. See Power Packing Casemakers v Faust
Fay v North Yorkshire County Council (1986) 85 LGR 87, [1986] ICR 133, sub nom North
    Yorkshire County Council v Fay [1985] IRLR 247, CA 44.7, 51.14
Fennelly v Connex South Eastern Ltd [2001] IRLR 390, [2000] All ER (D) 2233, CA 53.2
Fentiman v Fluid Engineering Products Ltd [1991] ICR 570, [1991] IRLR 150, EAT 52.12
Fenton v Stablegold Ltd (t/a Chiswick Court Hotel) [1986] ICR 236, [1986] IRLR 64,
    EAT 52.7
Ferenc-Batchelor v London Underground Ltd [2003] ICR 656, [2003] IRLR 252, [2003]
    All ER (D) 252 (Mar), EAT 48.22
Ferguson v Gateway Training Centre Ltd [1991] ICR 658, EAT 19.60
Ferguson v Prestwick Circuits Ltd [1992] IRLR 266, EAT 51.11
Ferguson v Welsh [1987] 3 All ER 777, [1987] 1 WLR 1553, 86 LGR 153, [1988] IRLR 112,
    131 Sol Jo 1552, [1987] LS Gaz R 3581, [1987] NLJ Rep 1037, HL 25.15
Fernandez v McDonald [2003] EWCA Civ 1219, [2003] 4 All ER 1033, [2004] 1 WLR
    1027, [2004] HLR 189, [2003] 42 EG 128, [2003] 34 LS Gaz R 33, (2003) Times, 9
    October, 147 Sol Jo LB 995, [2003] All ER (D) 94 (Aug) 40.6
Finalarte Sociedade de Construção Civil Lda v Urlaubs- und Lohnausgleichskasse der
    Bauwirtschaft: C-49/98, C-50/98, C-52/98 to C-54/98 and C-68/98 to C-71/98 [2001]
    ECR I-7831, [2003] 2 CMLR 333, [2001] All ER (D) 361 (Oct), ECJ 24.3
Financial Techniques (Planning Services) Ltd v Hughes [1981] IRLR 32, CA 50.7
Financial Times Ltd v Byrne (No 2) [1992] IRLR 163, EAT 22.11
Fire Brigades Union v Fraser [1998] IRLR 697, Ct of Sess 12.26
First Castle Electronics Ltd v West [1989] ICR 72, EAT 19.22
First Point International Ltd v Department of Trade and Industry (1999) 164 JP 89, [1999]
    All ER (D) 898, DC 44.3
Fisher v California Cake and Cookie Ltd [1997] IRLR 212, EAT 52.13
Fisscher v Voorhuis Hengelo BV: C-128/93 [1995] All ER (EC) 193, [1994] ECR I-4583,
    [1995] 1 CMLR 881, [1995] ICR 635, [1994] IRLR 662, ECJ 18.12, 22.18, 23.2
Fitzgerald v Hall, Russell & Co Ltd [1970] AC 984, [1969] 3 All ER 1140, [1969] 3 WLR
    868, [1969] 2 Lloyd's Rep 514, 7 KIR 263, 5 ITR 1, 113 Sol Jo 899, 1970 SC 1,
    1970 SLT 37, HL 44.8
Fitzgerald v University of Kent at Canterbury [2004] EWCA Civ 143, [2004] ICR 737,
    [2004] IRLR 300, [2004] 11 LS Gaz R 34, (2004) Times, 4 March, 148 Sol Jo LB
    237, [2004] All ER (D) 262 (Feb) 18.23, 50.13
Fitzpatrick v British Railways Board [1992] ICR 221, [1991] IRLR 376, CA 51.3
Flack v Kodak Ltd [1986] 2 All ER 1003, [1987] 1 WLR 31, [1986] ICR 775, [1986]
    IRLR 255, 130 Sol Jo 713, [1986] LS Gaz R 2238, CA 6.7
Fletcher v Clay Cross (Quarry Services) Ltd. See Clay Cross (Quarry Services) Ltd v Fletcher
Fogarty v United Kingdom (Application 37112/97) [2002] IRLR 148, 12 BHRC 132,
    ECtHR 12.20, 28.4

Table of cases

PARA

Folami v Nigerline (UK) Ltd [1978] ICR 277, EAT 8.3
Forbuoys Ltd v Rich EAT/144/01 .... 54.22
Ford v Milthorn Toleman Ltd [1980] IRLR 30, CA 50.7
Ford v Stakis Hotels and Inns Ltd [1987] ICR 943, [1988] IRLR 46, [1987] LS Gaz R 2192,
    EAT 18.21
Ford v Warwickshire County Council [1983] 2 AC 71, [1983] 1 All ER 753, [1983] 2
    WLR 399, 81 LGR 326, [1983] ICR 273, [1983] IRLR 126, 127 Sol Jo 154, HL 6.7, 44.8
Foreningen af Arbejdsledere i Danmark v Daddy's Dance Hall A/S: 324/86 [1988] ECR 739,
    [1989] 2 CMLR 517, [1988] IRLR 315, ECJ 38.22, 49.4, 49.24
Fosca Services (UK) Ltd v Birkett [1996] IRLR 325, EAT 7.23, 55.25
Foster v British Gas plc: C-188/89 [1991] 1 QB 405, [1990] 3 All ER 897, [1991] 2 WLR
    258, [1990] ECR I-3313, [1990] 2 CMLR 833, [1991] ICR 84, [1990] IRLR 353,
    ECJ; apld [1991] 2 AC 306, [1991] 2 All ER 705, [1991] 2 WLR 1075, [1991] 2
    CMLR 217, [1991] ICR 463, [1991] IRLR 268, [1991] 18 LS Gaz R 34, HL 23.2, 34.7
Foster v South Glamorgan Health Authority [1988] ICR 526, [1988] IRLR 277, [1988]
    15 LS Gaz R 37, EAT 18.30
Foster Clark Ltd's Indenture Trusts, Re, Loveland v Horscroft [1966] 1 All ER 43, [1966]
    1 WLR 125, 110 Sol Jo 108 .... 29.9, 55.9
Fozard v Greater Manchester Police Authority IDS Brief No 601 .... 9.12
Francovich and Bonifaci v Italy: C-6/90 and C-9/90 [1991] ECR I-5357, [1993] 2 CMLR
    66, [1995] ICR 722, [1992] IRLR 84, ECJ 23.2
Franks v Reuters Ltd [2003] EWCA Civ 417, [2003] ICR 1166, [2003] IRLR 423, [2003]
    25 LS Gaz R 45, (2003) Times, 23 April, 147 Sol Jo LB 474, [2003] All ER (D) 160
    (Apr) 7.3, 15.3, 44.2
Fraser v State Hospitals Board for Scotland 2001 SLT 1051, 2001 SCLR 357, Ct of Sess .. 26.24
Freeman v Sovereign Chicken Ltd [1991] ICR 853, [1991] IRLR 408, EAT 19.32
French v Barclays Bank plc [1998] IRLR 646, CA 52.12
Freud v Bentalls Ltd [1983] ICR 77, [1982] IRLR 443, EAT 51.11
Friend v Institution of Professional Managers and Specialists [1999] IRLR 173 .... 48.23
Frost v Chief Constable of South Yorkshire Police [1998] QB 254, [1997] 1 All ER 540,
    [1997] 3 WLR 1194, [1997] IRLR 173, 33 BMLR 108, [1996] NLJR 1651, CA; revsd
    sub nom White v Chief Constable of South Yorkshire Police [1999] 2 AC 455, [1999]
    1 All ER 1, [1998] 3 WLR 1509, [1999] ICR 216, [1999] IRLR 110, 45 BMLR 1,
    [1999] 02 LS Gaz R 28, [1998] NLJR 1844, [1999] 3 LRC 644, sub nom Frost v
    Chief Constable of South Yorkshire Police 143 Sol Jo LB 51, HL 25.8
Fry v Foreign and Commonwealth Office [1997] ICR 512, EAT 19.51
Fullarton Computer Industries Ltd v Central Arbitration Committee [2001] IRLR 752,
    Ct of Sess 47.10, 47.31
Fuller v Lloyds Bank plc [1991] ICR 336, EAT 51.4
Fyfe v Scientific Furnishings Ltd [1989] ICR 648, [1989] IRLR 331, EAT 52.13, 55.30
Fytche v Wincanton Logistics plc [2004] UKHL 31, [2004] 4 All ER 221, [2004] ICR
    975, [2004] IRLR 817, [2004] 31 LS Gaz R 25, (2004) Times, 2 July, 148 Sol Jo
    LB 825 .... 26.12

G
GEC Ferranti Defence Systems Ltd v MSF [1993] IRLR 101, EAT 36.4
GKN Sankey v National Society of Motor Mechanics [1980] ICR 148, [1980] IRLR 8,
    EAT 36.4
GMB v MAN Truck and Bus UK Ltd [2000] ICR 1101, [2000] IRLR 636, EAT 36.3
GMB v Susie Radin Ltd [2004] EWCA Civ 180, [2004] 2 All ER 279, [2004] ICR 893,
    [2004] 11 LS Gaz R 34, 148 Sol Jo LB 266, [2004] All ER (D) 353 (Feb), sub nom
    Susie Radin Ltd v GMB [2004] IRLR 400, (2004) Times, 16 March 36.6
GMB and Amicus v Beloit Walmsley Ltd [2004] IRLR 18, EAT 36.6
GMM v Hamm IDS Brief No 682 .... 18.25
Gale v Northern General Hospital NHS Trust [1994] IRLR 292, CA 6.9, 7.13
Gallagher v Alpha Catering Services Ltd (t/a Alpha Flight Services) [2004] All ER (D)
    262 (May), EAT; affd [2004] All ER (D) 121 (Nov), CA 54.2, 54.5, 54.29
Galt v Philp [1984] IRLR 156, 1984 SLT 28, JC 42.12
Ganase v Kent Community Housing Trust [2001] All ER (D) 07 (Jul), EAT 19.17

PARA

Gardiner v London Borough of Merton. See Merton London Borough Council v Gardiner
Gardiner-Hill v Roland Beiger Technics Ltd [1982] IRLR 498, EAT 52.13, 55.30
Garland v British Rail Engineering Ltd [1983] 2 AC 751, [1982] 2 WLR 918, [1981] 2
    CMLR 542, [1982] ICR 420, HL; refd 12/81: [1983] 2 AC 751, [1982] 2 All ER 402,
    [1982] 2 WLR 918, [1982] ECR 359, [1982] 1 CMLR 696, [1982] ICR 420, [1982]
    IRLR 111, ECJ; apld [1983] 2 AC 751, [1982] 2 All ER 402, [1982] 2 WLR 918,
    [1982] 2 CMLR 174, [1982] ICR 420, [1982] IRLR 257, 126 Sol Jo 309, HL 22.22, 39.5
Gascol Conversions Ltd v Mercer [1974] ICR 420, [1974] IRLR 155, [1975] KILR 149, 9 ITR
    282, 118 Sol Jo 219, CA 31.36
Gateway Hotels Ltd v Stewart [1988] IRLR 287, EAT 49.20
Gbaja-Biamila v DHL International (UK) Ltd [2000] ICR 730, EAT 13.8
Gee v Shell UK Ltd [2002] EWCA Civ 1479, [2003] IRLR 82, [2002] 49 LS Gaz R 19,
    (2002) Times, 4 November, 146 Sol Jo LB 245, [2002] All ER (D) 350 (Oct) 19.61
General Billposting Co Ltd v Atkinson [1909] AC 118, 78 LJ Ch 77, [1908-10] All ER
    Rep 619, 99 LT 943, 25 TLR 178, HL 38.20, 55.34
General Cleaning Contractors Ltd v Christmas [1953] AC 180, [1952] 2 All ER 1110,
    [1953] 2 WLR 6, 51 LGR 109, 97 Sol Jo 7, HL 25.3, 25.5
General Engineering Services Ltd v Kingston and St Andrew Corpn [1988] 3 All ER 867,
    [1989] 1 WLR 69, [1989] ICR 88, [1989] IRLR 35, 133 Sol Jo 20, [1989] 4 LS Gaz
    R 44, PC 53.2
General of the Salvation Army v Dewsbury [1984] ICR 498, [1984] IRLR 222, EAT 6.3,
                                                                                                    21.3, 50.11
General Rolling Stock Co, Re, Chapman's Case (1866) LR 1 Eq 346, 35 Beav 207, 12 Jur
    NS 44 .... 29.9, 55.9
Genower v Ealing, Hammersmith and Hounslow Area Health Authority [1980] IRLR 297,
    EAT 51.14
Georgiou v Colman Coyle (2002) IDS Brief No 705 .... 11.9
Gerster v Freistaat Bayern: C-1/95 [1997] ECR I-5253, [1998] 1 CMLR 303, [1998] ICR
    327, [1997] IRLR 699, ECJ 22.3, 22.11
Gesamtbetriebsrat Der Kühne & Nagel AG & Co KG v Kühne & Nagel AG & Co KG:
    C-440/00 [2004] 2 CMLR 1242, [2004] IRLR 332 , [2004] All ER (D) 31 (Jan),
    ECJ 16.6
Gibbons v Associated British Ports [1985] IRLR 376 .... 5.4
Gibson v East Riding of Yorkshire Council [2000] ICR 890, [2000] IRLR 598, [2000] All
    ER (D) 846, CA 27.2, 54.1
Gibson v Motortune Ltd [1990] ICR 740, EAT 6.9
Gilbert v Kembridge Fibres Ltd [1984] ICR 188, [1984] IRLR 52, EAT 2.4
Gilham v Kent County Council [1985] IRLR 16. See Kent County Council v Gilham
Gilham v Kent County Council (No 2) [1985] ICR 233, [1985] IRLR 18, CA 51.4
Gilham v Kent County Council (No 3) [1986] ICR 52, [1986] IRLR 56, EAT 52.12
Gill v Cremadez [2000] CLY 3876 .... 40.5
Gill v Ford Motor Co Ltd [2004] IRLR 840, [2004] 33 LS Gaz R 34, [2004] All ER (D)
    131 (Jul), EAT 31.6
Gillespie v Northern Health and Social Services Board: C-342/93 [1996] All ER (EC) 284,
    [1996] ECR I-475, [1996] 2 CMLR 969, [1996] ICR 498, [1996] IRLR 214, ECJ 22.9,
                                                                                               22.14, 30.14, 39.8
Gillespie v Northern Health and Social Services Board (No 2) [1997] IRLR 410, NICA 22.14
Gimber (W) & Sons Ltd v Spurrett (1967) 2 ITR 308, DC 35.7
Ging v Ellward Lancs Ltd [1991] ICR 222n, 13 ITR 265, EAT 52.12
Giraud UK Ltd v Smith [2000] IRLR 763, EAT 7.24, 45.16, 55.27
Glasgow City Council v Marshall [2000] 1 All ER 641, [2000] 1 WLR 333, [2000] LGR
    229, [2000] ICR 196, [2000] IRLR 272, [2000] 07 LS Gaz R 39, 2000 SC (HL) 67,
    2000 SLT 429, HL 22.11
Glasgow City Council v Zafar [1998] 2 All ER 953, [1997] 1 WLR 1659, [1998] ICR 120,
    [1997] 48 LS Gaz R 29, 1998 SC (HL) 27, 1998 SLT 135, 142 Sol Jo LB 30, sub nom
    Zafar v Glasgow City Council [1998] IRLR 36, HL 11.5
Glenboig Union Fireclay Co Ltd v Stewart (1971) 6 ITR 14, Ct of Sess 55.8
Glendale Managed Services v Graham [2003] EWCA Civ 773, [2003] IRLR 465, (2003)
    Times, 4 June, [2003] All ER (D) 225 (May) 49.14

Table of cases

PARA

Glennie v Independent Magazines (UK) Ltd [1999] IRLR 719, [1999] All ER (D) 637, CA 20.15
Glenrose (Fish Merchants) Ltd v Chapman IDS Brief No 438 .... 50.17
Gloystane & Co Ltd v Martin [2001] IRLR 15, EAT 19.32
Gogay v Hertfordshire County Council [2000] IRLR 703, [2001] 1 FCR 455, [2000] Fam Law 883, [2000] All ER (D) 1057, CA 7.13, 7.23
Goldman Sachs Services Ltd v Montali [2002] ICR 1251, CA 19.7
Gómez v Continental Industrias del Caucho SA: C-342/01 [2004] 2 CMLR 38, [2004] IRLR 407, [2004] All ER (D) 350 (Mar), ECJ 30.18
Goodeve v Gilsons [1985] ICR 401, 129 Sol Jo 283, CA 35.10
Goodwin v Cabletel UK Ltd [1998] ICR 112, [1997] IRLR 665, EAT 26.9, 51.3
Goodwin v Patent Office [1999] ICR 302, [1999] IRLR 4, EAT 9.2, 9.32
Goodwin v United Kingdom (Application 17488/90) (1996) 22 EHRR 123, 1 BHRC 81, ECtHR 28.5
Goodwin v United Kingdom (Application 28957/95) [2002] IRLR 664, [2002] 2 FCR 577, [2002] 2 FLR 487, [2002] Fam Law 738, 35 EHRR 447, 13 BHRC 120, 67 BMLR 199, [2002] NLJR 1171, (2002) Times, 12 July, [2002] All ER (D) 158 (Jul), ECtHR 11.6, 22.13, 28.4
Goold (W A) (Pearmak) Ltd v McConnell [1995] IRLR 516, EAT 7.13
Gorictree Ltd v Jenkinson [1985] ICR 51, [1984] IRLR 391, EAT 49.21
Goring v British Actors Equity Association [1987] IRLR 122 .... 48.12, 48.15
Gothard v Mirror Group Newspapers Ltd [1988] ICR 729, [1988] IRLR 396, CA 45.11, 55.21
Government Communications Staff Federation v Certification Officer [1993] ICR 163, [1993] IRLR 260, [1993] 5 LS Gaz R 41, EAT 47.22
Graf v Filzmoser Maschinenbau GmbH: C-190/98 [2000] All ER (EC) 170, [2000] ECR I-493, [2000] 1 CMLR 741, ECJ 24.2
Grant v South-West Trains Ltd: C-249/96 [1998] All ER (EC) 193, [1998] ECR I-621, [1998] 1 CMLR 993, [1998] ICR 449, [1998] IRLR 206, [1998] 1 FCR 377, [1998] 1 FLR 839, [1998] Fam Law 392, 3 BHRC 578, ECJ 28.5
Graphical, Paper and Media Union v Derry Print Ltd [2002] IRLR 380 .... 47.30
Gray v Canada Life Ltd. See Canada Life Ltd v Gray
Greater Manchester Police Authority v Lea [1990] IRLR 372, EAT 11.8
Green v Hackney London Borough Council EAT/182/98 .... 19.16
Green (E) & Son (Castings) Ltd v Association of Scientific, Technical and Managerial Staffs [1984] ICR 352, [1984] IRLR 135, EAT 36.4, 36.6
Greenaway Harrison Ltd v Wiles [1994] IRLR 380, 501 IRLIB 2, EAT 20.12, 50.7
Greenwood v British Airways plc [1999] ICR 969, [1999] IRLR 600 .... 9.4
Gregory v Tudsbury Ltd [1982] IRLR 267, IT 30.3
Gregory v Wallace [1998] IRLR 387, CA 55.21
Griffin v London Pensions Fund Authority [1993] 2 CMLR 571, [1993] ICR 564, [1993] IRLR 248, [1993] 11 LS Gaz R 44, EAT 22.18, 22.22
Griffin v South West Water Services Ltd [1995] IRLR 15 .... 34.7, 36.4
Griffiths v British Coal (23 January 1998, unreported) 25.8
Griffiths v Secretary of State for Social Services [1974] QB 468, [1973] 3 All ER 1184, [1973] 3 WLR 831, 117 Sol Jo 873 .... 29.9, 55.9
Grimaldi v Fonds des Maladies Professionnelles: 322/88 [1989] ECR 4407, [1991] 2 CMLR 265, [1990] IRLR 400, ECJ 23.1
Group 4 Nightspeed Ltd v Gilbert [1997] IRLR 398, 574 IRLB 13, EAT 18.31, 31.8
Gruber v Silhouette International Schmeid GmbH & Co: C-249/97 (1999) IDS Brief No 647 .... 22.14
Grundy (Teddington) Ltd v Plummer [1983] ICR 367, [1983] IRLR 98, EAT 51.11
Guinness plc v Saunders [1990] 2 AC 663, [1990] 1 All ER 652, [1990] 2 WLR 324, [1990] BCLC 402, 134 Sol Jo 457, [1990] 9 LS Gaz R 42, HL 8.4, 55.36
Guinness (Arthur) Son & Co (Great Britain) Ltd v Green [1989] ICR 241, [1989] IRLR 288, EAT 19.64, 52.12
Gunning v Mirror Group Newspapers Ltd [1986] 1 All ER 385, sub nom Mirror Group Newspapers Ltd v Gunning [1986] 1 WLR 546, [1986] ICR 145, [1986] IRLR 27, 130 Sol Jo 242, CA 11.12

PARA

Gunton v Richmond-upon-Thames London Borough Council [1981] Ch 448, [1980] 3
All ER 577, [1980] 3 WLR 714, 79 LGR 241, [1980] ICR 755, [1980] IRLR 321,
CA 45.19, 50.9, 55.7, 55.18, 55.25
Gutzmore v J Wardley (Holdings) Ltd [1993] ICR 581, CA 19.64

H

HSBC Bank plc (formerly Midland Bank plc) v Madden [2001] 1 All ER 550, [2000] ICR
1283, [2000] IRLR 827, [2000] All ER (D) 1137, CA 51.4, 51.9
Haddon v Van den Bergh Foods Ltd [1999] ICR 1150, [1999] IRLR 672, 628 IRLB 3,
EAT 51.4
Haden Ltd v Cowen. See Cowen v Haden Ltd
Hadjioannous v Coral Casinos Ltd [1981] IRLR 352, EAT 51.9
Haigh (Catherine) Harlequin Hair Design v Seed [1990] IRLR 175, EAT 45.15
Hair Colour Consultants Ltd v Mena [1984] ICR 671, [1984] IRLR 386, [1984] LS Gaz R
2147, EAT 6.9
Hairsine v Kingston upon Hull City Council [1992] ICR 212, [1992] IRLR 211, EAT 46.2
Halford v Sharples [1992] ICR 146, EAT; affd [1992] 3 All ER 624, [1992] 1 WLR 736,
[1992] ICR 583, CA 19.13, 19.50, 34.6
Halford v United Kingdom (Application 20605/92) (1997) 24 EHRR 523, [1997] IRLR
471, [1998] Crim LR 753, 94 LS Gaz R 24, 3 BHRC 31, ECtHR 28.4
Halfpenny v IGE Medical Systems Ltd [1999] ICR 834, [1999] IRLR 177, [1999] 1 FLR
944, 143 Sol Jo LB 38, [1998] All ER (D) 769, CA; revsd [2001] ICR 73, [2001]
IRLR 96, [2000] All ER (D) 2284, HL 11.12, 12.33, 30.21
Hall (Inspector of Taxes) v Lorimer [1994] 1 All ER 250, [1994] 1 WLR 209, [1994]
STC 23, 66 TC 349, [1994] ICR 218, [1994] IRLR 171, [1993] 45 LS Gaz R 45,
137 Sol Jo LB 256, CA 15.3
Hall v Woolston Hall Leisure Ltd [2000] 4 All ER 787, [2001] 1 WLR 225, [2001] ICR
99, [2000] IRLR 578, [2000] 24 LS Gaz R 39, [2000] NLJR 833, CA 7.15, 12.16
Hallam v Avery [2000] 1 WLR 966, [2000] LGR 452, [2000] ICR 583, [2000] 01 LS Gaz
R 23, 144 Sol Jo LB 32; affd [2001] UKHL 15, [2001] 1 WLR 655, [2001] LGR 278,
[2001] ICR 408, [2001] 21 LS Gaz R 39, 145 Sol Jo LB 116, [2001] IRLR 312 .... 11.13,
                                                                                                                                    12.36
Hallam Diocese Trustee v Connaughton [1996] 3 CMLR 93, [1996] IRLR 505, EAT 22.9,
                                                                                                                                    22.22
Hamill v EC Commission: 180/87 [1990] 1 All ER 982, [1988] ECR 6141, [1990] 1 CMLR
982, ECJ 34.8
Hamilton v Futura Floors Ltd [1990] IRLR 478, OH 5.3
Hamlet v General Municipal Boilermakers and Allied Trades Union [1987] 1 All ER 631,
[1987] 1 WLR 449, [1987] ICR 150, [1986] IRLR 293, 131 Sol Jo 470, [1987] LS
Gaz R 1327 .... 48.12, 48.15
Hammersmith and Fulham London Borough Council v Farnsworth [2000] IRLR 691,
[2000] All ER (D) 812, EAT 9.15
Hampson v Department of Education and Science [1990] 2 All ER 25, [1989] ICR 179,
[1989] IRLR 69, 133 Sol Jo 151, [1989] 13 LS Gaz R 43, CA; revsd [1991] 1 AC
171, [1990] 2 All ER 513, [1990] 3 WLR 42, [1990] ICR 511, [1990] IRLR 302,
134 Sol Jo 1123, [1990] 26 LS Gaz R 39, [1990] NLJR 853, HL 12.8, 12.18
Hancill v Marcon Engineering Ltd [1990] ICR 103, [1990] IRLR 51, EAT 6.9
Handels-og Kontorfunktionaerernes Forbund i Danmark v Dansk Arbejdsgiverforening,
acting on behalf of Danfoss: 109/88 [1989] ECR 3199, [1991] 1 CMLR 8, [1991]
ICR 74, [1989] IRLR 532, ECJ 22.11
Handels-og Kontorfunktionaerernes Forbund i Danmark (acting on behalf of Hoj Pedersen)
v Faellesforeningen for Danmarks Brugsforeninger (acting on behalf of Kvickly Skive):
C-66/96 [1998] ECR I-7327, [1999] 2 CMLR 326, [1999] IRLR 55, sub nom Pedersen
v Kvickly Skive [1999] All ER (EC) 138, [1998] All ER (D) 614, ECJ 22.14
Haniff v Robinson [1993] QB 419, [1993] 1 All ER 185, [1992] 3 WLR 875, 26 HLR 386,
[1992] 2 EGLR 111, [1992] 45 EG 145, CA 40.3
Hannah Blumenthal, The. See Wilson (Paal) & Co A/S v Partenreederei Hannah Blumenthal,
The Hannah Blumenthal

Table of cases

PARA

Hannan v TNT-IPEC (UK) Ltd [1986] IRLR 165, EAT 51.1
Hanover Insurance Brokers Ltd v Schapiro [1994] IRLR 82, CA 38.7
Harada Ltd (t/a Chequepoint UK) v Turner EAT/516/99 .... 24.11
Hardman v Mallon (t/a Orchard Lodge Nursing Home) [2002] IRLR 516 .... 11.5
Hardy v Polk (Leeds) Ltd [2004] IRLR 420, [2004] All ER (D) 282 (Mar), EAT 52.13
Harford v Swiftrim Ltd [1987] ICR 439, [1987] IRLR 360, [1987] LS Gaz R 820, EAT 6.9
Haringey Council (Haringey Design Partnership Directorate of Technical and Environmental
    Services) v Al-Azzawi (2002) IDS Brief No 703 .... 11.13, 12.35
Harmer v Cornelius (1858) 22 JP 724, 5 CBNS 236, 28 LJCP 85, 4 Jur NS 1110, 6 WR
    749, 141 ER 94, [1843-60] All ER Rep 624, 32 LTOS 62 .... 55.17
Harmony Healthcare plc v Drewery EAT/886/00 .... 19.17
Harper v Virgin Net Ltd [2004] EWCA Civ 271, [2004] IRLR 390, (2004) Times, 16
    March, 148 Sol Jo LB 353, [2004] All ER (D) 184 (Mar) 7.23, 50.11
Harris v Courage (Eastern) Ltd [1982] ICR 530, [1982] IRLR 509, CA 51.9
Harris v Shuttleworth [1994] ICR 991, [1994] IRLR 547, CA 39.3, 39.12
Harris & Russell Ltd v Slingsby [1973] 3 All ER 31, [1973] ICR 454, [1973] IRLR 221,
    15 KIR 157, 8 ITR 433, NIRC 50.5
Harrison v Boots the Chemist Ltd EAT/1098/97 .... 20.15
Harrison v Kent County Council [1995] ICR 434, EAT 48.2
Harrison v Norwest Holst Group Administration Ltd. See Norwest Holst Group Administration
    Ltd v Harrison
Harrison Bowden Ltd v Bowden [1994] ICR 186, EAT 49.10
Harrison (T C) (Newcastle-under-Lyme) Ltd v Ramsey [1976] IRLR 135, IT 25.36
Harrods Ltd v Remick [1998] 1 All ER 52, [1998] ICR 156, [1997] IRLR 583, CA 12.21
Harrow London Borough v Cunningham [1996] IRLR 256, EAT 51.9
Hart v A R Marshall & Sons (Bulwell) Ltd [1978] 2 All ER 413, [1977] 1 WLR 1067,
    [1977] ICR 539, [1977] IRLR 51, 12 ITR 190, 121 Sol Jo 677, EAT 45.3
Hartlebury Printers Ltd (in liquidation), Re [1993] 1 All ER 470, [1992] ICR 559, [1992]
    IRLR 516, [1993] BCLC 902, [1992] BCC 428 .... 23.2, 36.2, 36.4, 36.6
Hartwell v A-G of the British Virgin Islands [2004] UKPC 12, [2004] 1 WLR 1273, (2004)
    Times, 27 February, 148 Sol Jo LB 267, [2004] All ER (D) 372 (Feb) 53.2
Harvest Press Ltd v McCaffrey [1999] IRLR 778, EAT 26.9, 51.3
Harvest Town Circle Ltd v Rutherford [2001] 3 CMLR 691, [2002] ICR 123, [2001]
    IRLR 599, [2001] All ER (D) 112 (Jul), EAT 11.8, 22.10, 22.22, 50.14
Harvey v Institute of the Motor Industry (No 2) [1996] ICR 981, [1995] IRLR 416, EAT ... 13.8
Harvey v Port of Tilbury (London) Ltd [1999] ICR 1030, [1999] IRLR 693, EAT 19.10
Harvey's Household Linens Ltd v Benson [1974] ICR 306, 16 KIR 228, 9 ITR 234,
    NIRC 18.25
Haseltine Lake & Co v Dowler [1981] ICR 222, [1981] IRLR 25, EAT 50.5, 50.8, 55.5
Hasley v Fair Employment Agency [1989] IRLR 106, NICA 6.9, 22.9, 22.22
Hatton v Sutherland [2002] EWCA Civ 76, [2002] 2 All ER 1, [2002] ICR 613, 68
    BMLR 115, (2002) Times, 11 February, [2002] All ER (D) 53 (Feb), sub nom
    Sutherland v Hatton [2002] IRLR 263 .... 26.24
Hawkes v Southwark London Borough (20 February 1998, unreported), CA 26.18
Hawkins v Ball and Barclays Bank plc [1996] IRLR 258, EAT 13.3, 18.30,
                                                                              20.10, 20.14
Hay v George Hanson (Building Contractors) Ltd [1996] IRLR 427, EAT 49.12
Hayes v Malleable Working Men's Club and Institute [1985] ICR 703, [1985] IRLR 367,
    EAT 11.5
Hayward v Cammell Laird Shipbuilders Ltd [1988] AC 894, [1988] 2 All ER 257, [1988]
    2 WLR 1134, [1988] ICR 464, [1988] IRLR 257, 132 Sol Jo 750, [1988] NLJR 133,
    HL 22.5, 22.8
Healey v Française Rubastic SA [1917] 1 KB 946, 86 LJKB 1254, 117 LT 92, 33 TLR
    300 .... 8.16, 55.28
Health Development Agency v Parish [2004] IRLR 550, [2004] All ER (D) 106 (Jan),
    EAT 19.70
Heasmans v Clarity Cleaning Co Ltd [1987] ICR 949, [1987] IRLR 286, [1987] BTLC 174,
    [1987] NLJ Rep 101, CA 53.2
Hector v Untied Kingdom (1990) Guardian, 20 April, ECtHR 28.4

PARA

Hedley Byrne & Co Ltd v Heller & Partners Ltd [1964] AC 465, [1963] 2 All ER 575, [1963] 3 WLR 101, [1963] 1 Lloyd's Rep 485, 107 Sol Jo 454, HL 37.5

Heggie v Uniroyal Englebert Tyres Ltd [1998] IRLR 425, EAT; revsd [1999] IRLR 802, Ct of Sess 52.13

Heinz (H J) Co Ltd v Kenrick [2000] ICR 491, [2000] IRLR 144, 635 IRLB 10, EAT 9.11, 9.15, 51.8

Hellyer Bros Ltd v Atkinson and Dickinson [1992] IRLR 540, EAT; revsd [1994] IRLR 88, CA 45.2

Hellyer Bros Ltd v McLeod [1987] 1 WLR 728, [1987] ICR 526, 131 Sol Jo 805, [1987] LS Gaz R 1056, sub nom McLeod v Hellyer Bros Ltd [1987] IRLR 232, CA 15.3, 44.8

Hempell v W H Smith & Sons Ltd [1986] ICR 365, [1986] IRLR 95, EAT 35.12

Henderson v Henderson (1843) 3 Hare 100, [1843-60] All ER Rep 378, 1 LTOS 410 .... 13.4, 19.26

Hendricks v Metropolitan Police Comr [2002] EWCA Civ 1686, [2003] 1 All ER 654, [2003] ICR 530, [2003] IRLR 96, [2003] 05 LS Gaz R 30, (2002) Times, 6 December, 146 Sol Jo LB 274, [2002] All ER (D) 407 (Nov) 13.3, 18.29

Hendry v Scottish Liberal Club [1977] IRLR 5, IT 17.3

Henke v Gemeinde Schierke and Verwaltungsgemeinschaft Brocken: C-298/94 [1997] All ER (EC) 173, [1996] ECR I-4989, [1997] 1 CMLR 373, [1997] ICR 746, [1996] IRLR 701, ECJ 34.2, 49.3

Hennessy v Craigmyle & Co Ltd [1986] ICR 461, [1986] IRLR 300, 130 Sol Jo 633, [1986] LS Gaz R 2160, CA 2.4, 20.26

Henry v London General Transport Services Ltd [2002] EWCA Civ 488, [2002] IRLR 472, [2002] All ER (D) 322 (Mar) 5.3, 31.6

HM Prison Service v Beart [2003] EWCA Civ 119, [2003] ICR 1068, [2003] IRLR 238, (2003) Times, 7 March, [2003] All ER (D) 191 (Jan) 9.12

HM Prison Service v Davis (2000) IDS Brief No 666, EAT 11.13, 12.35

HM Prison Service v Dolby [2003] IRLR 694, [2003] All ER (D) 156 (Jul), EAT 19.17

HM Prison Service v Johnson [1997] ICR 275, [1997] IRLR 162, 567 IRLB 13, EAT 13.8

HM Prison Service v Salmon [2001] IRLR 425, [2001] All ER (D) 154 (Apr), EAT 13.8

Hereford and Worcester County Council v Neale. See Neale v Hereford and Worcester County Council

Heron v Citilink-Nottingham [1993] IRLR 372, EAT 51.11

Heron Corpn Ltd v Commis [1980] ICR 713, EAT 12.11

Hertaing v Benoidt: C-305/94 [1997] All ER (EC) 40, [1996] ECR I-5927, [1997] 1 CMLR 329, [1997] IRLR 127, ECJ 49.9

Hewcastle Catering Ltd v Ahmed and Elkamah [1992] ICR 626, [1991] IRLR 473, CA 7.15

Hewlett Packard Ltd v O'Murphy [2002] IRLR 4, [2001] All ER (D) 91 (Sep), EAT 15.3, 44.2

Hidalgo v Asociacion de Servicios Aser and Sociedad Cooperativa Minerva: C-173/96 [1998] ECR I-8237, [2002] ICR 73, [1999] IRLR 136, ECJ 49.5

High Table Ltd v Horst [1998] ICR 409, [1997] IRLR 513, sub nom Horst v High Table Ltd [1997] 28 LS Gaz R 25, 141 Sol Jo LB 161, CA 7.13, 19.63, 35.7

Higham v Horton. See Horton v Higham

Hill v Chapell [2003] IRLR 19, [2002] All ER (D) 461 (May), EAT 27.4

Hill v General Accident Fire and Life Assurance Corpn plc [1998] IRLR 641, 1999 SLT 1157, 1998 SCLR 1030, 609 IRLB 8, OH 7.13, 39.11, 41.15, 55.19

Hill v Revenue Comrs: C-243/95 [1998] All ER (EC) 722, [1998] ECR I-3739, [1998] 3 CMLR 81, [1999] ICR 48, [1998] IRLR 466, [1998] 34 LS Gaz R 33, [1998] All ER (D) 277, ECJ 22.3

Hill (William) Organisation Ltd v Tucker [1999] ICR 291, [1998] IRLR 313, [1998] 20 LS Gaz R 33, 142 Sol Jo LB 140, CA 7.13, 7.24, 55.21

Hillingdon London Borough Council v Commission for Racial Equality [1982] AC 779, [1982] 3 WLR 159, 80 LGR 737, [1982] IRLR 424, 126 Sol Jo 449, HL 13.12, 13.13

Hillman v London General Transport Services Ltd (14 April 1999, unreported), EAT 34.7

Hills v Co-operative Wholesale Society Ltd [1940] 2 KB 435, [1940] 3 All ER 233, 109 LJKB 972, 84 Sol Jo 658, 163 LT 167, 56 TLR 875, CA 7.23, 55.39

Hillsdown Holdings plc v Pensions Ombudsman [1997] 1 All ER 862, [1996] PLR 427 .... 39.11

Hilton v Shiner Ltd Builders Merchants [2001] IRLR 727, [2001] All ER (D) 316 (May), EAT 7.13

Table of cases

PARA

Hilton International Hotels (UK) Ltd v Faraji [1994] ICR 259, [1994] IRLR 267, EAT 52.12, 52.13
Hilton International Hotels (UK) Ltd v Protopapa [1990] IRLR 316, EAT 50.7
Hindle Gears Ltd v McGinty [1985] ICR 111, [1984] IRLR 477, EAT 50.5, 55.5
Hinton & Higgs (UK) Ltd v Murphy and Valentine [1989] IRLR 519, 1988 SC 353, 1989 SLT 450, 1989 SCLR 42, Ct of Sess 38.18
Hitchcock v Post Office [1980] ICR 100, EAT 15.3
Hivac Ltd v Park Royal Scientific Instruments Ltd [1946] Ch 169, [1946] 1 All ER 350, 115 LJ Ch 241, 90 Sol Jo 175, 174 LT 422, 62 TLR 231, CA 8.16
Hodgson v Scarlett (1818) 1 B & Ald 232 .... 37.4
Hoeffler v Kwik Save Stores Ltd EAT/803/97 .... 19.35
Hogg v Dover College [1990] ICR 39, EAT 7.22, 45.1
Holdsworth (Harold) & Co (Wakefield) Ltd v Caddies [1955] 1 All ER 725, [1955] 1 WLR 352, 99 Sol Jo 234, HL 8.5
Holland v Glendale Industries Ltd [1998] ICR 493, EAT 45.19, 50.7
Hollis & Co v Stocks [2000] UKCLR 658, [2000] IRLR 712 .... 38.15
Hollister v National Farmers' Union [1979] ICR 542, [1979] IRLR 238, CA 51.14
Homan v A1 Bacon Co Ltd [1996] ICR 721, EAT 52.6
Home Counties Dairies Ltd v Skilton [1970] 1 All ER 1227, [1970] 1 WLR 526, 114 Sol Jo 107, CA 38.15
Home Office v Ayres [1992] ICR 175, [1992] IRLR 59, EAT 31.6
Home Office v Bailey (27 July 2004, unreported), EAT 22.11
Home Office v Coyne [2000] ICR 1443, [2000] IRLR 838, [2000] All ER (D) 1081, CA 11.12
Home Office v Robinson [1982] ICR 31, [1981] IRLR 524, EAT 34.2
Hooper v British Railways Board [1988] IRLR 517, CA 7.10, 51.4
Hoover Ltd v Forde [1980] ICR 239, EAT 52.13
Hopkins v Norcros plc [1994] ICR 11, [1994] IRLR 18, CA 52.13, 55.30
Hopley Dodd v Highfield Motors (Derby) Ltd (1969) 4 ITR 289 .... 55.9
Horcal Ltd v Gatland [1984] IRLR 288, [1984] BCLC 549, CA 8.16
Horkulak v Cantor Fitzgerald International [2004] IRLR 756 .... 50.7
Horst v High Table Ltd. See High Table Ltd v Horst
Horton v Higham [2004] EWCA Civ 941, [2004] 3 All ER 852, [2004] All ER (D) 261 (Jul), sub nom 1 Pump Court Chambers v Horton [2004] 33 LS Gaz R 34, sub nom Higham v Meurig Lestyn Horton 148 Sol Jo LB 911 .... 12.9
Horton v Taplin Contracts Ltd [2002] EWCA Civ 1604, [2003] ICR 179, [2003] 01 LS Gaz R 24, [2003] PIQR P180, [2003] BLR 74, (2002) Times, 25 November, 146 Sol Jo LB 256, [2002] All ER (D) 122 (Nov) 26.12
Hotson v East Berkshire Area Health Authority [1987] AC 750, [1987] 1 All ER 210, [1987] 2 WLR 287, 130 Sol Jo 925, [1987] LS Gaz R 37, [1986] NLJ Rep 1163, CA; revsd [1987] AC 750, [1987] 2 All ER 909, [1987] 3 WLR 232, 131 Sol Jo 975, [1987] LS Gaz R 2365, [1987] NLJ Rep 638, HL 25.8
Hotson v Wisbech Conservative Club [1984] ICR 859, [1984] IRLR 422, EAT 18.35
Hough v Leyland DAF Ltd [1991] ICR 696, [1991] IRLR 194, EAT 20.17, 36.2, 36.4, 51.11
Hounslow London Borough Council v Bhatt [2001] IDS Brief No 692, EAT 11.10
Housing Corpn v Bryant [1999] ICR 123, sub nom Bryant v Housing Corpn [1998] 26 LS Gaz R 31, 142 Sol Jo LB 181, CA 13.4, 19.10
Housing Services Agency v Cragg [1997] ICR 1050, [1997] IRLR 380, 569 IRLB 8, EAT 50.15
Howlett Marine Services Ltd v Bowlam [2001] ICR 595, [2001] IRLR 201, [2000] All ER (D) 2494, EAT 18.25, 18.26, 18.33, 36.6
Howman & Son v Blyth [1983] ICR 416, [1983] IRLR 139, EAT 41.2
Hudson v GMB [1990] IRLR 67 .... 48.12
Hudson v Ridge Manufacturing Co Ltd [1957] 2 QB 348, [1957] 2 All ER 229, [1957] 2 WLR 948, 101 Sol Jo 409 .... 25.7
Hugh-Jones v St John's College Cambridge [1979] ICR 848, 123 Sol Jo 603, EAT 12.18
Hughes v Department of Health and Social Security [1985] AC 776, [1985] 2 WLR 866, [1985] ICR 419, 129 Sol Jo 315, sub nom Department of Health and Social Security v Hughes [1985] IRLR 263, HL 50.14

PARA

Hughes v Greenwich London Borough Council [1994] 1 AC 170, [1993] 4 All ER 577, [1993] 3 WLR 821, 92 LGR 61, 69 P & CR 487, [1994] ICR 48, 26 HLR 99, [1993] 46 LS Gaz R 38, [1993] NLJR 1571n, 137 Sol Jo LB 244, HL 40.7
Hughes v Southwark London Borough Council [1988] IRLR 55 .... 7.23
Hunter v British Coal Corpn [1999] QB 140, [1998] 2 All ER 97, [1998] 3 WLR 685, [1999] ICR 72, [1998] 12 LS Gaz R 27, 142 Sol Jo LB 85, CA 25.8
Hurley v Mustoe (No 2) [1983] ICR 422, EAT 13.8
Hurt v Sheffield Corpn (1916) 85 LJKB 1684 .... 27.8
Hussain v Elonex plc [1999] IRLR 420, CA 51.10
Hussain v HM Prison Service (2002) IDS Brief No 713, EAT 11.13, 12.39
Hussain v New Taplow Paper Mills Ltd [1987] 1 All ER 417, [1987] 1 WLR 336, [1987] ICR 28, 131 Sol Jo 358, [1987] LS Gaz R 1242, CA; affd [1988] AC 514, [1988] 1 All ER 541, [1988] 2 WLR 266, [1988] ICR 259, [1988] IRLR 167, 132 Sol Jo 226, [1988] 10 LS Gaz R 45, [1988] NLJR 45, HL 41.9
Hussman Manufacturing Ltd v Weir [1998] IRLR 288, 599 IRLB 5, EAT 31.6
Hutchinson v Westward Television Ltd [1977] ICR 279, [1977] IRLR 69, 12 ITR 125, EAT 18.30
Hyde v Lehman Bros Ltd [2004] All ER (D) 40 (Aug), EAT 18.31

I

ICTS (UK) Ltd v Tchoula [2000] IRLR 643, [2000] All ER (D) 614, EAT 13.8
Ibex Trading Co Ltd v Walton [1994] ICR 907, [1994] IRLR 564, [1994] BCC 982, EAT 49.20
Iceland Frozen Foods Ltd v Jones [1983] ICR 17, [1982] IRLR 439, EAT 51.4
Igbo v Johnson Matthey Chemicals Ltd [1986] ICR 505, [1986] IRLR 215, 130 Sol Jo 524, [1986] LS Gaz R 2089, CA 50.19
Iggesund Converters Ltd v Lewis [1984] ICR 544, [1984] IRLR 431, EAT 19.60
Imperial Group Pension Trust Ltd v Imperial Tobacco Ltd [1991] 2 All ER 597, [1991] 1 WLR 589, [1991] ICR 524, [1991] IRLR 66 .... 39.11
Income Tax Special Purposes Comrs v Pemsel [1891] AC 531, 3 TC 53, 55 JP 805, 61 LJQB 265, [1891-4] All ER Rep 28, 65 LT 621, 7 TLR 657, HL 11.6
Industrial Rubber Products v Gillon [1977] IRLR 389, 13 ITR 100, EAT 50.7
Ingham v ABC Contract Services Ltd (12 November 1993, unreported) 38.7
Ingram v Foxon [1984] ICR 685, [1985] IRLR 5, EAT 6.7
Initial Supplies Ltd v McCall 1992 SLT 67 .... 49.6
IRC v Bebb Travel plc [2002] 4 All ER 534, [2003] ICR 201, [2002] IRLR 783, [2002] NLJR 1350, (2002) Times, 30 October, [2002] All ER (D) 105 (Aug), EAT; affd [2003] EWCA Civ 563, [2003] 3 All ER 546, [2003] ICR 1271, [2003] NLJR 633, (2003) Times, 25 April, 147 Sol Jo LB 505, [2003] All ER (D) 291 (Apr) 31.13
IRC v Post Office Ltd [2003] ICR 546, [2003] IRLR 199, [2002] All ER (D) 282 (Dec), EAT 31.9
IRC v St Hermans Estate Co Ltd [2002] IRLR 788, [2002] All ER (D) 58 (Jul), EAT 31.13
Inner London Education Authority v Gravett [1988] IRLR 497, EAT 51.9
Insitu Cleaning Co Ltd v Heads [1995] IRLR 4, EAT 11.12
Institution of Professional Civil Servants v Secretary of State for Defence [1987] 3 CMLR 35, [1987] IRLR 373 .... 49.18
Intercity West Coast Ltd v National Union of Rail, Maritime and Transport Workers [1996] IRLR 583, CA 42.14
International Computers v Kennedy [1981] IRLR 28, EAT 55.5
International Consulting Services (UK) Ltd v Hart [2000] IRLR 227 .... 38.8
International Packaging Corpn (UK) Ltd v Balfour [2003] IRLR 11, [2002] All ER (D) 146 (Nov) 31.6
International Sports Co Ltd v Thomson [1980] IRLR 340, EAT 51.8
Investors' Compensation Scheme Ltd v West Bromwich Building Society [1998] 1 All ER 98, [1998] 1 WLR 896, [1998] 1 BCLC 493, [1997] NLJR 989, [1997] CLC 1243, [1997] PNLR 541, HL 7.9
Irani v Southampton and South West Hampshire Health Authority [1985] ICR 590, [1985] IRLR 203 .... 7.23

Table of cases

PARA

Ironmonger v Movefield Ltd (t/a Deering Appointments) [1988] IRLR 461, EAT 15.3, 44.2
Ironsides Ray & Vials v Lindsay [1994] ICR 384, [1994] IRLR 318, EAT 18.18, 19.75
Irving and Irving v Post Office [1987] IRLR 289, CA 12.35
Iske v P & O European Ferries (Dover) Ltd [1997] IRLR 401, EAT 11.5, 22.14
Isles of Scilly Council v Brintel Helicopters Ltd [1995] ICR 249, [1995] IRLR 6, EAT 49.5
Item Software (UK) Ltd v Fassihi [2002] EWHC 3116 (Ch), [2003] IRLR 769, [2003] 2
    BCLC 1, [2002] All ER (D) 62 (Dec); on appeal [2004] EWCA Civ 1244, [2004] 39
    LS Gaz R 34, [2004] All ER (D) 187 (Sep) 8.16
Ivory v Palmer [1975] ICR 340, 119 Sol Jo 405, CA 40.4
Iwanuszezak v General Municipal Boilermakers and Allied Trades Union [1988] IRLR 219,
    CA 48.2
Ixora Trading Inc v Jones [1990] FSR 251 .... 7.13

J
JMCC Holdings Ltd v Conroy [1990] ICR 179, EAT 19.22
Jackson v Ghost Ltd [2003] IRLR 824, [2003] All ER (D) 17 (Sep), EAT 50.15
Jackson v Invicta Plastics Ltd [1987] BCLC 329 .... 55.17
Jaffrey v Department of the Environment Transport, and the Regions [2002] IRLR 688,
    [2002] All ER (D) 111 (Jul), EAT 11.7
Jakeman v South West Thames Regional Health Authority and London Ambulance Service
    [1990] IRLR 62 .... 7.23, 31.14
James v Eastleigh Borough Council [1990] 2 AC 751, [1990] 2 All ER 607, [1990] 3 WLR
    55, 88 LGR 756, [1990] ICR 554, [1990] IRLR 288, [1990] 27 LS Gaz R 41, [1990]
    NLJR 926, HL 11.6
Jämställdhetsombudsmannen v Örebro läns landsting: C-236/98 [2000] ECR I-2189, [2000]
    2 CMLR 708, [2001] ICR 249, [2000] IRLR 421, ECJ 22.5
Janata Bank v Ahmed [1981] ICR 791, [1981] IRLR 457, CA 7.24
Janciuk v Winerite Ltd [1998] IRLR 63, EAT 7.23, 55.25
Janes Solicitors v Lamb-Simpson (1996) 541 IRLB 15, EAT 27.8
Jarnell v Department of the Environment [1985] AC 776, [1985] 2 WLR 866, [1985]
    ICR 419, [1985] IRLR 263, 129 Sol Jo 315, HL 50.14
Jeetle v Elster [1985] ICR 389, [1985] IRLR 227, EAT 6.9, 49.3
Jenkins v Kingsgate (Clothing Production) [1981] 1 WLR 1485, [1980] 1 CMLR 81,
    [1981] ICR 715, [1980] IRLR 6, 125 Sol Jo 587, EAT 22.10, 22.11
Jenkins v P & O European Ferries (Dover) Ltd [1991] ICR 652, EAT 20.25
Jenvey v Australian Broadcasting Corpn [2002] EWHC 927 (QB), [2003] ICR 79, [2002]
    IRLR 520, [2002] All ER (D) 179 (Apr) 7.13
Jepson and Dyas-Elliot v Labour Party [1996] IRLR 116, Ind Trib 12.27
Jeremiah v Ministry of Defence. See Ministry of Defence v Jeremiah
Jiad v Byford [2003] EWCA Civ 135, [2003] IRLR 232, [2003] All ER (D) 299 (Jan) 11.12
Jiminez v Southwark London Borough Council [2003] EWCA Civ 502, [2003] ICR 1176,
    [2003] IRLR 477, [2003] 23 LS Gaz R 37, (2003) Times, 1 May, 147 Sol Jo LB 476,
    [2003] All ER (D) 123 (Apr) 19.61
Jiménez Melgar v Ayuntamiento de Los Barrios: C-438/99 [2001] ECR I-6915, [2003] 3
    CMLR 67, [2004] ICR 610, [2001] IRLR 848, [2001] All ER (D) 42 (Oct), ECJ 11.5
John v Rees [1970] Ch 345, [1969] 2 All ER 274, [1969] 2 WLR 1294, 113 Sol Jo 487 .. 52.13
Johnson v Chief Adjudication Officer (No 2): C-410/92 [1995] All ER (EC) 258, [1994]
    ECR I-5483, [1995] 1 CMLR 725, [1995] ICR 375, [1995] IRLR 157, ECJ 23.2
Johnson v Coventry Churchill International Ltd [1992] 3 All ER 14 .... 24.10
Johnson v Ryan [2000] ICR 236, EAT 15.8
Johnson v Unisys Ltd [2001] UKHL 13, [2003] 1 AC 518, [2001] 2 All ER 801, [2001] 2
    WLR 1076, [2001] ICR 480, [2001] IRLR 279 .... 7.13, 7.23, 52.12,
                                                                                        55.18, 55.29
Johnson & Bloy (Holdings) Ltd and Johnson & Bloy Ltd v Wolstenholme Rink plc and
    Fallon [1989] FSR 135, [1987] IRLR 499, CA 38.24
Johnson Underwood Ltd v Montgomery [2001] EWCA Civ 318, [2001] ICR 819, [2001]
    20 LS Gaz R 40, [2001] All ER (D) 101 (Mar), sub nom Montgomery v Johnson
    Underwood Ltd [2001] IRLR 269, ... 15.3, 20.3, 44.2

PARA

Johnston v Chief Constable of the Royal Ulster Constabulary: 222/84 [1987] QB 129,
[1986] 3 All ER 135, [1986] 3 WLR 1038, [1986] ECR 1651, [1986] 3 CMLR 240,
[1987] ICR 83, [1986] IRLR 263, 130 Sol Jo 953, [1987] LS Gaz R 188, ECJ . 12.19, 23.6
Johnstone v Bloomsbury Health Authority [1992] QB 333, [1991] 2 All ER 293, [1991]
2 WLR 1362, [1991] ICR 269, [1991] IRLR 118, [1991] 2 Med LR 38, CA 7.13, 7.21
Jones v Associated Tunnelling Co Ltd [1981] IRLR 477, EAT 7.13, 7.22
Jones v DAS Legal Expenses Insurance Co Ltd [2003] EWCA Civ 1071, [2004] IRLR
218, 147 Sol Jo LB 932, [2003] All ER (D) 425 (Jul) 19.50, 20.12, 28.7
Jones v Friends Provident Life Office [2004] IRLR 783, NICA 12.21
Jones v Governing Body of Burdett Coutts School [1997] ICR 390, 571 IRLB 9, EAT;
revsd [1999] ICR 38, [1998] IRLR 521, [1998] 18 LS Gaz R 32, 142 Sol Jo LB 142,
CA 20.15, 35.12
Jones v Gwent County Council [1992] IRLR 521 .... 7.23
Jones v Mid-Glamorgan County Council [1997] ICR 815, [1997] IRLR 685, CA 50.8
Jones v Post Office [2001] EWCA Civ 558, [2001] ICR 805, [2001] IRLR 384, [2001]
All ER (D) 133 (Apr) 9.12
Jones v Secretary of State for Employment [1982] ICR 389, EAT 29.7
Jones v 3M Healthcare Ltd [2003] UKHL 33, [2003] 4 All ER 1113, [2003] 2 CMLR 1329,
[2003] ICR 867, [2003] IRLR 484, 74 BMLR 109, [2003] 30 LS Gaz R 30, (2003)
Times, 23 June, 147 Sol Jo LB 782, [2003] All ER (D) 258 (Jun) 9.17, 11.12
Jones v Tower Boot Co Ltd [1995] IRLR 529, EAT; revsd [1997] 2 All ER 406, [1997]
ICR 254, [1997] IRLR 168, [1997] NLJR 60, CA 11.13, 12.35, 53.1
Jones v University of Manchester [1993] ICR 474, [1993] IRLR 218, [1993] 10 LS Gaz
R 33, 137 Sol Jo LB 14, CA 11.8, 12.8
Jørgensen v Foreningen af Speciallæger: C-226/98 [2000] ECR I-2447, [2002] 1 CMLR
1151, [2000] IRLR 726, ECJ 12.8
Jowett (Angus) & Co Ltd v National Union of Tailors and Garment Workers [1985] ICR
646, [1985] IRLR 326, EAT 36.6, 49.15
Jowitt v Pioneer Technology (UK) Ltd [2003] EWCA Civ 411, [2003] ICR 1120, [2003]
IRLR 356, [2003] All ER (D) 263 (Mar) 41.14, 41.17
Jupiter General Insurance Co Ltd v Shroff [1937] 3 All ER 67, PC 55.17
Justfern Ltd v D'Ingerthorpe [1994] ICR 286, [1994] IRLR 164, EAT 6.9, 52.13

K

KB v National Health Service Pensions Agency: C-117/01 [2004] All ER (EC) 1089, [2004]
1 CMLR 931, [2004] ICR 781, [2004] IRLR 240, [2004] 1 FLR 683, (2004) Times, 15
January, [2004] All ER (D) 03 (Jan), ECJ 22.13, 39.6
Kachelmann v Bankhaus Hermann Lampe KG: C-322/98 [2000] ECR I-7505, [2002] 1
CMLR 155, [2001] IRLR 49, ECJ 11.9
Kalanke v Freie Hansestadt Bremen: C-450/93 [1996] All ER (EC) 66, [1995] ECR I-3051,
[1996] 1 CMLR 175, [1996] ICR 314, [1995] IRLR 660, ECJ 11.5, 11.12, 12.9, 34.2
Kalliope Schöning-Kougebetopoulou v Freie und Hansestadt Hamburg. See Schöning-
Kougebetopoulou v Freie und Hansestadt Hamburg
Kanapathiar v Harrow London Borough Council [2003] IRLR 571, [2003] All ER (D) 445
(Feb), EAT 20.5
Kapadia v Lambeth London Borough Council [2000] IRLR 14, EAT; affd [2000] IRLR
699, 57 BMLR 170, [2000] All ER (D) 785, CA 9.7
Kapur v Shields [1976] 1 All ER 873, [1976] 1 WLR 131, [1976] ICR 26, 120 Sol Jo 96 .... 50.15
Katsikas v Konstantinidis: C-132/91, C-138/91 and C-139/91 [1992] ECR I-6577, [1993]
1 CMLR 845, [1993] IRLR 179, ECJ 49.12
Kaur v MG Rover Group Ltd [2004] IRLR 279 .... 5.3
Kavanagh v Hiscock [1974] QB 600, [1974] 2 All ER 177, [1974] 2 WLR 421, [1974]
ICR 282, [1974] IRLR 121, 16 KIR 31, [1974] Crim LR 255, 118 Sol Jo 98 .... 42.10
Kells v Pilkington plc [2002] IRLR 693, [2002] All ER (D) 33 (May), EAT 22.9
Kelly v Northern Ireland Housing Executive [1999] 1 AC 428, [1998] 3 WLR 735, [1998]
ICR 828, [1998] IRLR 593, [1998] 36 LS Gaz R 31, 142 Sol Jo LB 254, HL 11.12
Kelly v Upholstery and Cabinet Works (Amesbury) Ltd [1977] IRLR 91, EAT 36.4, 51.11
Kelman v Care Contract Services Ltd [1995] ICR 260, EAT 49.5

Table of cases

PARA

Kenny v Hampshire Constabulary [1998] ICR 27, [1999] IRLR 76, EAT 9.12, 9.14
Kenny v South Manchester College [1993] ICR 934, [1993] IRLR 265 .... 49.5
Kent County Council v Gilham [1985] ICR 227, sub nom Gilham v Kent County Council
   [1985] IRLR 16, CA 45.14
Kent Free Press v NGA [1987] IRLR 267 .... 42.16
Kent Management Services Ltd v Butterfield [1992] ICR 272, [1992] IRLR 394, EAT 31.6
Kerr v Sweater Shop (Scotland) Ltd [1996] IRLR 424, EAT 31.6
Kerry Foods Ltd v Creber [2000] ICR 556, [2000] IRLR 10, EAT.............. 36.6, 49.18, 49.20
Keywest Club Ltd (t/a Veeraswamys Restaurant) v Choudhury [1988] IRLR 51, EAT 31.35
Khan v Chief Constable of West Yorkshire Police. See Chief Constable of West Yorkshire
   Police v Khan
Khan v General Medical Council [1996] ICR 1032, [1994] IRLR 646, CA 12.27, 13.2
Khan v Trident Safeguards Ltd [2004] EWCA Civ 624, 148 Sol Jo LB 634, (2004) Times,
   28 May 13.2
Khanum v Mid-Glamorgan Area Health Authority [1979] ICR 40, [1978] IRLR 215, 13
   ITR 303, EAT 51.10
Kidd v Axa Equity and Law Life Assurance Society plc [2000] IRLR 301 .... 37.4
Kidd v DRG (UK) Ltd [1985] ICR 405, [1985] IRLR 190, EAT.. 11.9
Kien Tran v Greenwich Vietnam Community Project [2002] EWCA Civ 553, [2002]
   ICR 1101, [2002] IRLR 735, [2002] 21 LS Gaz R 31, [2002] All ER (D) 238
   (Apr) 19.63, 20.11
Kigass Aero Components Ltd v Brown [2002] ICR 697, [2002] IRLR 312, [2002] All ER
   (D) 341 (Feb), EAT 27.3
King v Eaton Ltd [1996] IRLR 199, 1997 SLT 654, Ct of Sess 19.12, 51.11
King v Eaton Ltd (No 2) [1998] IRLR 686, 1999 SLT 656, Ct of Sess 52.13
King v Smith [1995] ICR 339, CA 25.5
King v University Court of the University of St Andrews [2002] IRLR 252, Ct of Sess 7.23
King's College London v Clark (2003) IDS Brief No 747 .... 22.11
Kingston v British Railways Board [1982] ICR 392, [1982] IRLR 274, EAT; affd [1984]
   ICR 781, [1984] IRLR 146, CA 11.13, 12.35, 51.14
Kingston-upon-Hull City Council v Dunnachie (No 3) [2004] ICR 227, [2003] IRLR 843,
   147 Sol Jo LB 992, EAT 19.69
Kirton v Tetrosyl Ltd [2003] EWCA Civ 619, [2003] ICR 1237, [2003] IRLR 353, (2003)
   Times, 28 April, 147 Sol Jo LB 474, [2003] All ER (D) 190 (Apr) 9.7
Knight v Central London Bus Co Ltd EAT/443/00 .... 20.12
Knight v Department of Social Security [2002] IRLR 249, [2001] All ER (D) 473 (Nov),
   EAT 19.12
Knowles v Liverpool City Council [1993] 4 All ER 321, [1993] 1 WLR 1428, 91 LGR
   629, [1994] 1 Lloyd's Rep 11, [1994] ICR 243, [1993] IRLR 588, [1993] NLJR
   1479n, [1994] PIQR P8, HL 25.6
Kopel v Safeway Stores plc [2003] IRLR 753, [2003] All ER (D) 05 (Sep), EAT . 19.36, 19.71,
                                                                                                                       52.22
Kording v Senator für Finanzen: C-100/95 [1997] ECR I-5289, [1998] 1 CMLR 395,
   [1997] IRLR 710, ECJ 22.3
Kovacs v Queen Mary and Westfield College [2002] EWCA Civ 352, [2002] ICR 919,
   [2002] IRLR 414, [2002] 19 LS Gaz R 29, (2002) Times, 12 April, 146 Sol Jo LB
   91, [2002] All ER (D) 368 (Mar) 18.3, 19.36, 19.69
Kowalska v Freie und Hansestadt Hamburg: C-33/89 [1990] ECR I-2591, [1992] ICR 29,
   [1990] IRLR 447, ECJ... 22.24, 22.25
Kraus v Penna plc [2004] IRLR 260, [2003] All ER (D) 275 (Nov), EAT 10.18
Kuddus v Chief Constable of Leicestershire Constabulary [2001] UKHL 29, [2002] 2 AC
   122, [2001] 3 All ER 193, [2001] 2 WLR 1789, [2001] 28 LS Gaz R 43, [2001]
   NLJR 936, 145 Sol Jo LB 166, [2001] All ER (D) 30 (Jun) 13.8
Kuratorium für Dialyse und Nierentransplantation eV v Lewark: C-457/93 [1996] ECR
   I-243, [1996] IRLR 637, ECJ.. 22.3, 46.4
Kutz-Bauer v Freie und Hansestadt Hamburg: C-187/00 [2003] ECR I-2741, [2003] IRLR
   368, [2003] All ER (D) 327 (Mar), ECJ 12.8
Kwamin v Abbey National plc [2004] ICR 841, [2004] IRLR 516, [2004] NLJR 418,
   [2004] All ER (D) 189 (Mar), EAT 18.13, 19.62, 28.7

PARA

Kwik-Fit (GB) Ltd v Lineham [1992] ICR 183, [1992] IRLR 156, [1992] 4 LS Gaz R 31,
EAT 45.5

L

LMC Drains Ltd v Waugh [1991] 3 CMLR 172, EAT 49.4
Labour Party v Oakley [1988] ICR 403, sub nom Oakley v Labour Party [1988] IRLR 34,
CA 51.14
Laher v Hammersmith and Fulham London Borough EAT/215/91, IDS Brief No 531 .... 19.52
Laird v A K Stoddart Ltd [2001] IRLR 591, [2001] All ER (D) 261 (Jan), EAT 31.12
Lambeth London Borough v D'Souza. See D'Souza v Lambeth London Borough
Lambeth London Borough Council v Commission for Racial Equality (1989) 87 LGR 862,
[1989] ICR 641, [1989] IRLR 379, [1989] 29 LS Gaz R 44, EAT; affd [1990] ICR
768, [1990] IRLR 231, CA 11.5, 11.8, 12.4, 12.9, 12.14
Lamont v Fry's Metals Ltd [1985] ICR 566, [1985] IRLR 470, CA 19.64
Lana v Positive Action Training In Housing (London) Ltd [2001] IRLR 501, [2001] All
ER (D) 23 (Jun), EAT 11.13, 12.38
Lancashire Fire Ltd v SA Lyons & Co Ltd [1997] IRLR 113, CA 38.9
Lancaster v DEK Printing Machines Ltd EAT/623/99 .... 18.25
Landeshauptstadt Kiel v Jaeger: C-151/02 [2004] All ER (EC) 604, [2003] 3 CMLR 493,
[2003] IRLR 804, 75 BMLR 201, [2003] All ER (D) 72 (Sep), ECJ 54.4, 54.14
Landsorganisationen i Danmark v Ny Molle Kro: 287/86 [1987] ECR 5465, [1989] ICR
330, [1989] IRLR 37, ECJ 49.4
Lane v Shire Roofing Co (Oxford) Ltd [1995] IRLR 493, [1995] PIQR P417, CA 25.2
Lange v Georg Schünemann GmbH: C-350/99 [2001] ECR I-1061, [2001] All ER (EC)
481, [2001] IRLR 244, [2001] All ER (D) 90 (Feb), ECJ 7.9
Langston v Amalgamated Union of Engineering Workers [1974] 1 All ER 980, [1974] 1
WLR 185, [1974] ICR 180, [1974] IRLR 15, 16 KIR 139, 118 Sol Jo 97, CA 7.13, 55.21
Lansing Linde Ltd v Kerr [1991] 1 All ER 418, [1991] 1 WLR 251, [1991] ICR 428,
[1991] IRLR 80, [1990] NLJR 1458, CA 7.23, 38.9
Landon v Lill EAT/1486/00 .... 18.18
Lanton Leisure Ltd v White and Gibson [1987] IRLR 119, EAT 50.13
Larsen v Henderson [1990] IRLR 512, sub nom Larsen's Executrix v Henderson 1990
SLT 498, Ct of Sess 29.10
Lasertop Ltd v Webster [1997] ICR 828, [1997] IRLR 498, 572 IRLB 14, EAT 12.3
Latchman v Reed Business Information Ltd [2002] ICR 1453 .... 9.6
Laurie v Holloway [1994] ICR 32, EAT 19.52
Lavarack v Woods of Colchester Ltd [1967] 1 QB 278, [1966] 3 All ER 683, [1966] 3
WLR 706, 1 KIR 312, 110 Sol Jo 770, CA 55.25
Law Hospital NHS Trust v Rush [2001] IRLR 611, Ct of Sess 9.2
Lawal v Northern Spirit Ltd [2003] UKHL 35, [2004] 1 All ER 187, [2003] ICR 856,
[2003] IRLR 538, [2003] 28 LS Gaz R 30, [2003] NLJR 1005, (2003) Times, 27
June, 147 Sol Jo LB 783, [2003] All ER (D) 255 (Jun) 20.2, 28.7
Lawrence v Regent Office Care Ltd [1999] ICR 654, [1999] IRLR 148, EAT; on appeal
[2000] IRLR 608, [2000] All ER (D) 842, CA; refd C-320/00: [2002] ECR I-7325,
[2002] 3 CMLR 761, [2003] ICR 1092, [2002] IRLR 822, (2002) Times, 10 October,
[2002] All ER (D) 84 (Sep), ECJ 22.9
Lawrie-Blum v Land Baden-Württemberg: 66/85 [1986] ECR 2121, [1987] 3 CMLR 389,
[1987] ICR 483, ECJ 22.4
Laws v London Chronicle (Indicator Newspapers) Ltd [1959] 2 All ER 285, [1959] 1 WLR
698, 103 Sol Jo 470, CA 55.17
Lawson v Serco Ltd [2004] EWCA Civ 12, [2004] 2 All ER 200, [2004] ICR 204, [2004]
IRLR 206, (2004) Times, 30 January, 148 Sol Jo LB 148, [2004] All ER (D) 217
(Jan) 24.3, 24.11, 50.15
Learoyd v Brook [1891] 1 QB 431, 55 JP 265, 60 LJQB 373, 39 WR 480, 64 LT 458, 7
TLR 236 .... 55.44
Ledernes Hovedorganisation (acting for Rygard) v Dansk Arbejdsgiverforening (acting for
Sto Molle Akustik A/S): C-48/94 [1995] ECR I-2745, [1996] 3 CMLR 45, [1996]
ICR 333, [1996] IRLR 51, ECJ 49.5
Lee v GEC Plessey Telecommunications [1993] IRLR 383 .... 5.4, 7.22

Table of cases

PARA

Lee v Showmen's Guild of Great Britain [1952] 2 QB 329, [1952] 1 All ER 1175, 96 Sol
    Jo 296, [1952] 1 TLR 1115, CA 48.12
Lee Ting Sang v Chung Chi-Keung [1990] 2 AC 374, [1990] 2 WLR 1173, [1990] ICR
    409, [1990] IRLR 236, 134 Sol Jo 909, [1990] 13 LS Gaz R 43, PC 15.3
Leech v Preston Borough Council [1985] ICR 192, [1985] IRLR 337, EAT 50.13
Leeds Private Hospital Ltd v Parkin [1992] ICR 571, EAT 11.5
Legal and General Assurance Ltd v Kirk [2001] EWCA Civ 1803, [2002] IRLR 124, [2001]
    All ER (D) 212 (Nov) 28.7
Legal and General Assurance Society Ltd v Pensions Ombudsman [2000] 2 All ER 577,
    [2000] 1 WLR 1524, [1999] 46 LS Gaz R 40, [1999] NLJR 1733, 144 Sol Jo LB 8 . 39.12
Leicester University v A [1999] ICR 701, [1999] IRLR 352, EAT 13.7, 19.18
Leighton v Charalambous [1995] ICR 1091, [1996] IRLR 67, EAT 7.15
Leighton v Construction Industry Training Board. See Construction Industry Training Board
    v Leighton
Leighton v Michael [1995] ICR 1091, [1996] IRLR 67, EAT 7.15, 12.16
Leisure Leagues UK Ltd v Maconnachie [2002] IRLR 600, (2002) Times, 3 May, [2002]
    All ER (D) 223 (Mar), EAT 31.14, 31.22
Lennon v Birmingham City Council [2001] EWCA Civ 435, [2001] IRLR 826, [2001] All
    ER (D) 321 (Mar) 7.23, 19.26
Leonard v Southern Derbyshire Chamber of Commerce [2001] IRLR 19, [2000] All ER
    (D) 1327, EAT 9.2
Leonard v Strathclyde Buses Ltd [1998] IRLR 693, 1999 SC 57, 1999 SLT 734, 606 IRLB
    8, Ct of Sess 52.13
Leonard (Cyril) & Co v Simo Securities Trust Ltd [1971] 3 All ER 1313, [1972] 1 WLR
    80, 115 Sol Jo 911, CA 55.20
Letheby & Christopher Ltd v Bond [1988] ICR 480, EAT 6.7
Leverton v Clwyd County Council [1989] AC 706, [1989] 2 WLR 47, [1988] 2 CMLR 811, 87
    LGR 269, [1989] ICR 33, [1988] IRLR 239, CA; affd [1989] AC 706, [1989] 1 All
    ER 78, [1989] 2 WLR 47, 87 LGR 269, [1989] ICR 33, [1989] IRLR 28, 133 Sol Jo
    45, [1989] 19 LS Gaz R 41, HL 22.7, 22.9,
                                                         22.11, 22.22
Levez v T H Jennings (Harlow Pools) Ltd: C-326/96 [1999] All ER (EC) 1, [1998] ECR I-
    7835, [1999] 2 CMLR 363, [1999] ICR 521, [1999] IRLR 36, 608 IRLB 3, [1998]
    All ER (D) 662, ECJ 18.12
Levez v T H Jennings (Harlow Pools) Ltd (No 2), Hicking v Basford Group Ltd [1999] 3
    CMLR 715, [2000] ICR 58, [1999] IRLR 764, 629 IRLB 7, EAT 22.9
Levy v Allied Dunbar Assurance plc (2000) 660 IRLB 12 .... 26.24
Lewen v Denda: C-333/97 [2000] All ER (EC) 261, [1999] ECR I-7243, [2000] 2 CMLR
    38, [2000] IRLR 67, ECJ 22.14
Lewicki v Brown & Root Wimpey Highland Fabricators Ltd 1996 STC 145, [1996] IRLR
    565, OH 41.16
Lewis v Motorworld Garages Ltd [1986] ICR 157, [1985] IRLR 465, CA 50.7
Lewis and Britton v E Mason & Sons [1994] IRLR 4, EAT 50.17
Lewis (John) plc v Coyne [2001] IRLR 139, EAT 51.9
Lewisham and Guys Mental NHS Trust v Andrews [2000] ICR 707, CA 13.2
Leyland DAF Ltd, Re. See Talbot v Cadge
Leyland Vehicles Ltd v Jones [1981] ICR 428, [1981] IRLR 269, EAT 48.5
Libyan Arab Foreign Bank v Bankers Trust Co [1989] QB 728, [1989] 3 All ER 252,
    [1989] 3 WLR 314, [1988] 1 Lloyd's Rep 259, 133 Sol Jo 568 .... 55.15
Lightfoot v D & J Sporting Ltd [1996] IRLR 64, EAT 7.15
Lightways (Contractors) Ltd v Associated Holdings Ltd [2000] IRLR 247, Ct of Sess 49.5
Linbourne v Constable [1993] ICR 698, EAT 19.10
Lincoln Mills (Australia) Ltd v Gough [1964] VR 193 .... 8.28
Lindsay v Alliance and Leicester plc [2000] ICR 1234, [2000] All ER (D) 282, EAT 11.10
Linfood Cash and Carry Ltd v Thomson [1989] ICR 518, [1989] IRLR 235, EAT 51.10
Lipkin Gorman (a firm) v Karpnale Ltd [1991] 2 AC 548, [1992] 4 All ER 512, [1991]
    3 WLR 10, [1991] NLJR 815, 135 Sol Jo LB 36, HL 31.15
Lisk-Carew v Birmingham City Council [2004] EWCA Civ 565, [2004] 20 LS Gaz R 35,
    2004) Times, 7 June, [2004] All ER (D) 215 (Apr) 13.8

PARA

List Design Group Ltd v Douglas [2002] ICR 686, [2003] IRLR 14, [2002] All ER (D) 215
(Mar), EAT 27.6, 31.6
Lister v Hesley Hall Ltd [2001] UKHL 22, [2002] 1 AC 215, [2001] 2 All ER 769, [2001] 1
WLR 1311, [2001] ICR 665, [2001] IRLR 472, [2001] 2 FCR 97, [2001] 2 FLR 307,
[2001] Fam Law 595, [2001] NPC 89, [2001] NLJR 728, (2001) Times, 10 May,
145 Sol Jo LB 126, [2001] All ER (D) 37 (May) 11.13, 12.35, 53.2
Litster v Forth Dry Dock and Engineering Co Ltd [1990] 1 AC 546, [1989] 1 All ER 1134,
[1989] 2 WLR 634, [1989] ICR 341, [1989] IRLR 161, 133 Sol Jo 455, [1989] NLJR
400, 1989 SC (HL) 96, HL 23.2, 49.4, 49.8, 49.10
Little v Charterhouse Magna Assurance Co Ltd [1980] IRLR 19, EAT 7.13
Littlewoods Organisation Ltd v Harris [1978] 1 All ER 1026, [1977] 1 WLR 1472, 121
Sol Jo 727, CA 38.12
Littlewoods Organisation plc v Traynor [1993] IRLR 154, EAT 13.3
Liverpool City Council v Irwin [1977] AC 239, [1976] 2 All ER 39, [1976] 2 WLR 562,
74 LGR 392, 32 P & CR 43, 13 HLR 38, 120 Sol Jo 267, 238 Estates Gazette 879,
963, HL 7.13
Living Design (Home Improvements) Ltd v Davidson [1994] IRLR 69, Ct of Sess 38.20
Livingstone v Hepworth Refractories Ltd [1992] 3 CMLR 601, [1992] ICR 287, [1992]
IRLR 63, [1992] 5 LS Gaz R 31, EAT 2.4, 18.12
Lloyd v Grace, Smith & Co [1912] AC 716, 81 LJKB 1140, [1911-13] All ER Rep 51,
56 Sol Jo 723, 107 LT 531, 28 TLR 547, HL 53.2
Lloyd v Taylor Woodrow Construction [1999] IRLR 782, EAT 51.11
Locabail (UK) Ltd v Bayfield Properties Ltd [2000] QB 451, [2000] 1 All ER 65, [2000]
2 WLR 870, [2000] IRLR 96, [2000] 3 LRC 482, 7 BHRC 583, [1999] All ER (D)
1279, CA 19.50
Lock v Cardiff Rly Co [1998] IRLR 358, 599 IRLB 6, EAT 51.4, 51.10
Lock v Connell Estate Agents [1994] ICR 983, [1994] IRLR 444, EAT 52.9, 52.13, 55.30
Lockwood v Crawley Warren Group (2001) IDS Brief No 680 .... 11.9
Lodwick v Southwark London Borough Council [2004] EWCA Civ 306, [2004] ICR 884,
[2004] IRLR 554, (2004) Times, 9 April, 148 Sol Jo LB 385, [2004] All ER (D) 349
(Mar) 19.71
Logan v Customs and Excise Comrs [2003] EWCA Civ 1068, [2004] ICR 1, [2004] IRLR
63, [2003] 37 LS Gaz R 31, (2003) Times, 4 September, [2003] All ER (D) 388
(Jul) 19.59
Lommers v Minister van Landbouw, Natuurbeheer en Visserij: C-476/99 [2002] ECR I-2891,
[2004] 2 CMLR 1141, [2002] IRLR 430, [2002] All ER (D) 280 (Mar), ECJ 22.3
London Ambulance Service v Charlton [1992] ICR 773, [1992] IRLR 510, EAT 46.2
London and Mashonaland Exploration Co Ltd v New Mashonaland Exploration Co Ltd
[1891] WN 165 .... 8.16
London Fire and Civil Defence Authority v Betty [1994] IRLR 384, EAT 51.8
London Fire and Civil Defence Authority v Samuels EAT/450/00, IDS Brief No 669 .... 19.38,
19.42
London International College v Sen [1993] IRLR 333, CA 18.25
London Transport Executive v Clarke [1981] ICR 355, [1981] IRLR 166, CA 45.19, 50.9,
55.7
London Underground Ltd v Edwards [1995] ICR 574, [1995] IRLR 355, EAT 11.8, 13.8
London Underground Ltd v Edwards (No 2) [1999] ICR 494, [1998] IRLR 364, [1998]
25 LS Gaz R 32, [1998] NLJR 905, 142 Sol Jo LB 182, [1998] All ER (D) 231,
CA 11.8
London Underground Ltd v National Union of Rail, Maritime and Transport Workers [2001]
EWCA Civ 211, [2001] ICR 647, [2001] IRLR 228, [2001] All ER (D) 191 (Feb) 42.14,
42.15
London Underground Ltd v National Union of Railwaymen [1989] IRLR 341 .... 42.14
London Underground Ltd v National Union of Railwaymen, Maritime and Transport
Workers [1996] ICR 170, CA 42.14
London Underground Ltd v Noel [2000] ICR 109, [1999] IRLR 621, sub nom Noel v
London Underground Ltd [1999] 31 LS Gaz R 38, CA 18.25
Longden v Ferrari Ltd [1994] ICR 443, [1994] BCC 250, sub nom Longden and Paisley v
Ferrari Ltd and Kennedy International Ltd [1994] IRLR 157, EAT 49.10

Table of cases

PARA

Lonrho Ltd v Shell Petroleum Co Ltd (No 2) [1982] AC 173, [1981] 2 All ER 456, [1981] 3 WLR 33, 125 Sol Jo 429, HL 42.2

Lonrho plc v Fayed [1992] 1 AC 448, [1991] 3 All ER 303, [1991] 3 WLR 188, [1991] BCLC 779, [1991] BCC 641, 135 Sol Jo LB 68, HL 42.2

Lord Chancellor v Coker and Osamor [2001] ICR 507, [2001] IRLR 116, [2001] All ER (D) 68 (Jan), EAT; affd sub nom Coker v Lord Chancellor [2001] EWCA Civ 1756, [2002] ICR 321, [2002] IRLR 80, (2001) Times, 3 December, 145 Sol Jo LB 268, [2001] All ER (D) 334 (Nov) 11.8, 11.9

Loughran v Northern Ireland Housing Executive [1999] 1 AC 428, [1998] 3 WLR 735, [1998] ICR 828, [1998] IRLR 593, [1998] 36 LS Gaz R 31, 142 Sol Jo LB 254, HL 11.12

Louies v Coventry Hood and Seating Co Ltd [1990] ICR 54, [1990] IRLR 324, EAT 51.10

Lubbe v Cape plc [2000] 4 All ER 268, [2000] 1 WLR 1545, [2000] 2 Lloyd's Rep 383, 144 Sol Jo LB 250, [2000] 5 LRC 605, HL 24.11

Lucas and Gandiya v Ministry of Defence (2004) IDS Brief No 763 ...... 12.15

Luce v Bexley London Borough Council (1990) 88 LGR 909, [1990] ICR 591, [1990] IRLR 422, [1990] 27 LS Gaz R 41, EAT 46.3

Lunt v Merseyside Tec Ltd [1999] ICR 17, [1999] IRLR 458, EAT 19.34

Lynock v Cereal Packaging Ltd [1988] ICR 670, [1988] IRLR 510, EAT 51.8

Lytlarch Ltd v Reid [1991] ICR 216, EAT 52.12

M

M v Vincent [1998] ICR 73, EAT 19.18

M and S Drapers (a firm) v Reynolds [1956] 3 All ER 814, [1957] 1 WLR 9, 101 Sol Jo 44, CA 38.10

MHC Consulting Services Ltd v Tansell [1999] ICR 1211, [1999] IRLR 677, EAT; affd [2000] ICR 789, 144 Sol Jo LB 205, sub nom Abbey Life Assurance Co Ltd v Tansell [2000] IRLR 387, [2000] All ER (D) 483, CA 9.25, 12.21

MPB Structure Ltd v Munro [2002] IRLR 601, [2002] All ER (D) 264 (Apr); affd sub nom Munro v MPB Structures Ltd [2004] 2 CMLR 1032, [2004] ICR 430, [2003] IRLR 350, (2003) Times, 24 April, 2003 SLT 551, 2003 SCLR 542 ...... 20.1, 27.4, 54.25

MRS Environmental Services Ltd v Marsh [1997] 1 All ER 92, [1997] 2 CMLR 842, [1997] ICR 995, [1996] 29 LS Gaz R 29, 140 Sol Jo LB 186, CA 6.1, 49.20

MSF v Refuge Assurance plc [2002] ICR 1365, [2002] IRLR 324, [2002] All ER (D) 209 (Feb), EAT 36.4

Mabey Plant Hire Ltd v Richens IDS Brief No 495 ...... 52.12

Mabirizi v National Hospital for Nervous Diseases [1990] ICR 281, [1990] IRLR 133, EAT 52.5

Macari v Celtic Football Athletic Co Ltd [1999] IRLR 787, 2000 SLT 80, 2000 SCLR 209 ...... 55.17

Macarthys Ltd v Smith [1979] 3 All ER 325, [1979] 1 WLR 1189, [1979] 3 CMLR 44, [1979] ICR 785, [1979] IRLR 316, 123 Sol Jo 603, CA; refd 129/79: [1981] QB 180, [1981] 1 All ER 111, [1980] 3 WLR 929, [1980] ECR 1275, [1980] 2 CMLR 205, [1980] ICR 672, [1980] IRLR 210, 124 Sol Jo 808, ECJ; apld [1981] QB 180, [1981] 1 All ER 111, [1980] 3 WLR 929, [1980] 2 CMLR 217, [1980] ICR 672, [1980] IRLR 210, 124 Sol Jo 808, CA 22.9, 22.22

McAuley v Eastern Health and Social Services Board [1991] IRLR 467, NICA 22.8

McBrearty v Thomson IDS Brief No 450 ...... 45.15

McCabe v Cornwall County Council [2004] UKHL 35, [2004] 3 All ER 991, [2004] 3 WLR 322, [2004] ICR 1064, [2004] IRLR 733, [2004] NLJR 1155, 148 Sol Jo LB 909, [2004] All ER (D) 268 (Jul) 7.13, 7.23

McCarthy v British Insulated Callenders Cables plc [1985] IRLR 94, EAT 52.10

McCausland v Dungannon District Council [1993] IRLR 583, NICA 11.8

McClaren v Home Office [1990] ICR 824, [1990] IRLR 338, CA 34.3, 34.4

McClelland v Northern Ireland General Health Services Board [1957] 2 All ER 129, [1957] 1 WLR 594, 55 LGR 281, [1957] NI 100, 101 Sol Jo 355, HL 55.15

McClory v Post Office [1993] 1 All ER 457, [1992] ICR 758, [1993] IRLR 159 ...... 7.13

McConnell v Police Authority for Northern Ireland [1997] IRLR 625, NICA 13.8

McCook v Lobo [2002] EWCA Civ 1760, [2003] ICR 89, [2002] All ER (D) 272 (Nov) .. 25.2

PARA

McDermid v Nash Dredging and Reclamation Co Ltd [1987] AC 906, [1987] 2 All ER 878, [1987] 3 WLR 212, [1987] 2 Lloyd's Rep 201, [1987] ICR 917, [1987] IRLR 334, 131 Sol Jo 973, [1987] LS Gaz R 2458, HL 53.1
McDonagh and Triesman v Ali [2002] EWCA Civ 93, [2002] ICR 1026, [2002] IRLR 489, (2002) Times, 11 March, [2002] All ER (D) 87 (Feb) 12.27
MacDonald v Ministry of Defence [2001] 1 All ER 620, [2001] ICR 1, [2000] IRLR 748, [2000] All ER (D) 1494, EAT; on appeal [2002] ICR 174, [2001] IRLR 431, 2002 SC 1, 2001 SLT 819, Ct of Sess; on appeal sub nom Macdonald v Advocate General for Scotland [2003] UKHL 34, [2004] 1 All ER 339, [2003] ICR 937, [2003] IRLR 512, [2003] 29 LS Gaz R 36, (2003) Times, 20 June, 2003 SLT 1158, 2003 SCLR 814, 147 Sol Jo LB 782, [2004] 2 LRC 111, [2003] All ER (D) 259 (Jun) 11.5, 11.6, 11.12, 11.13, 12.39, 28.5
Macer v Abafast Ltd [1990] ICR 234, [1990] IRLR 137, EAT 6.9, 49.8, 49.10
McFadden v Greater Glasgow Passenger Transport Executive [1977] IRLR 327, IT 30.6
McFarlane v Glasgow City Council [2001] IRLR 7, EAT 15.3
McGhee v Midlands British Road Services Ltd [1985] ICR 503, [1985] IRLR 198, EAT .. 48.13
McGuigan v T G Boynes & Sons (1999) IDS Brief No 633, EAT 11.5
Machine Tool Industry Research Association v Simpson [1988] ICR 558, [1988] IRLR 212, CA 18.25
McHugh v Hempsall Bulk Transport Ltd IDS Brief No 480 .... 35.12
McIntosh v John Brown Engineering Ltd IDS Brief No 441 .... 10.15
Mack Trucks (Britain) Ltd, Re [1967] 1 All ER 977, [1967] 1 WLR 780, 111 Sol Jo 435 .... 29.9, 55.9
McKechnie v UBM Building Supplies (Southern) Ltd [1991] 2 CMLR 668, [1991] ICR 710, [1991] IRLR 283, EAT 22.3
McLeod v Hellyer Bros Ltd. See Hellyer Bros Ltd v McLeod
McManus v Daylay Foods Ltd EAT/82/95 .... 23.2
McMaster v Manchester Airport plc [1998] IRLR 112, 593 IRLB 17, EAT 18.18, 18.23, 50.13
McMeechan v Secretary of State for Employment [1997] ICR 549, [1997] IRLR 353, CA 15.3, 44.2
Macmillan v Ministry of Defence (11 November 2003, unreported), EAT 12.8
Macmillan Inc v Bishopsgate Investment Trust plc [1993] 4 All ER 998, [1993] 1 WLR 837, [1993] IRLR 393, [1993] 11 LS Gaz R 44, sub nom Macmillan Inc v Bishopsgate Investment Trust plc (No 2) [1993] ICR 385; affd sub nom Macmillan Inc v Bishopsgate Investment Trust plc [1993] 4 All ER 998, [1993] 1 WLR 1372, [1993] 31 LS Gaz R 39, CA 7.13
McNicol v Balfour Beatty Rail Maintenance Ltd [2002] ICR 381, [2001] IRLR 644, [2001] All ER (D) 404 (Jul), EAT; affd [2002] EWCA Civ 1074, [2002] ICR 1498, [2002] IRLR 711, 71 BMLR 1, (2002) Times, 26 August, [2002] All ER (D) 407 (Jul) 9.2, 19.52
McPherson v BNP Paribas (London Branch) [2004] EWCA Civ 569, [2004] 3 All ER 266, [2004] IRLR 558, (2004) Times, 31 May, [2004] All ER (D) 175 (May) 19.17, 19.70, 19.71
MacPherson v London Borough of Lambeth [1988] IRLR 470 .... 7.23, 31.14
MacRae (Kenneth) & Co Ltd v Dawson [1984] IRLR 5, EAT 35.8
McShane and Ashton v Express Newspapers Ltd. See Express Newspapers Ltd v McShane
McVitae v UNISON [1996] IRLR 33 .... 48.15
Madden v Preferred Technical Group CHA Ltd [2004] EWCA Civ 1178, 148 Sol Jo LB 1064, [2004] All ER (D) 153 (Aug) 11.5
Magorrian v Eastern Health and Social Services Board: C-246/96 [1998] All ER (EC) 38, [1997] ECR I-7153, [1998] ICR 979, [1998] IRLR 86, ECJ 18.12
Mahlburg v Land Mecklenburg-Vorpommern: C-207/98 [2000] ECR I-549, [2001] 3 CMLR 887, [2001] ICR 1032, [2000] IRLR 276, [2000] All ER (D) 116, ECJ 11.5
Mailer v Austin Rover Group plc. See Austin Rover Group Ltd v HM Inspector of Factories
Mailway (Southern) Ltd v Willsher [1978] ICR 511, [1978] IRLR 322, 122 Sol Jo 79, EAT 31.24
Malik v BCCI SA (in liquidation) [1998] AC 20, [1997] 3 All ER 1, [1997] 3 WLR 95, [1997] ICR 606, [1997] IRLR 462, [1997] 94 LS Gaz R 33, [1997] NLJR 917, HL .. 7.13, 7.23, 52.12, 55.29

Table of cases

PARA

Malik v Post Office Counters Ltd [1993] ICR 93, EAT 12.27

Mandla v Dowell Lee [1983] 2 AC 548, [1983] 1 All ER 1062, [1983] 2 WLR 620, [1983]
ICR 385, [1983] IRLR 209, 127 Sol Jo 242, HL 11.6

Manel v Memon (2000) 33 HLR 235, [2000] 2 EGLR 40, [2000] 33 EG 74, 80 P & CR
D22, [2000] All ER (D) 481, CA 40.5

Mann v Secretary of State for Employment. See Secretary of State for Employment v
Mann

Manor Bakeries Ltd v Nazir [1996] IRLR 604, EAT 22.3, 46.4

Manpower Ltd v Hearne [1983] ICR 567, [1983] IRLR 281, EAT 52.12

Maresca v Motor Insurance Repair Research Centre [2004] 4 All ER 254, [2004] All ER
(D) 20 (Mar), EAT 19.16, 19.75

Market Force (UK) Ltd v Hunt [2002] IRLR 863, [2002] All ER (D) 06 (Jul), EAT 19.60

Market Investigations Ltd v Minister of Social Security [1969] 2 QB 173, [1968] 3 All
ER 732, [1969] 2 WLR 1, 112 Sol Jo 905 .... 15.3

Marleasing SA v La Comercial Internacional de Alimentacion SA: C-106/89 [1990] ECR I-
4135, [1992] 1 CMLR 305, [1993] BCC 421, 135 Sol Jo 15, ECJ 23.2

Marler (E T) Ltd v Robertson [1974] ICR 72, NIRC 19.71

Marley v Forward Trust Group Ltd [1986] ICR 891, [1986] IRLR 369, CA 5.3

Marley (UK) Ltd v Anderson [1996] ICR 728, [1996] IRLR 163, [1996] 02 LS Gaz R 28,
140 Sol Jo LB 26, CA 18.25, 18.26

Marley Tile Co Ltd v Shaw [1980] ICR 72, [1980] IRLR 25, 123 Sol Jo 803, CA 51.3

Marlow v East Thames Housing Group Ltd [2002] IRLR 798, [2002] All ER (D) 393
(May) 7.13, 41.14

Marriott v Oxford and District Co-operative Society Ltd (No 2) [1970] 1 QB 186, [1969]
3 All ER 1126, [1969] 3 WLR 984, 113 Sol Jo 655, CA 45.19

Marschall v Land Nordrhein-Westfalen: C-409/95 [1997] All ER (EC) 865, [1997] ECR I-
6363, [1998] 1 CMLR 547, [2001] ICR 45, [1998] IRLR 39, ECJ 11.12, 12.9

Marsh v National Autistic Society [1993] ICR 453 .... 45.19, 55.7

Marsh & McLennan Companies UK Ltd v Pensions Ombudsman [2001] IRLR 505, [2001]
All ER (D) 299 (Feb) 39.12

Marshall v Harland & Wolff Ltd [1972] 2 All ER 715, [1972] 1 WLR 899, [1972] ICR
101, [1972] IRLR 90, 7 ITR 150, 116 Sol Jo 484, NIRC 45.3

Marshall v Harland & Wolff Ltd (No 2) (Practice Note) [1972] ICR 97, 7 ITR 132, NIRC ... 20.6

Marshall v NM Financial Management Ltd [1995] 4 All ER 785, [1995] 1 WLR 1461,
[1995] ICR 1042, [1996] IRLR 20; on appeal [1997] 1 WLR 1527, [1997] ICR 1065,
[1997] IRLR 449, CA 38.2, 38.19

Marshall v Southampton and South West Hampshire Area Health Authority (Teaching):
152/84 [1986] QB 401, [1986] 2 All ER 584, [1986] 2 WLR 780, [1986] ECR 723,
[1986] 1 CMLR 688, [1986] ICR 335, [1986] IRLR 140, 130 Sol Jo 340, ECJ 18.12,
23.6, 34.7, 39.1

Marshall v Southampton and South West Hampshire Area Health Authority (No 2):
C-271/91 [1994] QB 126, [1993] 4 All ER 586, [1993] 3 WLR 1054, [1993] ECR I-
4367, [1993] 3 CMLR 293, [1993] ICR 893, [1993] IRLR 445, ECJ; apld sub nom
Marshall v Southampton and South-West Hampshire Area Health Authority (Teaching)
(No 2) [1994] 1 AC 530n, [1994] 1 All ER 736n, [1994] 2 WLR 392, [1994] ICR
242n, HL 13.8, 18.12, 19.67, 23.5

Marshall (Thomas) (Exports) Ltd v Guinle [1979] Ch 227, [1978] 3 All ER 193, [1978]
3 WLR 116, [1979] FSR 208, [1978] ICR 905, [1978] IRLR 174, 122 Sol Jo 295 ..... 8.16,
38.9, 45.19, 50.9, 55.7

Marshall (Cambridge) Ltd v Hamblin [1994] ICR 362, [1994] IRLR 260, EAT 7.13, 45.9,
50.5, 55.21

Marshalls Clay Products Ltd v Caulfield [2004] ICR 436, sub nom Caulfield v Marshalls
Clay Products Ltd [2003] IRLR 552, EAT; on appeal sub nom Caulfield v Marshalls Clay
Products Ltd [2004] EWCA Civ 422, [2004] 2 CMLR 1040, [2004] IRLR 564, 148
Sol Jo LB 539, [2004] All ER (D) 292 (Apr) 20.1, 27.4, 54.25

Martin v British Railways Board [1989] ICR 24, [1989] IRLR 198, EAT 20.5

Martin v Glynwed Distribution Ltd [1983] ICR 511, sub nom Martin v MBS Fastings
(Glynwed) Distribution Ltd [1983] IRLR 198, CA 50.8

Table of cases

PARA

Martin v South Bank University: C-4/01 [2004] 1 CMLR 472, [2004] ICR 1234, [2004]
IRLR 74, [2003] All ER (D) 85 (Nov), ECJ 39.3, 49.15, 49.24
Martin v Yeoman Aggregates Ltd [1983] ICR 314, [1983] IRLR 49, EAT 45.20, 50.10
Martin v Yorkshire Imperial Metals Ltd [1978] IRLR 440, EAT 25.23, 26.11
Martins v Marks & Spencer plc [1998] ICR 1005, [1998] IRLR 326, CA 11.5, 19.7
Masiak v City Restaurants (UK) Ltd [1999] IRLR 780, EAT 26.9, 51.3, 55.16
Mason v Provident Clothing and Supply Co Ltd [1913] AC 724, 82 LJKB 1153, [1911-13]
All ER Rep 400, 57 Sol Jo 739, 109 LT 449, 29 TLR 727, HL 38.19
Massey v Crown Life Insurance Co [1978] 2 All ER 576, [1978] 1 WLR 676, [1978] ICR
590, [1978] IRLR 31, 13 ITR 5, 121 Sol Jo 791, CA 15.3
Matthews v Kent and Medway Towns Fire Authority [2004] EWCA Civ 844, [2004] 3 All
ER 620, [2004] IRLR 697, (2004) Times, 8 July, 148 Sol Jo LB 876, [2004] All ER
(D) 47 (Jul) 22.15
Mattis v Pollock (t/a Flamingos Nightclub) [2003] EWCA Civ 887, [2004] 4 All ER 85,
[2003] 1 WLR 2158, [2003] ICR 1335, [2003] IRLR 603, (2003) Times, 16 July,
147 Sol Jo LB 816, [2003] All ER (D) 10 (Jul) 53.2
Matty v Tesco Stores IDS Brief No 609 .... 9.11
Maund v Penwith District Council [1984] ICR 143, [1984] IRLR 24, 134 NLJ 147, CA 51.1,
51.3
Maurissen and European Public Service Union v Court of Auditors of the European
Communities: 193/87 [1989] ECR 1045, ECJ 34.8
Maxwell Fleet and Facilities Management Ltd (in administration) (No 2), Re [2000] 2 All
ER 860, [2000] 2 BCLC 155, [2000] ICR 717, [2000] 06 LS Gaz R 35 .... 49.4
May (Greg) (Carpet Fitters and Contractors) Ltd v Dring [1990] ICR 188, [1990] IRLR 19,
EAT 31.6
Mayeur v Association Promotion de l'Information Messine (APIM): C-175/99 [2002] ICR
1316, [2000] IRLR 783, ECJ 49.3
Mayhew v Suttle (1854) 19 JP 38, 4 E & B 347, 24 LJQB 54, 1 Jur NS 303, 3 WR 108, 3
CLR 59, 24 LTOS 159, Ex Ch 40.2
Mazzoleni (criminal proceedings against): C-165/98 [2001] ECR I-2189, ECJ 24.3
Meacham v Amalgamated Engineering and Electrical Union [1994] IRLR 218 .... 48.15
Meade-Hill and National Union of Civil and Public Servants v British Council [1996] 1 All
ER 79, [1995] ICR 847, [1995] IRLR 478, CA 11.9
Mears v Safecar Security Ltd [1983] QB 54, [1982] 2 All ER 865, [1982] 3 WLR 366,
[1982] ICR 626, [1982] IRLR 183, 126 Sol Jo 496, [1982] LS Gaz R 921, CA 7.9, 41.2
Measures Bros Ltd v Measures [1910] 2 Ch 248, 79 LJ Ch 707, 18 Mans 40, 54 Sol Jo 521,
102 LT 794, 26 TLR 488, [1908-10] All ER Rep Ext 1188, CA 29.9
Meek v City of Birmingham District Council [1987] IRLR 250, CA 19.63, 20.18
Meer v Tower Hamlets London Borough Council [1988] IRLR 399, CA 11.8
Megner and Scheffel v Innungskrankenkasse Vorderpfalz: C-444/93 [1996] All ER (EC)
212, [1995] ECR I-4741, [1996] IRLR 236, ECJ 23.2
Meikle v Nottinghamshire County Council [2004] EWCA Civ 859, [2004] 4 All ER 97,
148 Sol Jo LB 908, [2004] All ER (D) 123 (Jul), sub nom Nottinghamshire County
Council v Meikle [2004] IRLR 703, ... 9.21, 18.29
Mennell v Newell & Wright (Transport Contractors) Ltd [1997] ICR 1039, [1997] IRLR
519, [1997] 33 LS Gaz R 26, CA 31.6, 51.3
Mensah v East Hertfordshire NHS Trust [1998] IRLR 531, [1998] All ER (D) 260, CA 13.4,
19.52
Merckx v Ford Motors Co Belgium SA: C-171/94 and C-172/94 [1996] All ER (EC) 667,
[1996] ECR I-1253, [1997] ICR 352, [1996] IRLR 467, ECJ 49.5, 49.12
Mercury Communications Ltd v Scott-Garner [1984] Ch 37, [1984] 1 All ER 179, [1983]
3 WLR 914, [1984] ICR 74, [1983] IRLR 485; revsd [1984] Ch 37, [1984] 1 All ER
179, [1983] 3 WLR 914, [1984] ICR 74, [1983] IRLR 494, 127 Sol Jo 764, CA 42.4
Merkur Island Shipping Corpn v Laughton [1983] 2 AC 570, [1983] 2 All ER 189, [1983]
2 WLR 778, [1983] 2 Lloyd's Rep 1, [1983] ICR 490, [1983] IRLR 218, 127 Sol Jo
306, HL 42.2
Mersey Dock and Harbour Co v Verrinder [1982] IRLR 152 .... 42.2
Mersey Docks and Harbour Board v Coggins & Griffiths (Liverpool) Ltd [1947] AC 1, [1946]
2 All ER 345, 115 LJKB 465, 90 Sol Jo 466, 175 LT 270, 62 TLR 533, HL 44.2, 53.3

lxxxvii

Table of cases

PARA

Merseyside and North Wales Electricity Board v Taylor [1975] ICR 185, [1975] IRLR 60, 10 ITR 52, 119 Sol Jo 272 .... 51.8
Merton London Borough Council v Gardiner [1981] QB 269, [1981] 2 WLR 232, 79 LGR 374, [1981] ICR 186, sub nom Gardiner v London Borough of Merton [1980] IRLR 472, 125 Sol Jo 97, CA 6.9
Meteorological Office v Edgar [2002] ICR 149, [2001] All ER (D) 06 (Aug), EAT 10.18
Methven v Cow Industrial Polymers Ltd [1980] ICR 463, [1980] IRLR 289, 124 Sol Jo 374, CA 22.11
Metropolitan Police Comr v Harley [2001] ICR 927, [2001] IRLR 263, [2001] All ER (D) 216 (Feb), EAT 18.29
Metropolitan Police Comr v Locker [1993] 3 All ER 584, [1993] ICR 440, [1993] IRLR 319, [1993] NLJR 543, EAT 34.6
Metropolitan Police Comr v Lowrey-Nesbitt [1999] ICR 401, EAT 34.2
Metropolitan Police Service v Hendricks (2002) IDS Brief No 707 .... 13.3
Metropolitan Police Service v Hendricks [2003] ICR 999 .... 13.3
Metropolitan Police Service v Shoebridge EAT/0234/03, (2004) IDS Brief No 765 .... 12.33
Mettoy Pension Trustees Ltd v Evans [1991] 2 All ER 513, [1990] 1 WLR 1587 .... 39.11
Meyers v Adjudication Officer: C-116/94 [1995] All ER (EC) 705, [1995] ECR I-2131, [1996] 1 CMLR 461, [1995] IRLR 498, ECJ 23.5
Michael (John) Design plc v Cooke [1987] 2 All ER 332, [1987] ICR 445, 131 Sol Jo 595, [1987] LS Gaz R 1492, CA 38.4
Mid-Staffordshire General Hospitals NHS Trust v Cambridge [2003] IRLR 566, [2003] All ER (D) 06 (Sep), EAT 9.15
Middlebrook Mushrooms Ltd v Transport and General Workers' Union [1993] ICR 612, [1993] IRLR 232, CA 28.4, 42.2
Middlesbrough Borough Council v Transport and General Workers Union [2002] IRLR 332, [2001] All ER (D) 79 (May), EAT 36.4
Midland Bank plc v Madden [2000] IRLR 288 .... 51.4
Midland Counties District Bank Ltd v Attwood [1905] 1 Ch 357, 74 LJ Ch 286, 12 Mans 20, [1904-7] All ER Rep 648, 92 LT 360, 21 TLR 175 .... 29.9, 55.9
Midland Mainline Ltd v National Union of Rail, Maritime and Transport Workers [2001] EWCA Civ 1206, [2001] IRLR 813, [2001] 38 LS Gaz R 37, [2001] All ER (D) 352 (Jul) 42.14
Mihlenstedt v Barclays Bank International Ltd and Barclays Bank plc [1989] IRLR 522, [1989] PLR 124, CA 39.3, 39.11
Mikeover Ltd v Brady [1989] 3 All ER 618, 59 P & CR 218, 21 HLR 513, [1989] 2 EGLR 61, [1989] 40 EG 92, CA 40.2
Miles v Wakefield Metropolitan District Council [1987] AC 539, [1987] 1 All ER 1089, [1987] 2 WLR 795, 85 LGR 649, [1987] ICR 368, [1987] IRLR 193, 131 Sol Jo 408, [1987] LS Gaz R 1239, [1987] NLJ Rep 266, HL 7.24, 31.14, 42.16
Miller v Harry Thornton (Lollies) Ltd [1978] IRLR 430, IT 31.24
Miller v Karlinski (1945) 62 TLR 85, CA 7.15
Miller Bros and F P Butler Ltd v Johnston [2002] ICR 744, [2002] IRLR 386, (2002) Times, 18 April, [2002] All ER (D) 220 (Mar), EAT 7.23, 18.32, 19.34
Milligan v Securicor Cleaning Ltd [1995] ICR 867, [1995] IRLR 288, EAT 6.1, 6.12, 49.20
Milsom v Leicestershire County Council [1978] IRLR 433, IT 31.20
Mingeley v Pennock and Ivory (t/a Amber Cars) [2004] EWCA Civ 328, [2004] ICR 727, [2004] IRLR 373, [2004] 11 LS Gaz R 33, (2004) Times, 4 March, [2004] All ER (D) 132 (Feb) 11.12
Mining Supplies (Longwall) Ltd v Baker [1988] ICR 676, [1988] IRLR 417, EAT 52.13
Ministry of Defence v Anderson [1996] IRLR 39, EAT 13.8
Ministry of Defence v Armstrong [2004] IRLR 672, [2004] All ER (D) 146 (Apr), EAT 22.10
Ministry of Defence v Cannock [1995] 2 All ER 449, [1994] ICR 918, [1994] IRLR 509, EAT 13.8
Ministry of Defence v Hunt [1996] ICR 544, EAT 13.8
Ministry of Defence v Jeremiah [1980] QB 87, [1979] 3 All ER 833, [1979] 3 WLR 857, [1980] ICR 13, 123 Sol Jo 735, sub nom Jeremiah v Ministry of Defence [1979] IRLR 436, CA 11.12
Ministry of Defence v Meredith [1995] IRLR 539, EAT 13.8, 19.12, 34.5

PARA

Ministry of Defence v O'Hare (No 2) [1997] ICR 306, EAT 13.8
Ministry of Defence v Pope [1997] ICR 296, EAT 11.5
Ministry of Defence v Wheeler [1998] 1 All ER 790, [1998] 1 WLR 637, [1998] ICR 242,
  [1998] IRLR 23, [1997] 45 LS Gaz R 27, 142 Sol Jo LB 13, CA 13.8
Miriki v General Council of the Bar [2001] EWCA Civ 1973, [2002] ICR 505, (2002)
  Times, 22 January, [2001] All ER (D) 364 (Dec) 20.9
Mirror Group Newspapers Ltd v Gunning. See Gunning v Mirror Group Newspapers Ltd
Mitchell v Arkwood Plastics (Engineering) Ltd [1993] ICR 471, EAT 51.8
Mitie Managed Services Ltd v French [2002] ICR 1395 .... 49.14
Mock v IRC [1999] IRLR 785, EAT 20.6
Monie v Coral Racing Ltd [1981] ICR 109, [1980] IRLR 464, CA 51.9
Mono Pumps Ltd v Froggatt and Radford [1987] IRLR 368, EAT 52.12
Monsanto plc v Transport and General Workers' Union [1987] 1 All ER 358, [1987] 1
  WLR 617, [1987] ICR 269, [1986] IRLR 406, 131 Sol Jo 690, [1987] LS Gaz R 1572,
  [1986] NLJ Rep 917, CA 42.14
Mont (J A) (UK) Ltd v Mills [1993] FSR 577, [1993] IRLR 172, CA 38.17
Montgomery v Johnson Underwood Ltd. See Johnson Underwood Ltd v Montgomery
Montgomery v Lowfield Distribution Ltd (1996) IDS Brief No 576 .... 22.11
Moore v Duport Furniture Products Ltd [1982] ICR 84, [1982] IRLR 31, 126 Sol Jo 98,
  HL 2.4, 19.32
Moore's (Wallisdown) Ltd v Pensions Ombudsman [2002] 1 All ER 737, [2002] 1 WLR
  1649, [2002] ICR 773, (2002) Times, 1 March, [2001] All ER (D) 372 (Dec) 39.12
Moores v Bude Stratton Town Council [2001] LGR 129, [2001] ICR 271, [2000] IRLR
  676, [2000] All ER (D) 404, EAT 7.13, 53.1
Morgan v Brith Gof Cyf [2001] ICR 978, [2000] All ER (D) 2540, EAT 18.9
Morgan v Electrolux Ltd [1991] ICR 369, [1991] IRLR 89, CA 20.19
Morgan v Staffordshire University [2002] ICR 475, [2002] IRLR 190, [2001] All ER (D)
  119 (Dec), EAT 9.2
Morgan v West Glamorgan County Council [1995] IRLR 68, EAT 31.6
Morganite Electrical Carbon Ltd v Donne [1988] ICR 18, [1987] IRLR 363, EAT 52.15
Morley v Heritage plc [1993] IRLR 400, CA 7.5, 27.8
Moroni v Collo GmbH: C-110/91 [1993] ECR I-6591, [1995] 2 CMLR 357, [1995] ICR
  137, [1994] IRLR 130, [1995] 42 LS Gaz R 23, ECJ 22.18
Morris (Herbert) Ltd v Saxelby [1916] 1 AC 688, 85 LJ Ch 210, [1916-17] All ER Rep
  305, 60 Sol Jo 305, 114 LT 618, 32 TLR 297, HL 38.1
Morris v Acco Ltd [1985] ICR 306, EAT 52.13
Morris v Breaveglen Ltd (t/a Anzac Construction Co) [1993] ICR 766, [1993] IRLR 350,
  [1993] PIQR P294, 137 Sol Jo LB 13, CA 53.3
Morris v C W Martin & Sons Ltd [1966] 1 QB 716, [1965] 2 All ER 725, [1965] 3 WLR
  276, [1965] 2 Lloyd's Rep 63, 109 Sol Jo 451, CA 53.2
Morris v John Grose Group Ltd [1998] ICR 655, [1998] IRLR 499, EAT 49.20
Morris v Secretary of State for Employment [1985] ICR 522, [1985] IRLR 297, EAT 29.5
Morris v Walsh Western UK Ltd [1997] IRLR 562, EAT 6.5, 6.7
Morrison v Amalgamated Transport and General Workers Union [1989] IRLR 361,
  NICA 51.10, 52.13
Morrison (William B) & Son Ltd (1999) IDS Brief No 648 .... 11.5
Morrow v Safeway Stores plc [2002] IRLR 9, [2001] All ER (D) 63 (Sep), EAT 7.13, 50.7,
  55.6
Morse v Wiltshire County Council [1998] ICR 1023, [1998] IRLR 352, 44 BMLR 58,
  EAT 9.12
Morton Sundour Fabrics Ltd v Shaw (1966) 2 KIR 1, 2 ITR 84, DC 45.5, 55.5
Motorola Ltd v Davidson [2001] IRLR 4, EAT 15.3, 44.2
Mowat-Brown v University of Surrey [2002] IRLR 235, [2001] All ER (D) 115 (Dec),
  EAT 9.7
Mowlem Northern Ltd v Watson [1990] ICR 751, [1990] IRLR 500, EAT 45.5
Muffett (S H) Ltd v Head [1987] ICR 1, [1986] IRLR 488, [1986] LS Gaz R 2653, EAT 52.12
Mugford v Midland Bank plc [1997] ICR 399, [1997] IRLR 208, EAT 51.11
Mulox IBC Ltd v Geels: C-125/92 [1993] ECR I-4075, [1994] IRLR 422, ECJ 24.11
Munir v Jang Publications [1989] ICR 1, [1989] IRLR 224, CA 19.22

Table of cases

PARA

Munro v MPB Structures Ltd. See MPB Structure Ltd v Munro
Murphy v Bord Telecom Eireann: 157/86 [1988] ECR 673, [1988] 1 CMLR 879, [1988]
    ICR 445, [1988] IRLR 267, ECJ 22.6, 22.8
Murphy v Slough Borough Council [2004] ICR 1163, [2004] All ER (D) 393 (May), EAT 9.24
Murray v Foyle Meats Ltd [2000] 1 AC 51, [1999] 3 All ER 769, [1999] 3 WLR 356,
    [1999] ICR 827, [1999] IRLR 562, [1999] 31 LS Gaz R 36, 143 Sol Jo LB 214,
    HL 35.7
Murray v Powertech (Scotland) Ltd [1992] IRLR 257, EAT 13.8

N

NACODS v Gluchowski [1996] IRLR 252, EAT 48.13
NALGO v Secretary of State for the Environment (1992) 5 Admin LR 785 .... 28.4
NRG Victory Reinsurance Ltd v Alexander [1992] ICR 675, EAT 52.1
NUPE and COHSE's Application, Re [1989] IRLR 202 .... 34.4
NWL Ltd v Woods, The Nawala [1979] 3 All ER 614, [1979] 1 WLR 1294, [1980] 1
    Lloyd's Rep 1, [1979] ICR 867, [1979] IRLR 478, 123 Sol Jo 751, HL 42.4, 42.16
Nagarajan v London Regional Transport [1998] IRLR 73, CA; revsd [2000] 1 AC 501,
    [1999] 4 All ER 65, [1999] 3 WLR 425, [1999] ICR 877, [1999] IRLR 572, [1999]
    31 LS Gaz R 36, 143 Sol Jo LB 219, HL 11.6, 11.10, 18.17
Nagle v Feilden [1966] 2 QB 633, [1966] 1 All ER 689, [1966] 2 WLR 1027, 110 Sol Jo
    286, CA 48.12
Nairne v Highland and Islands Fire Brigade [1989] IRLR 366, 1989 SLT 754, Ct of Sess .. 52.13
Napier v National Business Agency Ltd [1951] 2 All ER 264, 30 ATC 180, 44 R & IT 413,
    95 Sol Jo 528, CA 7.15
National and Local Government Officers' Association v Courtney-Dunn [1991] ICR 784,
    [1992] IRLR 114, EAT 48.16
National and Local Government Officers' Association v Killorn [1991] ICR 1, [1990] IRLR
    464, EAT 48.16
National Coal Board v Galley [1958] 1 All ER 91, [1958] 1 WLR 16, 102 Sol Jo 31, CA 42.16
National Coal Board v National Union of Mineworkers [1986] ICR 736, [1986] IRLR 439 . 5.3
National Coal Board v Sherwin [1978] ICR 700, [1978] IRLR 122, EAT 22.6
National Dock Labour Board v Pinn & Wheeler Ltd [1989] BCLC 647, 5 BCC 75 .... 6.9
National Federation of Self-Employed and Small Businesses Ltd v Philpott [1997] ICR 518,
    [1997] IRLR 340, EAT 12.26
National Grid Co plc v Mayes [2001] UKHL 20, [2001] 2 All ER 417, [2001] 1 WLR 864,
    [2001] ICR 544, [2001] IRLR 394, [2001] NLJR 572, (2001) Times, 10 April, 145
    Sol Jo LB 98, [2001] All ER (D) 28 (Apr) 39.11
National Grid Co plc v Virdee [1992] IRLR 555, EAT 19.16
National Union of Gold, Silver and Allied Trades v Albury Bros Ltd [1979] ICR 84, [1978]
    IRLR 504, 122 Sol Jo 662, CA 36.4, 47.20
National Union of Mineworkers (Yorkshire Area) v Millward [1995] ICR 482, [1995] IRLR
    411, EAT 47.39
National Union of Teachers v Avon County Council (1978) 76 LGR 403, [1978] ICR 626,
    [1978] IRLR 55, EAT 36.4, 51.11
National Union of Teachers v St Mary's Church of England (Aided) Junior School (Governing
    Body) [1997] ICR 334, [1997] IRLR 242, [1997] ELR 169, CA 23.2, 34.7
National Vulcan Engineering Insurance Group Ltd v Wade [1979] QB 132, [1978] 3 All
    ER 121, [1978] 3 WLR 214, [1978] ICR 800, [1978] IRLR 225, 13 ITR 212, 122
    Sol Jo 470, CA 22.11
Nawala, The. See NWL Ltd v Woods, The Nawala
Neale v Hereford and Worcester County Council [1986] ICR 471, sub nom Hereford and
    Worcester County Council v Neale [1986] IRLR 168, CA 20.17, 51.4
Neary v Dean of Westminster [1999] IRLR 288 .... 55.17
Neath v Hugh Steeper Ltd: C-152/91 [1994] 1 All ER 929, [1993] ECR I-6935, [1995] 2
    CMLR 357, [1995] ICR 158, [1994] IRLR 91, [1995] 42 LS Gaz R 23, ECJ .. 20.27, 22.18
Neil v Strathclyde Borough Council. See Strathclyde Regional Council v Neil
Nelhams v Sandells Maintenance Ltd (1995) Times, 15 June, CA 25.10
Nelson v BBC (No 2) [1980] ICR 110, [1979] IRLR 346, 123 Sol Jo 552, CA 52.13

PARA

Nelson v Carillion Services Ltd [2003] EWCA Civ 544, [2003] ICR 1256, [2003] IRLR 428, [2003] 26 LS Gaz R 36, (2003) Times, 2 May, 147 Sol Jo LB 504 .... 22.10, 22.23
Nelson v James Nelson & Sons Ltd [1914] 2 KB 770, 83 LJKB 823, 110 LT 888, 30 TLR 368, CA 8.4
Nerva v RL & G Ltd [1997] ICR 11, [1996] IRLR 461, [1996] 23 LS Gaz R 35, 140 Sol Jo LB 140, CA 31.21
Nerva v United Kingdom (Application 42295/98) [2002] IRLR 815, 13 BHRC 246, (2002) Times, 10 October, [2002] All ER (D) 137 (Sep), ECtHR 28.7, 31.9, 31.21
Nethermere (St Neots) Ltd v Gardiner [1984] ICR 612, sub nom Nethermere (St Neots) Ltd v Taverna and Gardiner [1984] IRLR 240, CA 15.3
New Century Cleaning Co Ltd v Church [2000] IRLR 27, [1999] All ER (D) 345, CA 31.6
New Victoria Hospital v Ryan [1993] ICR 201, [1993] IRLR 202, [1993] 5 LS Gaz R 41, EAT 19.13
Newell v Gillingham Corpn [1941] 1 All ER 552, 39 LGR 191, 165 LT 184 ...... 55.44
Newham London Borough Council v National and Local Government Officers' Association [1993] ICR 189, [1993] IRLR 83, CA 42.4
Newham London Borough Council v Skingle [2003] EWCA Civ 280, [2003] 2 All ER 761, [2003] ICR 1008, [2003] IRLR 359, 147 Sol Jo LB 300, [2003] All ER (D) 287 (Feb) 39.6
Newland v Simons & Willer (Hairdressers) Ltd [1981] ICR 521, [1981] IRLR 359, EAT 7.15
Newman v Polytechnic of Wales Students Union [1995] IRLR 72, EAT 18.23
Newns v British Airways plc [1992] IRLR 575, CA 49.20
News Group Newspapers Ltd v Society of Graphical and Allied Trades 1982 [1986] ICR 716, [1986] IRLR 227, 130 Sol Jo 407, [1986] LS Gaz R 1726, CA 42.16
News Group Newspapers Ltd v Society of Graphical and Allied Trades '82 (No 2) [1987] ICR 181, [1986] IRLR 337 ...... 42.2, 47.1
Nicoll v Cutts [1985] BCLC 322, 1 BCC 99,427, [1985] PCC 311, CA 29.9
Nimz v Freie und Hansestadt Hamburg: C-184/89 [1991] ECR I-297, [1992] 3 CMLR 699, [1991] IRLR 222, ECJ 5.6, 22.3, 22.11, 22.24, 22.25
Noel v London Underground Ltd. See London Underground Ltd v Noel
Noel (Auguste) Ltd v Curtis [1990] ICR 604, [1990] IRLR 326, EAT 51.9
Nolte v Landesversicherungsanstalt Hannover: C-317/93 [1996] All ER (EC) 212, [1995] ECR I-4625, [1996] IRLR 225, ECJ 23.2
Noone v North West Thames Regional Health Authority (No 2). See North West Thames Regional Health Authority v Noone
Noorani v Merseyside Tec Ltd [1999] IRLR 184, CA 19.14
Nordenfelt v Maxim Nordenfelt Guns and Ammunition Co Ltd [1894] AC 535, 63 LJ Ch 908, 11 R 1, [1891-4] All ER Rep 1, 71 LT 489, 10 TLR 636, HL 38.1
Norris v Checksfield [1991] 4 All ER 327, [1991] 1 WLR 1241, 63 P & CR 38, [1991] ICR 632, 23 HLR 425, [1992] 1 EGLR 159, [1991] NLJR 707, [1992] 01 EG 97, CA ... 40.2, 40.4
North East Midlands Co-operative Society Ltd v Allen [1977] IRLR 212, EAT 36.4, 51.11
North West Thames Regional Health Authority v Noone [1988] ICR 813, sub nom Noone v North West Thames Regional Health Authority (No 2) [1988] IRLR 530, CA 13.8
North Yorkshire County Council v Fay. See Fay v North Yorkshire County Council
North Yorkshire County Council v Ratcliffe [1994] ICR 810, [1994] IRLR 342, CA; revsd sub nom Ratcliffe v North Yorkshire County Council [1995] 3 All ER 597, 93 LGR 571, 159 LG Rev 1009, [1995] IRLR 439, [1995] 30 LS Gaz R 34, [1995] NLJR 1092, 139 Sol Jo LB 196, sub nom North Yorkshire County Council v Ratcliffe [1995] ICR 833, HL 22.9, 22.10, 22.11, 34.2
Northern General Hospital NHS Trust v Gale [1994] ICR 426, CA 49.11
Northern Joint Police Board v Power [1997] IRLR 610, EAT 11.6
Norton Tool Co Ltd v Tewson [1973] 1 All ER 183, [1973] 1 WLR 45, [1972] ICR 501, [1972] IRLR 86, 117 Sol Jo 33, NIRC 52.12
Norwest Holst Group Administration Ltd v Harrison [1985] ICR 668, sub nom Harrison v Norwest Holst Group Administration Ltd [1985] IRLR 240, CA 50.7, 50.8
Norwich Pharmacal Co v Customs and Excise Comrs [1974] AC 133, [1972] 3 All ER 813, [1972] 3 WLR 870, [1972] RPC 743, 116 Sol Jo 823, CA; revsd [1974] AC 133, [1973] 2 All ER 943, [1973] 3 WLR 164, [1973] FSR 365, [1974] RPC 101, 117 Sol Jo 567, HL 7.23

Table of cases

PARA

Notcutt v Universal Equipment Co (London) Ltd [1986] 3 All ER 582, [1986] 1 WLR 641, [1986] ICR 414, [1986] IRLR 218, 130 Sol Jo 392, [1986] LS Gaz R 1314, [1986] NLJ Rep 393, CA 45.3
Nottingham University v Fishel [2000] ICR 1462, [2000] IRLR 471, [2000] ELR 385, [2001] RPC 367, [2000] All ER (D) 269 .... 7.13
Nottinghamshire County Council v Bowly [1978] IRLR 252, EAT 51.9
Nottinghamshire County Council v Meikle. See Meikle v Nottinghamshire County Council
Nu-Swift International Ltd v Mallinson [1979] ICR 157, [1978] IRLR 537, 122 Sol Jo 744, EAT 30.5

O
Oakley v Labour Party. See Labour Party v Oakley
O'Brien v Associated Fire Alarms Ltd [1969] 1 All ER 93, [1968] 1 WLR 1916, 3 KIR 223, 3 ITR 182, 112 Sol Jo 232, CA 7.13
O'Brien v Barclays Bank plc [1995] 1 All ER 438, sub nom Barclays Bank plc v O'Brien [1994] ICR 865, [1994] IRLR 580, CA 39.2, 50.14
O'Brien v Sim-Chem Ltd [1980] 3 All ER 132, [1980] 1 WLR 1011, [1980] ICR 573, [1980] IRLR 373, 124 Sol Jo 560, HL 22.7
O'Brien v Transco plc (formerly BG plc). See BG plc v O'Brien
O'Donoghue v Redcar and Cleveland Borough Council [2001] EWCA Civ 701, [2001] IRLR 615, [2001] All ER (D) 192 (May) 13.8, 52.13
Office Angels Ltd v Rainer-Thomas and O'Connor [1991] IRLR 214, CA 38.14
Ojutiku v Manpower Services Commission [1982] ICR 661, [1982] IRLR 418, CA 12.8
O'Kelly v Trusthouse Forte plc [1984] QB 90, [1983] 3 All ER 456, [1983] 3 WLR 605, [1983] ICR 728, [1983] IRLR 369, 127 Sol Jo 632, [1983] LS Gaz R 2367, CA 15.3
O'Laoire v Jackel International Ltd (No 2) [1991] ICR 718, [1991] IRLR 170, CA, CA .. 55.33
Oliver v J P Malnick & Co [1983] 3 All ER 795, [1983] ICR 708, [1983] IRLR 456, 127 Sol Jo 646, EAT 14.2
O'Neill v DSG Retail Ltd [2002] EWCA Civ 1139, [2003] ICR 222, [2002] 40 LS Gaz R 32, (2002) Times, 9 September, [2002] All ER (D) 500 (Jul) 26.18
O'Neill v Governors of St Thomas More RCVA Upper School [1997] ICR 33, [1996] IRLR 372, EAT 11.5
O'Neill v Symm & Co Ltd [1998] ICR 481, [1998] IRLR 232, EAT 9.15
Optikinectics Ltd v Whooley [1999] ICR 984 .... 52.13
O'Reilly v Mackman [1983] 2 AC 237, [1982] 3 All ER 680, [1982] 3 WLR 604, 126 Sol Jo 311; on appeal AC 237, [1982] 3 All ER 680, [1982] 3 WLR 604, 126 Sol Jo 578, CA; affd [1983] 2 AC 237, [1982] 3 All ER 1124, [1982] 3 WLR 1096, 126 Sol Jo 820, HL 34.4
Orlando v Didcot Power Station Sports and Social Club [1996] IRLR 262, EAT 13.8
Osborn & Co Ltd v Dior [2003] HLR 649, [2003] EWCA Civ 281, [2003] 05 EGCS 144, [2003] All ER (D) 185 (Jan), CA 40.5
Osborne v Valve (Engineering) Services Ltd (24 November 2000, unreported) 7.23
Osterreichischer Gewerkschaftsbund v Wirtschaftskammer Osterreich (2004) IDS Brief No 760 .... 22.14
Outram v Academy Plastics [2001] ICR 367, [2000] IRLR 499, CA 39.11
Owusu v London Fire and Civil Defence Authority [1995] IRLR 574, EAT 13.3, 18.29
Oxford v Department of Health and Social Security [1977] ICR 884, [1977] IRLR 225, 12 ITR 436, EAT 13.5
Oy Liikenne Ab v Liskojärvi: C-172/99 [2001] All ER (EC) 544, [2001] ECR I-745, [2001] 3 CMLR 807, [2002] ICR 155, [2001] IRLR 171, [2001] All ER (D) 168 (Jan), ECJ 49.5

P
P (a minor) v National Association of Schoolmasters/Union of Women Teachers [2003] UKHL 8, [2003] 2 AC 663, [2003] 1 All ER 993, [2003] 2 WLR 545, [2003] ICR 386, [2003] IRLR 307, [2003] ELR 357, (2003) Times, 6 March, [2003] NLJR 350, [2003] All ER (D) 384 (Feb) 42.4, 42.14
P v Nottinghamshire County Council [1992] ICR 706, [1992] IRLR 362, CA 51.9

PARA

P v S: C-13/94 [1996] All ER (EC) 397, [1996] ECR I-2143, [1996] 2 CMLR 247, [1996] ICR 795, [1996] IRLR 347, [1997] 2 FCR 180, [1996] 2 FLR 347, ECJ 1.2, 11.6, 20.27, 22.2
P & O European Ferries (Dover) Ltd v Iverson (1999) IDS Brief No 640 .... 22.14
P & O Property Ltd v Allen [1997] ICR 436, EAT 49.12
P & O Trans European Ltd v Initial Transport Service Ltd [2003] IRLR 128, [2002] All ER (D) 116 (Nov), EAT 49.5
PR Consultants Scotland Ltd v Mann [1996] IRLR 188, 1997 SLT 437, OH 38.20
PSM International plc v Whitehouse [1992] FSR 489, [1992] IRLR 279, CA 38.24
Page v Freight Hire (Tank Haulage) Ltd [1981] 1 All ER 394, [1981] ICR 299, [1981] IRLR 13, EAT 12.18
Page v Hull University Visitor. See R v Hull University Visitor, ex p Page
Page v Smith [1996] AC 155, [1995] 2 All ER 736, [1995] 2 WLR 644, [1995] RTR 210, [1995] 2 Lloyd's Rep 95, 28 BMLR 133, [1995] PIQR P329, [1995] 23 LS Gaz R 33, [1995] NLJR 723, ... 25.8
Paggetti v Cobb [2002] IRLR 861, (2002) Times, 12 April, [2002] All ER (D) 394 (Mar), EAT 31.12
Paine v Colne Valley Electricity Supply Co Ltd and British Insulated Cables Ltd [1938] 4 All ER 803, 37 LGR 200, 83 Sol Jo 115, 160 LT 124, 55 TLR 181 .... 25.3
Palfrey v Greater London Council [1985] ICR 437 .... 41.9
Palmer v Southend-on-Sea Borough Council [1984] 1 All ER 945, [1984] 1 WLR 1129, [1984] ICR 372, [1984] IRLR 119, 128 Sol Jo 262, CA 18.25
Palmer, Wyeth and National Union of Rail, Maritime and Transport Workers v United Kingdom [2002] IRLR 568, ECtHR 28.4
Pambakian v Brentford Nylons Ltd [1978] ICR 665, 122 Sol Jo 177, EAT 29.9
Panama v London Borough of Hackney [2003] EWCA Civ 273, [2003] IRLR 278, [2003] All ER (D) 224 (Feb) 51.9
Paramount Airways Ltd (No 3), Re. See Powdrill v Watson
Parkins v Sodexho Ltd [2002] IRLR 109, [2001] All ER (D) 377 (Jun), EAT 10.18
Parkinson v March Consulting Ltd [1998] ICR 276, [1997] IRLR 308, CA 51.1
Parliamentary Comr for Administration v Fernandez [2004] 2 CMLR 59, [2004] ICR 123, [2004] IRLR 22, [2003] All ER (D) 115 (Oct), EAT 22.11, 22.12
Parr v Whitbread & Co plc [1990] ICR 427, [1990] IRLR 39, EAT 51.9
Parsons v Albert J Parsons & Sons Ltd [1979] FSR 254, [1979] ICR 271, [1979] IRLR 117, 122 Sol Jo 812, CA 8.3, 15.3
Parsons v BNM Laboratories Ltd [1964] 1 QB 95, [1963] 2 All ER 658, [1963] 2 WLR 1273, 42 ATC 200, [1963] TR 183, 107 Sol Jo 294, CA 55.30
Patefield v Belfast City Council [2000] IRLR 664, NICA 12.21
Patel v Nagesan [1995] ICR 989, [1995] IRLR 370, CA 18.23
Patel v RCMS Ltd [1999] IRLR 161, EAT 18.32
Paterson v Islington London Borough (23 April 2004, unreported), EAT 22.7, 22.11
Patterson v Legal Services Commission [2003] EWCA Civ 1558, [2004] ICR 312, [2004] IRLR 153, [2004] 02 LS Gaz R 28, (2003) Times, 20 November, 147 Sol Jo LB 1364, [2003] All ER (D) 140 (Nov) 12.27
Paul v East Surrey District Health Authority [1995] IRLR 305, 30 BMLR 41, CA 51.9
Paul v National and Local Government Officers' Association [1987] IRLR 43 .... 47.12
Pay v Lancashire Probation Service [2004] ICR 187, [2004] IRLR 129, (2003) Times, 27 November, [2003] All ER (D) 468 (Oct), EAT 28.7
Payne v Secretary of State for Employment [1989] IRLR 352, CA 6.9
Peace v City of Edinburgh Council [1999] IRLR 417, 1999 SLT 712, OH 7.23
Peach Grey & Co (a firm) v Sommers [1995] 2 All ER 513, [1995] ICR 549, [1995] IRLR 363, [1995] 13 LS Gaz R 31 .... 19.14
Pearson v Kent County Council [1993] IRLR 165, CA 6.7
Pedersen v Camden London Borough Council [1981] ICR 674, [1981] IRLR 173, CA 50.7
Pedersen v Kvickly Skive See Handels-og Kontorfunktionaerernes Forbund i Danmark (acting on behalf of Hoj Pedersen) v Faellesforeningen for Danmarks Brugsforeninger (acting on behalf of Kvickly Skive)
Peninsula Business Services Ltd v Sweeney [2004] IRLR 49, EAT 7.21, 7.23

Table of cases

PARA

Pepper (Inspector of Taxes) v Hart [1993] AC 593, [1993] 1 All ER 42, [1992] 3 WLR 1032, [1992] STC 898, 65 TC 421, [1993] ICR 291, [1993] IRLR 33, [1993] NLJR 17, [1993] RVR 127, HL 43.20

Percival-Price v Department of Economic Development [2000] NI 141, [2000] IRLR 380, NICA 22.4, 22.22, 23.2

Perera v Civil Service Commission [1983] ICR 428, [1983] IRLR 166, CA 11.7

Pertemps Groups plc v Nixon IDS Brief No 506 .... 44.2

Petch v Customs and Excise Comrs [1993] ICR 789, 137 Sol Jo LB 120, CA 39.11

Peterborough Regional College v Gidney IDS Brief No 644 .... 18.23

Peters v Sat Katar Co Ltd [2003] ICR 1574, [2003] IRLR 574, [2003] 33 LS Gaz R 28, (2003) Times, 1 July, [2003] All ER (D) 271 (Jun), CA 20.6

Peters (Michael) Ltd v Farnfield [1995] IRLR 190, EAT 49.11

Pfaffinger v City of Liverpool Community College [1997] ICR 142, [1996] IRLR 508, EAT 35.7, 50.7

Photostatic Copiers (Southern) Ltd v Okuda and Japan Office Equipment Ltd (in liquidation) [1995] IRLR 11, EAT 49.9

Pickford v Imperial Chemical Industries plc [1998] 3 All ER 462, [1998] 1 WLR 1189, [1998] ICR 673, [1998] IRLR 435, [1998] 31 LS Gaz R 36, [1998] NLJR 978, 142 Sol Jo LB 198, [1998] All ER (D) 302, HL 26.29

Pickstone v Freemans plc [1989] AC 66, [1987] 3 All ER 756, [1987] 3 WLR 811, [1987] 2 CMLR 572, [1987] ICR 867, [1987] IRLR 218, 131 Sol Jo 538, [1987] LS Gaz R 1409, [1987] NLJ Rep 315, CA; affd [1989] AC 66, [1988] 2 All ER 803, [1988] 3 WLR 265, [1988] 3 CMLR 221, [1988] ICR 697, [1988] IRLR 357, 132 Sol Jo 994, [1988] NLJR 193, HL 18.12, 22.22

Pickwell v Lincolnshire County Council (1993) 91 LGR 509, [1993] ICR 87, [1992] 41 LS Gaz R 36, EAT 35.6, 49.14

Piggott Bros & Co Ltd v Jackson [1992] ICR 85, [1991] IRLR 309, CA .. 20.7, 20.14, 20.17, 26.11

Pinkney v Sandpiper Drilling Ltd [1989] ICR 389, [1989] IRLR 425, EAT 6.9

Polentarutti v Autokraft Ltd [1991] ICR 757, [1991] IRLR 457, EAT 52.13

Polkey v A E Dauton (or Dayton) Services Ltd [1988] AC 344, [1987] 3 All ER 974, [1987] 3 WLR 1153, [1988] ICR 142, [1987] IRLR 503, 131 Sol Jo 1624, [1988] 1 LS Gaz R 36, [1987] NLJ Rep 1109, HL 36.4, 51.4, 51.10, 51.11, 52.13

Porcelli v Strathclyde Regional Council [1986] ICR 564, sub nom Strathclyde Regional Council v Porcelli [1986] IRLR 134, Ct of Sess 11.12

Port of London Authority v Payne [1994] ICR 555, [1994] IRLR 9, CA 52.2, 52.5, 52.17

Porter v Bandridge Ltd [1978] 1 WLR 1145, [1978] ICR 943, [1978] IRLR 271, 13 ITR 340, 122 Sol Jo 592, CA 18.25

Porter v Cannon Hygiene Ltd [1993] IRLR 329, NICA 23.2

Porter v Magill [2001] UKHL 67, [2002] 2 AC 357, [2002] 1 All ER 465, [2002] 2 WLR 37, [2002] LGR 51, [2001] All ER (D) 181 (Dec) 28.7

Porter and Nanyakkara v Queen's Medical Centre (Nottingham University Hospital) [1993] IRLR 486 .... 49.20

Portsea Island Mutual Co-operative Society Ltd v Leyland (1978) 77 LGR 164, [1978] ICR 1195, [1978] IRLR 556, [1978] Crim LR 554, 122 Sol Jo 486, DC 3.3

Portugaia Construções Lda, Re: C-164/99 [2002] ECR I-787, [2003] 2 CMLR 1093, ECJ .. 24.3

Post Office v Adekeye [1997] ICR 110, 140 Sol Jo LB 262, sub nom Adekeye v Post Office (No 2) [1997] IRLR 105, CA 11.12, 37.4

Post Office v Fennell [1981] IRLR 221, CA 51.9

Post Office v Foley 2001] 1 All ER 550, [2000] ICR 1283, [2000] IRLR 827, [2000] All ER (D) 1137, CA 51.4, 51.9

Post Office v Footitt [2000] IRLR 243 .... 26.27

Post Office v Howell [2000] ICR 913, [2000] IRLR 224, EAT 18.9

Post Office v Marney [1990] IRLR 170, EAT 51.4, 51.9, 51.15

Post Office v Moore [1981] ICR 623, EAT 18.21

Post Office v Mughal [1977] ICR 763, [1977] IRLR 178, 12 ITR 130, EAT 33.2

Post Office v Roberts [1980] IRLR 347, EAT 7.13

Post Office v Strange [1981] IRLR 515, EAT 50.7

Post Office v Union of Communication Workers [1990] 3 All ER 199, [1990] 1 WLR 981, [1990] ICR 258, [1990] IRLR 143, CA 42.14

PARA

Postcastle Properties Ltd v Perridge (1985) 18 HLR 100, [1985] 2 EGLR 107, 276 Estates Gazette 1063, CA 40.2
Potter v Arafa [1995] IRLR 316, sub nom Arafa v Potter [1994] PIQR Q73, CA 55.30
Potter v Hunt Contracts Ltd [1992] ICR 337, [1992] IRLR 108, EAT 31.6, 31.8
Potter v R J Temple plc (in liquidation) (2004) Times, 11 February, [2003] All ER (D) 327 (Dec), EAT 18.23
Powdrill v Watson [1994] 2 BCLC 118, sub nom Re Paramount Airways Ltd (No 3) [1993] BCC 662; affd sub nom Powdrill v Watson [1994] 2 All ER 513, [1994] ICR 395, [1994] IRLR 295, [1994] 2 BCLC 118, 138 Sol Jo LB 76, [1994] 15 LS Gaz R 35, sub nom Powdrill v Watson, Re Paramount Airways Ltd (No 3) [1994] BCC 172, CA; on appeal sub nom Powdrill v Watson [1995] 2 AC 394, [1995] 2 All ER 65, [1995] 2 WLR 312, [1995] ICR 1100, [1995] 1 BCLC 386, [1995] NLJR 449, [1995] 17 LS Gaz R 47, sub nom Powdrill and Atkinson (as joint administrators of Paramount Airways Ltd) v Watson [1995] IRLR 269, sub nom Powdrill v Watson (Paramount Airways Ltd) [1995] BCC 319, HL 8.28, 29.10
Powell v Brent London Borough Council [1988] ICR 176, [1987] IRLR 466, CA 7.23
Power Packing Casemakers v Faust [1983] QB 471, [1983] 2 All ER 166, [1983] 2 WLR 439, [1983] ICR 292, 127 Sol Jo 187, sub nom Faust v Power Packing Casemakers [1983] IRLR 117, CA 50.17
Powerhouse Retail Ltd v Burroughs [2004] EWCA Civ 1281 .... 22.19
Practice Direction [2003] IRLR 65 .... 20.3
Premier Motors (Medway) Ltd v Total Oil Great Britain Ltd [1984] 1 WLR 377, [1984] ICR 58, [1983] IRLR 471, 128 Sol Jo 151, EAT 49.20
Presley v Llanelli Borough Council [1979] ICR 419, [1979] IRLR 381, EAT 18.23
Prestige Group plc, Re, Commission for Racial Equality v Prestige Group plc [1984] 1 WLR 335, [1984] ICR 473, [1984] IRLR 166, 128 Sol Jo 131, HL 13.12
Preston v Wolverhampton Healthcare NHS Trust [2004] ICR 993, [2004] IRLR 96, [2004] All ER (D) 175 (Feb), EAT; revsd sub nom Preston v Wolverhampton Healthcare Trust (No 2) [2004] EWCA Civ 1281, [2004] All ER (D) 73 (Oct) 22.19
Preston v Wolverhampton Healthcare NHS Trust and Secretary of State for Health [1996] IRLR 484, EAT; affd [1997] 2 CMLR 754, [1997] ICR 899, [1997] IRLR 233, CA; on appeal [1998] 1 All ER 528, [1998] 1 WLR 280, [1998] ICR 227, [1998] IRLR 197, [1998] 08 LS Gaz R 33, 142 Sol Jo LB 82, 566 IRLB 12, HL; refd sub nom Preston v Wolverhampton Healthcare NHS Trust: C-78/98 [2001] 2 AC 415, [2000] All ER (EC) 714, [2001] 2 WLR 408, [2000] ECR I-3201, [2000] 2 CMLR 837, [2000] ICR 961, [2000] IRLR 506, ECJ; apld sub nom Preston v Wolverhamptom Healthcare NHS Trust (No 2) [2001] UKHL 5, [2001] 2 AC 455, [2001] 3 All ER 947, [2001] 2 WLR 448, [2001] ICR 217, [2001] IRLR 237, (2001) Times, 8 February, 145 Sol Jo LB 55 .... 18.28, 22.19, 22.20, 22.22, 23.2
Prestwick Circuits Ltd v McAndrew [1990] IRLR 191, 1990 SLT 654, Ct of Sess 7.13
Price v Civil Service Commission (No 2) [1978] IRLR 3, IT 11.9
Printers and Finishers Ltd v Holloway [1964] 3 All ER 731, [1965] 1 WLR 1, [1965] RPC 239, 109 Sol Jo 47 .... 38.9
Procter v British Gypsum Ltd [1992] IRLR 7, EAT 51.9
Property Guards Ltd v Taylor and Kershaw [1982] IRLR 175, EAT 17.3
Provident Financial Group plc v Hayward [1989] 3 All ER 298, [1989] ICR 160, [1989] IRLR 84, CA 7.24
Pruden v Cunard Ellerman Ltd [1993] IRLR 317, EAT 18.18
Prudential Assurance Co Ltd v London Residuary Body [1992] 2 AC 386, [1992] 3 All ER 504, [1992] 3 WLR 279, 64 P & CR 193, [1992] 2 EGLR 56, [1992] 33 LS Gaz R 36, [1992] NLJR 1087, [1992] 36 EG 129, 136 Sol Jo LB 229, HL 40.2
Prudential Assurance Co Ltd v Lorenz (1971) 11 KIR 78 .... 42.3
Puglia v James & Sons [1996] ICR 301, [1996] IRLR 70, EAT 52.12, 52.13
Puttick v Eastbourne Borough Council (COIT 3106/2) (1995) unreported 11.9

Q

Qualcast (Wolverhampton) Ltd v Haynes [1959] AC 743, [1959] 2 All ER 38, [1959] 2 WLR 510, 103 Sol Jo 310, HL 25.5
Quarcoopome v Sock Shop Holdings Ltd [1995] IRLR 353, EAT 13.4, 19.10

Table of cases

PARA

Quinn v Ministry of Defence [1998] PIQR P387, HL 34.2
Quinn v Schwarzkopf Ltd [2001] IRLR 67, [2000] All ER (D) 1607, EAT; revsd [2002]
   IRLR 602, Ct of Sess 9.15
Quirk v Burton Hospital NHS Trust [2002] EWCA Civ 149, [2002] IRLR 353, (2002)
   Times, 19 February, [2002] All ER (D) 149 (Feb) 22.18

R

R v Associated Octel Co Ltd [1996] 4 All ER 846, [1996] 1 WLR 1543, [1996] ICR 972,
   [1997] IRLR 123, [1997] Crim LR 355, [1996] NLJR 1685, HL 25.19
R v A-G for Northern Ireland, ex p Burns [1999] IRLR 315 .... 18.12,
   54.9
R v Boal [1992] QB 591, [1992] 3 All ER 177, [1992] 2 WLR 890, 95 Cr App Rep 272,
   [1992] ICR 495, [1992] IRLR 420, 156 JP 617, [1992] BCLC 872, [1992] 21 LS
   Gaz R 26, 136 Sol Jo LB 100, CA 25.38, 26.13
R v Bow Street Metropolitan Stipendiary Magistrate, ex p Pinochet Ugarte (No 2) [2000]
   1 AC 119, [1999] 1 All ER 577, [1999] 2 WLR 272, 6 BHRC 1, [1999] 1 LRC 1,
   sub nom Re Pinochet Ugarte [1999] NLJR 88, [1999] All ER (D) 18, HL 20.12
R v BBC, ex p Lavelle [1983] 1 All ER 241, [1983] 1 WLR 23, [1983] ICR 99, [1982]
   IRLR 404, 126 Sol Jo 836 .... 7.23, 34.4, 55.18
R v British Coal Corpn, ex p Vardy [1993] 1 CMLR 721, [1993] ICR 720, sub nom R v
   British Coal Corpn and Secretary of State for Trade and Industry, ex p Vardy [1993]
   IRLR 104 .... 34.4, 36.4
R v British Coal Corpn and Secretary of State for Trade and Industry, ex p Price [1994]
   IRLR 72, DC 34.4, 36.4
R v British Steel plc [1995] 1 WLR 1356, [1995] ICR 586, [1995] IRLR 310, [1995]
   Crim LR 654, CA 25.19, 25.38
R v Burke [1991] 1 AC 135, [1990] 2 All ER 385, [1990] 2 WLR 1313, 90 Cr App Rep
   384, 154 JP 798, [1990] Crim LR 877, 22 HLR 433, 134 Sol Jo 1106, [1990] 24
   LS Gaz R 43, [1990] NLJR 742, HL 40.3
R v Central Arbitration Committee, ex p BTP Tioxide Ltd [1981] ICR 843, [1982] IRLR
   60 .... 10.3, 47.8
R (on the application of the BBC) v Central Arbitration Committee [2003] EWHC 1375
   (Admin), [2003] ICR 1542, [2003] IRLR 460, (2003) Times, 12 June, [2003] All ER
   (D) 71 (Jun) 47.26
R (on the application of Kwik-Fit (GB) Ltd) v Central Arbitration Committee [2002]
   EWCA Civ 512, [2002] ICR 1212, [2002] IRLR 395, (2002) Times, 29 March,
   [2002] All ER (D) 272 (Mar) 47.30
R v Certification Officer for Trade Unions and Employers' Associations, ex p Electrical
   Power Engineers' Association [1990] ICR 682, [1990] IRLR 398, HL 47.14
R v Chief Constable of West Midlands Police, ex p Wiley [1995] 1 AC 274, [1994] 3 All
   ER 420, [1994] 3 WLR 433, 159 LG Rev 181, [1995] 1 Cr App Rep 342, [1994]
   40 LS Gaz R 35, [1994] NLJR 1008, 138 Sol Jo LB 156, HL 19.13, 34.6
R v Civil Service Appeal Board, ex p Bruce [1988] 3 All ER 686, [1988] ICR 649, DC;
   affd sub nom R v Civil Service Appeal Board, ex p Bruce (A-G intervening) [1989]
   2 All ER 907, [1989] ICR 171, CA 34.3
R v Civil Service Appeal Board, ex p Chance [1993] COD 116 .... 34.4
R v Civil Service Appeal Board, ex p Cunningham [1991] 4 All ER 310, [1992] ICR 816,
   [1991] IRLR 297, [1991] NLJR 455, CA 34.4
R v Commission for Racial Equality, ex p Cottrell and Rothon [1980] 3 All ER 265, [1980]
   1 WLR 1580, 124 Sol Jo 882, 255 Estates Gazette 783 .... 13.13
R v Commission for Racial Equality, ex p Westminster City Council [1984] ICR 770, [1984]
   IRLR 230; affd [1985] ICR 827, [1985] IRLR 426, CA 11.6, 13.13
R v Crown Prosecution Service, ex p Hogg (1994) Times, 14 April, [1994] 6 Admin LR
   778, CA 34.4
R v Davies (David Janway) [2003] ICR 586 .... 25.37
R v Department of Health, ex p Gandhi [1991] 4 All ER 547, [1991] 1 WLR 1053, [1991]
   ICR 805, [1991] IRLR 431, DC 12.27, 13.2
R v Derbyshire County Council, ex p Noble (1990) 154 LG Rev 575, [1990] ICR 808,
   [1990] IRLR 332, 4 BMLR 103, CA 34.4

Table of cases

PARA

R v Director of Government Communications Headquarters, ex p Hodges [1988] COD 123, (1988) Times, 26 July, DC 34.4

R v DPP, ex p Jones [2000] IRLR 373, [2000] Crim LR 858 .... 25.42

R v East Berkshire Health Authority, ex p Walsh [1985] QB 152, [1984] 3 All ER 425, [1984] 3 WLR 818, [1984] ICR 743, [1984] IRLR 278, CA 34.4

R v F Howe & Son (Engineers) Ltd [1999] 2 All ER 249, [1999] 2 Cr App Rep (S) 37, [1999] IRLR 434, 163 JP 359, [1999] Crim LR 238, [1998] 46 LS Gaz R 34, [1998] All ER (D) 552, CA 25.37

R v Gateway Foodmarkets Ltd [1997] 3 All ER 78, [1997] 2 Cr App Rep 40, [1997] ICR 382, [1997] IRLR 189, [1997] Crim LR 512, [1997] 03 LS Gaz R 28, 141 Sol Jo LB 28, CA 25.18

R v Ghosh [1982] QB 1053, [1982] 2 All ER 689, [1982] 3 WLR 110, 75 Cr App Rep 154, 146 JP 376, [1982] Crim LR 608, 126 Sol Jo 429, CA 51.9

R v Gough [1993] AC 646, [1993] 2 All ER 724, [1993] 2 WLR 883, 97 Cr App Rep 188, 157 JP 612, [1993] Crim LR 886, [1993] NLJR 775, 137 Sol Jo LB 168, HL 20.12

R v Greater London Council, ex p Westminster City Counil (1984) Times, 27 December ... 34.2

R v Hammersmith and Fulham London Borough Council, ex p NALGO [1991] IRLR 249, [1991] COD 397 .... 34.4

R v Hull University Visitor, ex p Page [1991] 4 All ER 747, [1991] 1 WLR 1277, [1992] ICR 67, CA; on appeal sub nom R v Lord President of the Privy Council, ex p Page [1993] AC 682, [1992] 3 WLR 1112, [1993] ICR 114, [1993] 10 LS Gaz R 33, 137 Sol Jo LB 45, sub nom Page v Hull University Visitor [1993] 1 All ER 97, [1993] NLJR 15, HL 7.12

R (on the application of Professional Contractors Group) v IRC [2001] EWCA Civ 1945, [2002] STC 165, 74 TC 393, [2002] 09 LS Gaz R 31, 146 Sol Jo LB 21, [2001] All ER (D) 356 (Dec) 43.35

R v Islington London Borough, ex p Building Employers' Confederation [1989] IRLR 382, 45 BLR 45, DC 13.17

R v Kirk: 63/83 [1985] 1 All ER 453, [1984] ECR 2689, [1984] 3 CMLR 522, ECJ 28.5

R v Liverpool City Corpn, ex p Ferguson and Ferguson [1985] IRLR 501 .... 34.4

R v London (North) Industrial Tribunal, ex p Associated Newspapers Ltd [1998] ICR 1212, [1998] IRLR 569, [1998] All ER (D) 181 .... 13.7, 19.18, 19.51

R v Lord Chancellor's Department, ex p Nangle [1992] 1 All ER 897, [1991] ICR 743, [1991] IRLR 343 .... 34.2, 34.3

R v Lord President of the Privy Council, ex p Page. See R v Hull University Visitor, ex p Page

R v Mara [1987] 1 All ER 478, [1987] 1 WLR 87, [1987] ICR 165, [1987] IRLR 154, 131 Sol Jo 132, [1986] LS Gaz R 3751, CA 25.19, 25.38

R v Nelson Group Services (Maintenance) Ltd [1998] 4 All ER 331, [1999] 1 WLR 1526, [1999] ICR 1004, [1999] IRLR 646, CA 25.19

R v North Thames Regional Health Authority, ex p L (an infant) [1996] 7 Med LR 385 ... 34.2

R v Registrar General, ex p Segerdal [1970] 2 QB 697, [1970] 3 All ER 886, [1970] 3 WLR 479, [1970] RA 439, 114 Sol Jo 703, CA 11.6

R v Rhone-Poulenc Rorer Ltd [1996] ICR 1054, [1996] Crim LR 656, [1996] 02 LS Gaz R 27, 140 Sol Jo LB 39, CA 25.19

R v Rollco Screw and Rivet Co Ltd [1999] 2 Cr App Rep (S) 436, [1999] IRLR 439, CA 25.37, 25.38

R v Science Museum (Board of Trustees) [1994] IRLR 25, 158 JP 39, CA 25.19

R (on the application of Williamson) v Secretary of State for Education and Employment [2001] EWHC Admin 960, [2002] 1 FLR 493, [2002] Fam Law 257, [2002] ELR 214, [2001] All ER (D) 405 (Nov); affd [2002] EWCA Civ 1926, [2003] QB 1300, [2003] 1 All ER 385, [2003] 3 WLR 482, [2003] 1 FCR 1, [2003] 1 FLR 726, [2003] 09 LS Gaz R 27, (2002) Times, 18 December, [2002] All ER (D) 192 (Dec) 11.6

R v Secretary of State for Education and Science, ex p Prior [1994] ICR 877, [1994] ELR 231, [1994] COD 197 .... 34.4

R v Secretary of State for Employment, ex p Equal Opportunities Commission [1995] 1 AC 1, [1994] 2 WLR 409, [1995] 1 CMLR 391, 92 LGR 360, [1994] IRLR 176, [1994] NLJR 358, sub nom Equal Opportunities Commission v Secretary of State for Employment [1994] 1 All ER 910, [1994] ICR 317, HL 6.1, 11.9, 13.10, 22.11, 22.22, 23.2, 23.6, 34.4, 35.4

Table of cases

PARA

R v Secretary of State for Employment, ex p Seymour-Smith: C-167/97 [1999] 2 AC 554, [1999] All ER (EC) 97, [1999] 3 WLR 460, [1999] ECR I-623, [1999] 2 CMLR 273, [1999] ICR 447, [1999] IRLR 253, ECJ; apld sub nom R v Secretary of State for Employment, ex p Seymour-Smith (No 2) [2000] 1 All ER 857, [2000] 1 WLR 435, [2000] 1 CMLR 770, [2000] ICR 244, [2000] IRLR 263, [2000] 09 LS Gaz R 40, HL 6.1, 11.8, 12.8, 22.3, 22.10, 23.2, 50.11

R v Secretary of State for Foreign and Commonwealth Affairs, ex p Council of Civil Service Unions. See Council of Civil Service Unions v Minister for the Civil Service

R v Secretary of State for the Environment, ex p Oldham Metropolitan Borough Council [1998] ICR 367, 96 LGR 287 ...... 34.2

R v Secretary of State for the Environment, ex p Oswestry Borough Council [1995] COD 357 ...... 34.2

R v Secretary of State for the Home Department, ex p Attard [1990] COD 261, CA 34.4

R v Secretary of State for the Home Department, ex p Brind [1991] 1 AC 696, [1990] 1 All ER 469, [1990] 2 WLR 787, [1989] NLJR 1751, CA; affd [1991] 1 AC 696, [1991] 2 WLR 588, 135 Sol Jo 250, sub nom Brind v Secretary of State for the Home Department [1991] 1 All ER 720, HL 28.5

R v Secretary of State for the Home Department, ex p Moore [1994] COD 67 ...... 34.4

R v Secretary of State for the Home Department, ex p Narin [1990] 2 CMLR 233, [1990] Imm AR 403, [1990] COD 417, CA 24.2

R (on the application of Amicus – MSF section) v Secretary of State for Trade and Industry [2004] EWHC 860 (Admin), [2004] IRLR 430, [2004] All ER (D) 238 (Apr) 12.7, 12.13, 28.7

R (on the application of the Broadcasting, Entertainment, Cinematographic and Theatre Union) v Secretary of State for Trade and Industry: C-173/99 [2001] All ER (EC) 647, [2001] 1 WLR 2313, [2001] ECR I-4881, [2001] 3 CMLR 109, [2001] ICR 1152, [2001] IRLR 559, [2001] All ER (D) 272 (Jun), ECJ 23.11, 27.2, 54.2

R v Secretary of State for Trade and Industry, ex p Trades Union Congress [2001] 1 CMLR 5, [2000] Eu LR 698, [2000] IRLR 565; affd [2001] 1 CMLR 8, CA 23.6

R v Secretary of State for Trade and Industry, ex p UNISON [1997] 1 CMLR 459, [1996] ICR 1003, [1996] IRLR 438 ...... 6.1, 36.6, 49.18

R v Secretary of State for Transport, ex p Factortame Ltd: C-48/93 [1996] QB 404, [1996] All ER (EC) 301, [1996] 2 WLR 506, [1996] ECR I-1029, [1996] 1 CMLR 889, [1996] IRLR 267, ECJ; apld [1998] 1 All ER 736n, [1998] 1 CMLR 1353, [1997] Eu LR 475, DC; on appeal [1999] 2 All ER 640n, [1998] 3 CMLR 192, [1998] NPC 68, [1998] Eu LR 456, CA; affd [2000] 1 AC 524, [1999] 4 All ER 906, [1999] 3 WLR 1062, [1999] 3 CMLR 597, [1999] 43 LS Gaz R 32, HL 23.2

R v Securities and Futures Authority Ltd, ex p Fleurose [2001] EWCA Civ 2015, [2002] IRLR 297 ...... 28.7

R v Southampton Industrial Tribunal, ex p INS News Group Ltd [1995] IRLR 247 . 19.18, 19.51

R v Walsall Metropolitan Borough Council, ex p Yapp [1994] ICR 528, 92 LGR 110, CA . 34.2

RCO Support Services Ltd v UNISON [2000] ICR 1502, [2000] IRLR 624, EAT; affd [2002] EWCA Civ 464, [2002] ICR 751, [2002] IRLR 401, [2002] All ER (D) 50 (Apr) 49.5

RS Components Ltd v Irwin [1974] 1 All ER 41, [1973] ICR 535, [1973] IRLR 239, NIRC 51.14

Radin (Susie) Ltd v GMB. See GMB v Susie Radin Ltd

Rai v Somerfield Stores Ltd [2004] ICR 656, [2004] IRLR 124, EAT 18.23, 45.5

Rainey v Greater Glasgow Health Board [1987] AC 224, [1987] 1 All ER 65, [1986] 3 WLR 1017, [1987] 2 CMLR 11, [1987] ICR 129, [1987] IRLR 26, 130 Sol Jo 954, [1987] LS Gaz R 188, [1986] NLJ Rep 1161, 1987 SC (HL) 1, 1987 SLT 146, HL ... 12.8, 22.11

Ralton v Havering College of Further and Higher Education [2001] 3 CMLR 1452, [2001] IRLR 738, [2001] All ER (D) 297 (Jun), EAT 49.24

Rank Xerox Ltd v Churchill [1988] IRLR 280, EAT 7.13

Rank Xerox (UK) Ltd v Stryczek [1995] IRLR 568, EAT 52.3

Rankin v British Coal Corpn [1995] ICR 774, [1993] IRLR 69, EAT 23.2

Rao v Civil Aviation Authority [1994] ICR 495, [1994] IRLR 240, CA 52.13

Rask and Christensen v ISS Kantineservice A/S: C-209/91 [1992] ECR I-5755, [1993] IRLR 133, ECJ 49.5

PARA

Raspin v United News Shops Ltd [1999] IRLR 9, 611 IRLB 4, EAT 55.33
Ratcliffe v North Yorkshire County Council. See North Yorkshire County Council v Ratcliffe
Ravenseft Properties Ltd v Hall [2001] EWCA Civ 2034, [2002] HLR 624, [2002] 11 EG
    156, (2002) Times, 15 January, [2001] All ER (D) 318 (Dec) 40.5
Rayware Ltd v Transport and General Workers' Union [1989] 3 All ER 583, [1989] 1 WLR
    675, [1989] ICR 457, [1989] IRLR 134, [1989] 29 LS Gaz R 44, CA 42.9
Read v Astoria Garage (Streatham) Ltd [1952] Ch 637, [1952] 2 All ER 292, [1952] 2 TLR
    130, CA 8.4, 55.10
Read v Phoenix Preservation Ltd [1985] ICR 164, [1985] IRLR 93, [1985] LS Gaz R 43,
    EAT 51.9
Read (Richard) (Transport) Ltd v National Union of Mineworkers (South Wales Area)
    [1985] IRLR 67 .... 42.16
Ready Mixed Concrete (South East) Ltd v Minister of Pensions and National Insurance
    [1968] 2 QB 497, [1968] 1 All ER 433, [1968] 2 WLR 775, 112 Sol Jo 14 .... 15.3
Red Bank Manufacturing Co Ltd v Meadows [1992] ICR 204, [1992] IRLR 209, EAT 20.12,
                                                                                                                                          52.13
Reda v Flag Ltd [2002] UKPC 38, [2002] IRLR 747, [2002] All ER (D) 201 (Jul) 7.13, 45.6
Reddington v Straker & Sons Ltd [1994] ICR 172, EAT 19.3, 19.10, 19.41
Redmond (Dr Sophie) Stichting v Bartol: C-29/91 [1992] ECR I-3189, [1994] 3 CMLR
    265, [1992] IRLR 366, ECJ 49.3, 49.5
Reed and Bull Information Systems v Stedman [1999] IRLR 299 .... 11.12
Rees v Apollo Watch Repairs plc [1996] ICR 466, EAT 11.5
Refreshment Systems Ltd v Wolstenholme EAT/608/03 .... 20.1
Reid v Camphill Engravers [1990] ICR 435, [1990] IRLR 268, EAT 18.31, 31.8
Reid v Explosives Co Ltd (1887) 19 QBD 264, 56 LJQB 388, 35 WR 509, [1886-90] All
    ER Rep 712, 57 LT 439, 3 TLR 588, CA 29.9, 55.9
Reid v Rush & Tompkins Group plc [1989] 3 All ER 228, [1990] 1 WLR 212, [1990] RTR
    144, [1989] 2 Lloyd's Rep 167, [1990] ICR 61, [1989] IRLR 265, CA 26.16
Relaxion Group plc v Rhys-Harper [2003] UKHL 33, [2003] 4 All ER 1113, [2003] 2
    CMLR 1329, [2003] ICR 867, [2003] IRLR 484, 74 BMLR 109, [2003] 30 LS Gaz
    R 30, (2003) Times, 23 June, 147 Sol Jo LB 782, [2003] All ER (D) 258 (Jun)9.17, 11.12
Rentokil Ltd v Mackin [1989] IRLR 286, EAT 51.9
Retarded Children's Aid Society Ltd v Day [1978] 1 WLR 763, [1978] ICR 437, [1978]
    IRLR 128, 122 Sol Jo 385, CA 20.17
Rewe-Zentralfinanz GmbH v Landwirtschaftskammer für Saarland: 33/76 [1976] ECR 1989,
    [1977] 1 CMLR 533, CMR 8382, ECJ 23.2
Rhys Harper v Relaxion Group plc [2003] UKHL 33, [2003] 4 All ER 1113, [2003] 2
    CMLR 1329, [2003] ICR 867, [2003] IRLR 484, 74 BMLR 109, [2003] 30 LS Gaz
    R 30, 147 Sol Jo LB 782 .... 12.33, 37.5
Richardson (Inspector of Taxes) v Delaney [2001] STC 1328, 74 TC 167, [2001] IRLR
    663, [2001] All ER (D) 74 (Jun) 45.10, 55.32
Richardson v Koefod [1969] 3 All ER 1264, [1969] 1 WLR 1812, 113 Sol Jo 898, CA 55.15
Richmond Precision Engineering Ltd v Pearce [1985] IRLR 179, EAT 51.14
Rickard v PB Glass Supplies Ltd [1990] ICR 150, CA 31.8
Ridout v T C Group [1998] IRLR 628, EAT 9.12, 9.15, 9.32
Rigby v Ferodo Ltd [1988] ICR 29, [1987] IRLR 516, HL 7.22, 45.19, 55.7, 55.24
Riley v Tesco Stores Ltd [1980] ICR 323, [1980] IRLR 103, CA 18.25
Rinner-Kühn v FWW Spezial-Gebäudereinigung GmbH & Co KG: 171/88 [1989] ECR 2743,
    [1993] 2 CMLR 932, [1989] IRLR 493, ECJ 22.3
Riordan v War Office [1959] 3 All ER 552, [1959] 1 WLR 1046, 103 Sol Jo 921; affd
    [1960] 3 All ER 774n, [1961] 1 WLR 210, CA 45.20, 50.5, 50.10, 55.5, 55.43
Roach v CSB (Moulds) Ltd [1991] ICR 349, [1991] IRLR 200, EAT 6.6
Robb v Hammersmith and Fulham London Borough Council [1991] ICR 514, [1991]
    IRLR 72 .... 7.23
Roberts v Birds Eye Walls Ltd. See Birds Eye Walls Ltd v Roberts
Roberts v Skelmersdale College [2003] EWCA Civ 954, [2003] ICR 1127, [2004] IRLR
    69, [2003] All ER (D) 272 (Jun) 19.54
Robertson v Bexley Community Centre (t/a Leisure Link) [2003] EWCA Civ 576, [2003]
    IRLR 434, [2003] All ER (D) 151 (Mar) 13.3, 18.30

Table of cases

PARA

Robertson v Blackstone Franks Investment Management Ltd [1998] IRLR 376, CA . 31.6, 31.8
Robertson v British Gas Corpn [1983] ICR 351, [1983] IRLR 302, CA 5.4, 7.5
Robertson v Magnet Ltd (Retail Division) [1993] IRLR 512, EAT 51.4, 52.13
Robertson and Rough v Forth Road Bridge Joint Board [1995] IRLR 251, Ct of Sess 25.8
Robinson v Oddbins Ltd [1996] 27 DCLD 1 .... 11.9
Robinson v Post Office [2000] IRLR 804 , [2000] All ER (D) 1304, EAT 13.3, 18.30
Robinson v Ulster Carpet Mills Ltd [1991] IRLR 348, NICA 51.4, 51.11
Rock-it Cargo Ltd v Green [1997] IRLR 581, EAT 7.23, 19.34
Rock Refrigeration Ltd v Jones [1997] 1 All ER 1, [1997] ICR 938, [1996] IRLR 675,
    [1996] 41 LS Gaz R 29, 140 Sol Jo LB 226, CA 38.20, 55.34
Rockfon A/S v Specialarbejderforbundet i Danmark: C-449/93 [1995] ECR I-4291, [1996]
    ICR 673, [1996] IRLR 168, ECJ 36.4
Roebuck v National Union of Mineworkers (Yorkshire Area) [1977] ICR 573, 121 Sol Jo
    709 .... 48.15
Roith (W & M) Ltd, Re [1967] 1 All ER 427, [1967] 1 WLR 432, 110 Sol Jo 963 .... 55.36
Rolls Royce Ltd v Walpole [1980] IRLR 343, EAT 51.8
Rolls-Royce Motor Cars Ltd v Price [1993] IRLR 203, EAT 51.11
Rolls-Royce Motors Ltd v Dewhurst [1985] ICR 869, [1985] IRLR 184, EAT 51.11
Rolls-Royce plc v Doughty. See Doughty v Rolls-Royce plc
Rookes v Barnard [1964] AC 1129, [1964] 1 All ER 367, [1964] 2 WLR 269, [1964] 1
    Lloyd's Rep 28, 108 Sol Jo 93, HL 34.5
Rose v Plenty [1976] 1 All ER 97, [1976] 1 WLR 141, [1976] 1 Lloyd's Rep 263, [1975]
    ICR 430, [1976] IRLR 60, 119 Sol Jo 592, CA 53.2
Ross v Delrosa Caterers Ltd [1981] ICR 393, EAT 6.12
Rossiter v Pendragon plc [2002] EWCA Civ 745, [2002] ICR 1063, [2002] IRLR 483,
    (2002) Times, 28 May, [2002] All ER (D) 143 (May) 49.20
Rovenska v General Medical Council [1998] ICR 85, [1997] IRLR 367, CA 13.3, 18.29
Rowan v Machinery Installations (South Wales) Ltd [1981] ICR 386, [1981] IRLR 122,
    EAT 6.12
Rowell v Hubbard Group Services Ltd [1995] IRLR 195, EAT 51.11
Rowley v Cerberus Software Ltd. See Cerberus Software Ltd v Rowley
Roy v Kensington and Chelsea and Westminster Family Practitioner Committee [1992]
    1 AC 624, [1992] 1 All ER 705, [1992] 2 WLR 239, [1992] IRLR 233, 8 BMLR 9,
    [1992] 17 LS Gaz R 48, 136 Sol Jo LB 62, HL 34.4
Royal National Orthopaedic Hospital Trust v Howard [2002] IRLR 849, [2002] All ER
    (D) 54 (Aug), EAT 19.32
Royal Ordnance plc v Pilkington [1989] ICR 737, [1989] IRLR 489, CA 35.13
Royal Philanthropic Society v County (1985) 18 HLR 83, 129 Sol Jo 854, [1985] 2 EGLR
    109, 276 Estates Gazette 1068, CA 40.2
Royal Society for the Prevention of Cruelty to Animals v Cruden [1986] ICR 205, [1986]
    IRLR 83, EAT 51.10
Royal Society for the Protection of Birds v Croucher [1984] ICR 604, [1984] IRLR 425,
    EAT 51.10
Rubenstein and Roskin (t/a McGuffies Dispensing Chemists) v McGloughlin [1996] ICR 318,
    [1996] IRLR 557, EAT 20.25, 52.13
Rummler v Dato-Druck GmbH: 237/85 [1987] ICR 774, [1987] IRLR 32, ECJ 22.7
Runciman v Walter Runciman plc [1992] BCLC 1084, [1993] BCC 223 .... 8.7, 55.28, 55.36
Rushton v Harcros Timber and Building Supplies Ltd [1993] ICR 230, [1993] IRLR 254,
    [1993] 8 LS Gaz R 40, EAT 52.13
Russell v Elmdon Freight Terminal Ltd [1989] ICR 629, EAT 6.9
Rutherford v Radio Rentals Ltd 1993 SLT 221 .... 41.14
Rutherford v Secretary of State for Trade and Industry [2003] 3 CMLR 933, [2003] 42
    LS Gaz R 31, [2003] NLJR 1633, sub nom Secretary of State for Trade and Industry
    v Rutherford [2003] IRLR 858, EAT; on appeal sub nom Rutherford v Secretary of
    State for Trade and Industry [2004] EWCA Civ 1156 .... 12.8, 22.10, 22.22, 39.2, 50.14
Rutherford v Towncircle Ltd (t/a Harvest) (in liquidation) and Secretary of State for Trade
    and Industry (No 2) [2003] 2 CMLR 877, [2002] IRLR 768, EAT 35.13
Rutten v Cross Medical Ltd: C-383/95 [1997] All ER (EC) 121, [1997] ECR I-57, [1997]
    ICR 715, [1997] IRLR 249, ECJ 24.11

c

Table of cases

PARA
Ryan v Shipboard Maintenance Ltd [1980] ICR 88, [1980] IRLR 16, EAT 50.10
Rybak v Jean Sorelle Ltd [1991] ICR 127, sub nom Jean Sorelle Ltd v Rybak [1991] IRLR
    153, EAT 18.25
Ryford Ltd v Drinkwater [1996] IRLR 16, EAT 46.2, 46.6
Rygard v Sto Molle Akustik. See Ledernes Hovedorganisation (acting for Rygard) v Dansk
    Arbejdsgiverforening (acting for Sto Molle Akustik A/S)

S
S and U Stores Ltd v Wilkes [1974] 3 All ER 401, [1974] ICR 645, [1974] IRLR 283,
    [1975] KILR 117, 9 ITR 415, NIRC 31.39
SBJ Stephenson Ltd v Mandy (1999) Times, 21 July 38.21
SIP Industrial Products Ltd v Swinn [1994] ICR 473, [1994] IRLR 323, EAT 31.6
SSAFA v McClymont UKEAT/0164/02/DA 24.11
ST v North Yorkshire County Council. See Trotman v North Yorkshire County Council
Sadler v Imperial Life Assurance Co of Canada Ltd [1988] IRLR 388 .... 38.19
Safeway Stores plc v Burrell [1997] ICR 523, [1997] IRLR 200, 567 IRLB 8, EAT 35.7
Sainsbury (J) Ltd v Savage [1981] ICR 1, [1980] IRLR 109, CA 18.23, 50.13, 51.15
Sainsbury (J) plc v Moger [1994] ICR 800, EAT 20.20
St Anne's Board Mill Co Ltd v Brien [1973] ICR 444, [1973] IRLR 309, NIRC 51.10
St John of God (Care Services) Ltd v Brooks [1992] ICR 715, [1992] IRLR 546, [1992]
    29 LS Gaz R 24, EAT 51.14
St Matthias Church of England School (Board of Governors) v Crizzle [1993] ICR 401,
    [1993] IRLR 472, [1993] 15 LS Gaz R 39, EAT 12.8
Sajid v Sussex Muslim Society [2001] EWCA Civ 1684, [2002] IRLR 113, [2001] All ER
    (D) 19 (Oct) 7.23, 19.26, 55.39
Salgueiro da Silva Mouta v Portugal [2001] 1 FCR 653, ECtHR 28.4
Salton v Durham County Council [1989] IRLR 99, EAT 50.19
Salvesen v Simons [1994] ICR 409, [1994] IRLR 52, EAT 7.15
Salvesen (Christian) Food Services Ltd v Ali. See Ali v Christian Salvesen Food Services Ltd
Sampson v Wilson [1996] Ch 39, [1995] 3 WLR 455, 70 P & CR 359, 29 HLR 18, CA 40.3
Sanni v SmithKline Beecham Ltd EAT/656/98 .... 19.16
Santamera v Express Cargo Forwarding (t/a IEC Ltd) [2003] IRLR 273, (2003) Times, 13
    January, [2002] All ER (D) 379 (Nov), EAT 51.10
Sarker v South Tees Acute Hospitals NHS Trust [1997] ICR 673, [1997] IRLR 328, EAT ... 7.23,
    21.5
Saunders v Richmond-upon-Thames London Borough Council [1978] ICR 75, [1977] IRLR
    362, 12 ITR 488, EAT 11.12
Savage v British India Steam Navigation Co Ltd (1930) 46 TLR 294 .... 55.17
Savoia v Chiltern Herb Farms Ltd [1982] IRLR 166, CA 50.7
Sayers v International Drilling Co NV [1971] 3 All ER 163, [1971] 1 WLR 1176, [1971]
    2 Lloyd's Rep 105, 115 Sol Jo 466, CA 24.10
Scally v Southern Health and Social Services Board [1992] 1 AC 294, [1991] 4 All ER 563,
    [1991] 3 WLR 778, [1991] ICR 771, [1991] IRLR 522, 135 Sol Jo LB 172, HL 7.9,
    7.13, 22.19, 39.11
Scanfuture UK Ltd v Secretary of State for the Department of Trade and Industry [2001]
    ICR 1096, [2001] IRLR 416, [2001] All ER (D) 296 (Mar), EAT 18.7, 28.7, 29.7
Schmidt v Austicks Bookshops Ltd [1978] ICR 85, [1977] IRLR 360, EAT 11.5
Schmidt v Spar und Leihkasse der früheren Amter Bordesholm, Kiel und Cronshagen:
    C-392/92 [1994] ECR I-1311, [1995] 2 CMLR 331, [1995] ICR 237, [1994] IRLR
    302, ECJ 49.5
Schöning-Kougebetopoulou v Freie und Hansestadt Hamburg: C-15/96 [1998] All ER (EC)
    97, [1998] 1 CMLR 931, sub nom Kalliope Schöning-Kougebetopoulou v Freie und
    Hansestadt Hamburg [1998] ECR I-47, ECJ 24.2
Schuler-Zgraggen v Switzerland (Application 14518/89) (1993) 16 EHRR 405, [1994] 1
    FCR 453, ECtHR 28.4
Schultz v Esso Petroleum Ltd [1999] 3 All ER 338, [1999] ICR 1202, [1999] IRLR 488,
    CA 18.25
Science Research Council v Nassé [1980] AC 1028, [1979] 3 All ER 673, [1979] 3 WLR
    762, [1979] IRLR 465, [1979] ICR 921, 123 Sol Jo 768, HL 13.5, 19.12

Table of cases

PARA

Scotch Premier Meat Ltd v Burns [2000] IRLR 639, EAT 36.4
Scott v Coalite Fuels and Chemicals Ltd [1988] ICR 355, [1988] IRLR 131, EAT ... 45.2, 50.19
Scott v Creager [1979] ICR 403, [1979] IRLR 162, EAT 31.20
Scott v IRC [2004] EWCA Civ 400, [2004] IRLR 713, (2004) Times, 19 April, 148 Sol
    Jo LB 474, [2004] All ER (D) 46 (Apr) 13.8, 19.11
Scottbridge Construction Ltd v Wright [2003] IRLR 21, Ct of Sess 31.12
Scottish Daily Record and Sunday Mail (1986) Ltd v Laird [1996] IRLR 665, 1997 SLT
    345, Ct of Sess 51.9
Scullard v Knowles [1996] ICR 399, [1996] IRLR 344, EAT 22.9, 22.22, 23.2, 23.6
Scully UK Ltd v Lee [1998] IRLR 259, CA 38.14
Sealy v Consignia plc [2002] EWCA Civ 878, [2002] 3 All ER 801, [2002] ICR 1193,
    [2002] IRLR 624, (2002) Times, 3 July, [2002] All ER (D) 129 (Jun) 18.21, 18.25
Secretary of State for Employment v Associated Society of Locomotive Engineers and
    Firemen (No 2) [1972] 2 QB 455, [1972] 2 All ER 949, [1972] 2 WLR 1370, [1972]
    ICR 19, 13 KIR 1, 116 Sol Jo 467, CA 7.13, 42.16
Secretary of State for Employment v Banks [1983] ICR 48, EAT 35.11
Secretary of State for Employment v Chapman [1989] ICR 771, CA 6.9
Secretary of State for Employment v Clark [1997] 1 CMLR 613, sub nom Clark v Secretary
    of State for Employment [1997] ICR 64, [1996] IRLR 578, CA 22.3, 22.14
Secretary of State for Employment v Cooper [1987] ICR 766, EAT 29.5
Secretary of State for Employment v Doulton Sanitaryware Ltd [1981] ICR 477, [1981]
    IRLR 365, EAT 30.11
Secretary of State for Employment v Globe Elastic Thread Co Ltd [1980] AC 506, [1979]
    2 All ER 1077, [1979] 3 WLR 143, [1979] ICR 706, [1979] IRLR 327, 123 Sol Jo
    504, HL 6.5, 6.7, 35.13
Secretary of State for Employment v Helitron Ltd [1980] ICR 523, EAT 36.7
Secretary of State for Employment v John Woodrow & Sons (Builders) Ltd [1983] ICR
    582, [1983] IRLR 11, EAT 31.39
Secretary of State for Employment v Mann [1996] ICR 197, [1996] IRLR 4, EAT; on appeal
    [1997] ICR 209, [1997] IRLR 21, CA; affd sub nom Mann v Secretary of State for
    Employment [1999] ICR 898, [1999] IRLR 566, HL 18.12, 23.2, 29.5
Secretary of State for Employment v Reeves [1993] ICR 508, EAT 29.7
Secretary of State for Employment v Spence [1987] QB 179, [1986] 3 All ER 616, [1986]
    3 WLR 380, [1986] 3 CMLR 647, [1986] ICR 651, [1986] IRLR 248, 130 Sol Jo 407,
    [1986] LS Gaz R 2084, CA 49.8, 49.10
Secretary of State for Employment v Staffordshire County Council. See Staffordshire County
    Council v Secretary of State for Employment
Secretary of State for Employment v Stewart [1996] IRLR 334, EAT 29.5
Secretary of State for Employment v Wilson [1997] ICR 408, [1996] IRLR 330, EAT 29.5
Secretary of State for Scotland v Taylor [2000] 3 All ER 90, [2000] ICR 595, 2000 SC
    (HL) 139, 2000 SLT 708, sub nom Taylor v Secretary of State for Scotland [2000]
    IRLR 502, HL 7.11, 39.1
Secretary of State for Scotland and Greater Glasgow Health Board v Wright and Hannah
    [1993] 2 CMLR 257, [1991] IRLR 187, EAT 22.22, 23.2, 34.4
Secretary of State for Trade and Industry v Bottrill [2000] 1 All ER 915, [1999] ICR 592,
    [1999] IRLR 326, [2000] 2 BCLC 448, [1999] BCC 177, 143 Sol Jo LB 73, CA 8.3,
                                                                                                                          15.3, 29.4
Secretary of State for Trade and Industry v Cook [1997] 3 CMLR 1465, [1997] ICR 288,
    [1997] IRLR 150, 562 IRLB 12, EAT 49.9
Secretary of State for Trade and Industry v Forde [1997] ICR 231, [1997] IRLR 387, EAT 29.5
Secretary of State for Trade and Industry v Lassman (Pan Graphics Industries Ltd, in
    receivership) [2000] ICR 1109, [2000] IRLR 411, CA 6.12
Secretary of State for Trade and Industry v Rutherford. See Rutherford v Secretary of State
    for Trade and Industry
Secretary of State for Trade and Industry v Walden [2000] IRLR 168, EAT 29.5
Securicor Guarding Ltd v R [1994] IRLR 633, EAT 19.18
Securicor Omega Express Ltd v GMB [2004] IRLR 9, [2003] All ER (D) 181 (Sep), EAT .. 36.4
Seide v Gillette Industries [1980] IRLR 427, EAT 11.6

PARA

Selfridges Ltd v Malik [1998] ICR 268, [1997] IRLR 577, EAT 52.5
Selkent Bus Co Ltd v Moore [1996] ICR 836, [1996] IRLR 661, EAT 19.10, 19.41
Senior Heat Treatment Ltd v Bell [1997] IRLR 614, EAT 6.12, 49.12
Setiya v East Yorkshire Health Authority [1995] ICR 799, [1995] IRLR 348, EAT 20.6
Sevince v Staatssecretaris van Justitie: C-192/89 [1990] ECR I-3461, [1992] 2 CMLR 57,
    ECJ 24.2
Shakespeare v British Coal Corpn (1988) Times, 5 April, CA 4.3
Shamoon v Chief Constable of the Royal Ulster Constabulary [2003] UKHL 11, [2003] 2
    All ER 26, [2003] ICR 337, [2003] IRLR 285, (2003) Times, 4 March, 147 Sol Jo
    LB 268, [2003] All ER (D) 410 (Feb) 11.4, 11.5, 11.12
Sharifi v Strathclyde Regional Council [1992] IRLR 259, EAT 13.8
Sharma v Hindu Temple IDS Brief No 464 .... 7.15
Sharp (G F) & Co Ltd v McMillan [1998] IRLR 632, EAT 45.3
Shawkat v Nottingham City Hospital Trust [2001] EWCA Civ 954, [2002] ICR 7, [2001]
    IRLR 555, [2001] All ER (D) 214 (Jun) 35.7
Sheffield v Oxford Controls Co Ltd [1979] ICR 396, [1979] IRLR 133, EAT 45.2, 50.8
Sheikh v Chief Constable of Greater Manchester Police [1990] 1 QB 637, [1989] 2 All ER
    684, [1989] 2 WLR 1102, [1989] ICR 373, 133 Sol Jo 784, CA 11.12, 34.2
Sheiky v Argos Distributions Ltd (1997) IDS Brief No 597 .... 11.12
Shepherd (F C) & Co Ltd v Jerrom [1987] QB 301, [1986] 3 All ER 589, [1986] 3 WLR
    801, [1986] ICR 802, [1986] IRLR 358, 130 Sol Jo 665, CA 45.3
Sheridan v Stanley Cole (Wainfleet) Ltd [2003] ICR 297, [2003] IRLR 52, [2002] All ER
    (D) 11 (Nov), EAT; affd [2003] EWCA Civ 1046, [2003] 4 All ER 1181, [2003]
    ICR 1449, [2003] IRLR 885, [2003] 38 LS Gaz R 33, (2003) Times, 5 September .. 19.52,
                                                                                                                                   50.7
Sheriff v Klyne Tugs (Lowestoft) Ltd [1999] ICR 1170, [1999] IRLR 481, 625 IRLB 6,
    [1999] All ER (D) 666, CA 13.8, 19.26
Shillcock v Uppingham School [1997] Pens LR 207 .... 22.17
Shillito v Van Leer (UK) Ltd [1997] IRLR 495, EAT 26.9
Shindler v Northern Raincoat Co Ltd [1960] 2 All ER 239, [1960] 1 WLR 1038 ..... 8.4, 55.10,
                                                                                                                                   55.30
Shipping Co Uniform Inc v International Transport Workers' Federation, The Uniform
    Star [1985] 1 Lloyd's Rep 173, [1985] ICR 245, [1985] IRLR 71 .... 42.14
Shomer v B & R Residential Lettings Ltd [1992] IRLR 317, CA 11.5
Shove v Downs Surgical plc [1984] 1 All ER 7, [1984] ICR 532, [1984] IRLR 17 .... 52.12,
                                                                                                                            55.28, 55.32
Showboat Entertainment Centre Ltd v Owens [1984] 1 All ER 836, [1984] 1 WLR 384,
    [1984] ICR 65, [1984] IRLR 7, 128 Sol Jo 152, [1983] LS Gaz R 3002, 134 NLJ 37,
    EAT 11.6
Sian v Abbey National plc [2004] ICR 55, [2004] IRLR 185, [2003] All ER (D) 247 (Oct),
    EAT 20.5
Sibson v United Kingdom (Application 14327/88) (1993) 17 EHRR 193, ECtHR 28.4
Sidhu v Aerospace Composite Technology Ltd [2001] ICR 167, [2000] IRLR 602, [2000]
    25 LS Gaz R 38, [2000] All ER (D) 744, CA 11.6, 11.13, 12.35
Sigurjonsson v Iceland (Application 16130/90) (1993) 16 EHRR 462, ECtHR 28.4
Sillars v Charringtons Fuels Ltd [1989] ICR 475, [1989] IRLR 152, CA 6.7, 44.8
Silvey v Pendragon plc [2001] EWCA Civ 784, [2001] IRLR 685 .... 7.23, 55.21
Sim v Rotherham Metropolitan Borough Council [1987] Ch 216, [1986] 3 All ER 387,
    [1986] 3 WLR 851, 85 LGR 128, [1986] ICR 897, [1986] IRLR 391, 130 Sol Jo
    839, [1986] LS Gaz R 3746 .... 7.24, 31.14,
                                                                                                                                   42.16
Sime v Sutcliffe Catering Scotland Ltd [1990] IRLR 228, 1990 SLT 687n, Ct of Sess 53.3
Simmons v Hoover Ltd [1977] QB 284, [1977] 1 All ER 775, [1976] 3 WLR 901, [1977]
    ICR 61, [1976] IRLR 266, 10 ITR 234, 120 Sol Jo 540, EAT 55.17
Simms v Transco plc [2001] All ER (D) 245 (Jan), EAT 13.3
Simon v Brimham Associates [1987] ICR 596, [1987] IRLR 307, CA 11.6
Simper (Peter) & Co Ltd v Cooke [1986] IRLR 19, EAT 20.12
Simrad Ltd v Scott [1997] IRLR 147, EAT 52.13
Sinclair Roche & Temperley v Heard [2004] IRLR 763 .... 11.9, 11.13, 12.36, 19.58

Table of cases

PARA

Sindicato de Médicos de Asistencia Pública (Simap) v Conselleria de Sanidad y Consumo de la Generalidad Valenciana: C-303/98 [2001] All ER (EC) 609, [2000] ECR I-7963, [2001] 3 CMLR 932, [2001] ICR 1116, [2000] IRLR 845, [2000] All ER (D) 1236, ECJ 54.5, 54.7

Singh v British Rail Engineering Ltd [1986] ICR 22, EAT 12.8

Singh v Guru Nanak Gurdwara [1990] ICR 309, CA 15.3

Sirdar v Army Board and Secretary of State for Defence: C-273/97 [1999] All ER (EC) 928, [1999] ECR I-7403, [1999] 3 CMLR 559, [2000] ICR 130, [2000] IRLR 47, 7 BHRC 459, [1999] All ER (D) 1156, ECJ 12.10, 12.19

Sisley v Britannia Security Systems Ltd [1983] ICR 628, [1983] IRLR 404, EAT 12.3

Sita (GB) Ltd v Burton [1998] ICR 17, [1997] IRLR 501, EAT 49.20

Skyrail Oceanic Ltd v Coleman [1981] ICR 864, sub nom Coleman v Skyrail Oceanic Ltd (t/a Goodmos Tours) [1981] IRLR 398, 125 Sol Jo 638, CA 11.9, 13.8

Slack v Greenham (Plant Hire) Ltd [1983] ICR 617, [1983] IRLR 271, EAT 2.4

Slater v Leicestershire Health Authority [1989] IRLR 16, CA 51.10

Slaughter v C Brewer & Sons Ltd [1990] ICR 730, [1990] IRLR 426, EAT 52.13

Slaven v Thermo Engineers Ltd [1992] ICR 295, HC 46.20

Smith v Avdel Systems Ltd: C-408/92 [1995] All ER (EC) 132, [1994] ECR I-4435, [1995] 3 CMLR 543, [1995] ICR 596, [1994] IRLR 602, ECJ 20.27, 22.18, 39.4

Smith v Bexley London Borough Council IDS Brief No 448 .... 31.14

Smith v City of Glasgow District Council [1987] ICR 796, [1987] IRLR 326, 1987 SC (HL) 175, 1987 SLT 605, HL 51.4

Smith v Gardner Merchant Ltd [1998] 3 All ER 852, [1999] ICR 134, [1998] IRLR 510, [1998] 32 LS Gaz R 29, 142 Sol Jo LB 244, [1998] All ER (D) 338, CA 11.5

Smith v Gwent District Health Authority [1996] ICR 1044, EAT 19.41

Smith v Hayle Town Council [1978] ICR 996, [1978] IRLR 413, 77 LGR 52, 122 Sol Jo 642, CA 51.3

Smith v Safeway plc [1996] ICR 868, [1996] IRLR 456, CA 11.5

Smith v Secretary of State for Trade and Industry [2000] ICR 69, [2000] IRLR 6, EAT 18.7, 28.7

Smith v Seghill Overseers (1875) LR 10 QB 422, 40 JP 228, 44 LJMC 114, 23 WR 745, [1874-80] All ER Rep 373, 32 LT 859 .... 40.2

Smith v Stages [1989] AC 928, [1989] 1 All ER 833, [1989] 2 WLR 529, [1989] ICR 272, [1989] IRLR 177, 133 Sol Jo 324, [1989] 15 LS Gaz R 42, [1989] NLJR 291, HL 53.2

Smith v United Kingdom [1999] IRLR 734 .... 11.6

Smith v Zeneca (Agrochemicals) Ltd [2000] ICR 800, [2000] All ER (D) 163, EAT 13.4, 19.10

Smith and Grady v United Kingdom (Applications 33985/96 and 33986/96) (1999) 29 EHRR 493, [1999] IRLR 734, 11 Admin LR 879, ECtHR 28.4

Smiths Industries Aerospace and Defence Systems v Rawlings [1996] IRLR 656, EAT 51.11

Snoxell v Vauxhall Motors Ltd [1978] QB 11, [1977] 3 All ER 770, [1977] 3 WLR 189, [1977] 1 CMLR 487, [1977] ICR 700, [1977] IRLR 123, 12 ITR 235, 121 Sol Jo 354, EAT 22.11

Sogbetun v Hackney London Borough [1998] ICR 1264, [1998] IRLR 676, EAT 18.9

Solectron Scotland Ltd v Roper [2004] IRLR 4, EAT 7.13, 7.22, 49.23

Solihull Metropolitan Borough v National Union of Teachers [1985] IRLR 211 .... 42.16

Somjee v United Kingdom (Application 42116/98) [2002] IRLR 886, [2002] All ER (D) 214 (Oct), ECtHR 18.13, 28.4

Sorelle (Jean) Ltd v Rybak. See Rybak v Jean Sorelle Ltd

Soros v Davison [1994] ICR 590, [1994] IRLR 264, EAT 52.13

Soteriou v Ultrachem Ltd [2004] IRLR 870 .... 19.16, 19.22

Sothern v Franks Charlesly & Co [1981] IRLR 278, CA 45.5, 50.10

Sougrin v Haringey Health Authority [1992] ICR 650, [1992] IRLR 416, CA 13.3

South Ayrshire Council v Morton [2001] IRLR 28, [2000] All ER (D) 1899, EAT; affd [2002] IRLR 256, (2002) Times, 1 March, Ct of Sess 22.9

South Durham Health Authority v UNISON [1995] ICR 495, [1995] IRLR 407, EAT . 18.33, 49.18

South East Sheffield Citizens Advice Bureau v Grayson [2004] ICR 1138, [2004] IRLR 353, [2004] All ER (D) 398 (Feb), EAT 15.3

PARA

South Holland District Council v Stamp EAT/1097/02 .... 54.5
South Place Ethical Society, Re, Barralet v A-G. See Barralet v A-G
South Tyneside Metropolitan Borough Council v Toulson [2003] 1 CMLR 867, [2002]
    All ER (D) 437 (Nov), EAT 27.2
South West Launderettes Ltd v Laidler [1986] ICR 455, [1986] IRLR 305, CA 6.9
Southern Foundries (1926) Ltd v Shirlaw [1940] AC 701, [1940] 2 All ER 445, 109 LJKB
    461, 84 Sol Jo 464, 164 LT 251, 56 TLR 637, HL 8.4, 55.10
Southwark London Borough v O'Brien [1996] IRLR 420, EAT 31.6
Southwark London Borough Council v Bartholomew [2004] ICR 358, EAT 19.54
Sovereign Distribution Services Ltd v Transport and General Workers' Union [1990] ICR
    31, [1989] IRLR 334, EAT 36.4, 36.6
Sovereign House Security Services Ltd v Savage [1989] IRLR 115, CA 45.5, 55.5
Spano v Fiat Geotech SpA and Fiat Hitachi Excavators SpA: C-472/93 [1995] ECR I-4321,
    ECJ 49.23
Speciality Care plc v Pachela [1996] ICR 633, [1996] IRLR 248, EAT 51.3
Spencer v Marchington [1988] IRLR 392 .... 7.13, 38.13, 55.21
Spencer v Paragon Wallpapers Ltd [1977] ICR 301, [1976] IRLR 373, EAT 51.8
Spencer and Griffin v Gloucestershire County Council [1985] IRLR 393, CA 35.12
Spijkers v Gebroeders Benedik Abbatoir CV and Alfred Benedik en Zonen BV: 24/85 [1986]
    ECR 1119, [1986] 2 CMLR 296, ECJ 49.5
Spillers-French (Holdings) Ltd v Union of Shop, Distributive and Allied Workers [1980] 1
    All ER 231, [1980] ICR 31, [1979] IRLR 339, 123 Sol Jo 654, EAT 36.6
Sports Club v HM Inspector of Taxes [2000] STC (SCD) 443 .... 43.35
Spring v Guardian Assurance plc [1995] 2 AC 296, [1994] 3 All ER 129, [1994] 3 WLR
    354, [1994] ICR 596, [1994] IRLR 460, [1994] 40 LS Gaz R 36, [1994] NLJR 971,
    138 Sol Jo LB 183, HL 37.4, 39.11
Spring Grove Service Group plc v Hickinbottom [1990] ICR 111, EAT 19.64
Springboard Sunderland Trust v Robson [1992] ICR 554, [1992] IRLR 261, EAT 22.7
Square D Ltd v Cook. See Cook v Square D Ltd
Squibb UK Staff Association v Certification Officer [1979] 2 All ER 452, [1979] 1 WLR
    523, [1979] ICR 235, [1979] IRLR 75, 123 Sol Jo 352, CA 47.22
Stacey v Babcock Power Ltd [1986] QB 308, [1986] 2 WLR 207, [1986] ICR 221, [1986]
    IRLR 3, 130 Sol Jo 71, EAT 51.4, 51.11
Stadt Lengerich v Helmig: C-399/92, C-409/92, C-425/92, C-34/93, C-50/93, and C-78/93
    [1994] ECR I-5727, [1995] 2 CMLR 261, [1996] ICR 35, [1995] IRLR 216, ECJ ... 22.11
Staffordshire County Council v Barber. See Barber v Staffordshire County Council
Staffordshire County Council v Black [1995] IRLR 234, EAT 22.10
Staffordshire County Council v Secretary of State for Employment [1989] ICR 664, sub
    nom Secretary of State for Employment v Staffordshire County Council [1989] IRLR
    117, CA 50.13
Stankovic v Westminster City Council (17 October 2001, unreported) 35.7
Stannard v Fisons Pension Trust Ltd [1992] IRLR 27, [1991] PLR 225, CA 39.11
Stannard & Co (1969) Ltd v Wilson [1983] ICR 86, EAT 20.25
Stansbury v Datapulse plc [2003] EWCA Civ 1951, [2004] ICR 523, [2004] IRLR 466,
    [2004] 06 LS Gaz R 32, (2004) Times, 28 January, 148 Sol Jo LB 145 ... 19.52, 19.56, 20.12
Stapp v Shaftesbury Society [1982] IRLR 326, CA 50.13
Stark v Post Office [2000] ICR 1013, [2000] PIQR P105, [2000] 14 LS Gaz R 41, 144
    Sol Jo LB 150, CA 26.12
Steel Stockholders (Birmingham) Ltd v Kirkwood [1993] IRLR 515, EAT 52.13
Steenhorst-Neerings v Bestuur van de Bedrijfsvereniging voor Detailhandel, Ambachten en
    Huisvrouwen: C-338/91 [1993] ECR I-5475, [1995] 3 CMLR 323, [1994] IRLR 244,
    ECJ 23.2
Steinicke v Bundesanstalt fur Arbeit: C-77/02 [2003] IRLR 892, [2003] All ER (D) 87
    (Sep), ECJ 22.3
Stephenson v Delphi Diesel Systems Ltd [2003] ICR 471, [2003] All ER (D) 84 (Mar),
    EAT 15.3
Stephenson (S B J) Ltd v Mandy [2000] FSR 286, [2000] IRLR 233 .... 55.21
Stevedoring and Haulage Services Ltd v Fuller [2001] EWCA Civ 651, [2001] IRLR 627,
    [2001] All ER (D) 106 (May) 15.3

Table of cases

PARA

Stevens v Bexley Health Authority [1989] ICR 224, [1989] IRLR 240, EAT 13.3, 22.22

Stevenson v United Road Transport Union [1977] 2 All ER 941, [1977] ICR 893, CA 48.15

Stewart v Cleveland Guest (Engineering) Ltd [1994] ICR 535, [1994] IRLR 440, EAT 20.17

Stewart v Glentaggart (1963) 42 ATC 318, [1963] TR 345, 1963 SC 300, 1963 SLT 119, Ct of Sess 55.32

Stewart (Rex) Jeffries Parker Ginsberg Ltd v Parker [1988] IRLR 483, CA 38.19, 55.21

Stocker v Lancashire County Council [1992] IRLR 75, CA 51.4, 51.10

Stokes v Guest, Keen and Nettlefold (Bolts and Nuts) Ltd [1968] 1 WLR 1776, 5 KIR 401, 112 Sol Jo 821 .... 25.8

Stolt Offshore Ltd v Miklaszewicz [2002] IRLR 344, 2002 SC 232, 2002 SLT 103 .... 10.18, 51.3

Stonehill Furniture Ltd v Phillippo [1983] ICR 556, EAT 19.74

Storer v British Gas plc [2000] 2 All ER 440, [2000] 1 WLR 1237, [2000] ICR 603, [2000] IRLR 495, CA 18.8, 19.51

Stratford (J T) & Son Ltd v Lindley [1965] AC 269, [1964] 2 All ER 209, [1964] 2 WLR 1002, [1964] 1 Lloyd's Rep 237, 108 Sol Jo 298, CA; revsd [1965] AC 269, [1964] 3 All ER 102, [1964] 3 WLR 541, [1964] 2 Lloyd's Rep 133, 108 Sol Jo 636, HL 42.2

Strathclyde Regional Council v Neil [1984] IRLR 11; affd sub nom Neil v Strathclyde Borough Council [1984] IRLR 14, 1983 SLT (Sh Ct) 89 .... 14.3

Strathclyde Regional Council v Porcelli. See Porcelli v Strathclyde Regional Council

Strathclyde Regional Council v Wallace [1998] 1 All ER 394, [1998] 1 WLR 259, [1998] ICR 205, [1998] IRLR 146, [1998] 07 LS Gaz R 32, 1998 SC (HL) 72, 142 Sol Jo LB 83, sub nom West Dunbartonshire Council v Wallace 1998 SLT 421, HL . 22.11, 22.12

Street v Derbyshire Unemployed Workers Centre [2004] EWCA Civ 964, [2004] IRLR 687, [2004] All ER (D) 377 (Jul) 10.18

Street v Mountford [1985] AC 809, [1985] 2 All ER 289, [1985] 2 WLR 877, 50 P & CR 258, 17 HLR 402, 129 Sol Jo 348, [1985] 1 EGLR 128, [1985] LS Gaz R 2087, [1985] NLJ Rep 460, 274 Estates Gazette 821, HL 40.2

Stribling v Wickham (1989) 21 HLR 381, [1989] 2 EGLR 35, [1989] 27 EG 81, CA 40.2

Strouthos v London Underground Ltd [2004] EWCA Civ 402, [2004] IRLR 636, [2004] All ER (D) 366 (Mar) 51.9

Strudwick v Iszatt Bros Ltd (or IBL) [1988] ICR 796, [1988] IRLR 457, EAT 6.9

Suffritti v Istituto Nazionale della Previdenza Sociale (INPS): C-140/91, C-141/91, C-278/91 and C-279/91 [1992] ECR I-6337, [1993] IRLR 289, ECJ 23.2

Sun Alliance and London Insurance Ltd v Dudman [1978] ICR 551, [1978] IRLR 169, EAT 22.5

Sunderland Polytechnic v Evans [1993] ICR 392, [1993] IRLR 196, EAT 31.6

Sunley Turriff Holdings Ltd v Thomson [1995] IRLR 184, EAT 49.11

Surrey County Council v Lamond (1998) 31 HLR 1051, [1999] 1 EGLR 32, [1999] 12 EG 170, [1998] EGCS 185, 78 P & CR D3, CA 40.7

Sutcliffe v Big C's Marine Ltd [1998] ICR 913, [1998] IRLR 428, EAT 18.9, 18.18, 20.13

Sutherland v British Telecommunications plc (1989) Times, 30 January 37.4

Sutherland v Hatton. See Hatton v Sutherland

Sutherland v Network Appliance Ltd [2001] IRLR 12, [2000] All ER (D) 1000, EAT 19.35, 55.42

Suzen v Zehnacker Gebaudereinigung GmbH Krankenhausservice: C-13/95 [1997] All ER (EC) 289, [1997] ECR I-1259, [1997] 1 CMLR 768, [1997] ICR 662, [1997] IRLR 255, ECJ 49.5

Swain v Denso Marston Ltd [2000] ICR 1079, [2000] PIQR P129, CA 26.18

Swain v Hillman [2001] 1 All ER 91, [2000] PIQR P51, (1999) Times, 4 November, CA 19.15, 19.17

Swainston v Hetton Victory Club Ltd [1983] 1 All ER 1179, [1983] ICR 341, [1983] IRLR 164, 127 Sol Jo 171, CA 18.21

Sweater Shop (Scotland) Ltd v Park [1996] IRLR 424, EAT 31.6

Sweeney v J & S Henderson (Concessions) Ltd [1999] IRLR 306, EAT 6.6

Sweetlove v Redbridge and Waltham Forest Area Health Authority [1979] ICR 477, [1979] IRLR 195, EAT 52.13

Swift v Chief Constable of Wiltshire Constabulary [2004] ICR 909, [2004] IRLR 540, [2004] All ER (D) 299 (Feb), EAT 9.4, 9.6

PARA

Swithland Motors plc v Clarke [1994] ICR 231, [1994] IRLR 275, EAT 13.3, 18.29
Sybron Corpn v Rochem Ltd [1984] Ch 112, [1983] 2 All ER 707, [1983] 3 WLR 713,
    [1983] ICR 801, [1983] IRLR 253, [1983] BCLC 43, 127 Sol Jo 391, CA 7.13, 8.16
Symbian Ltd v Christensen [2001] IRLR 77 .... 38.23
Sysdeco v Atkins UKEAT/0080/04/DA 24.11
Systems Reliability Holdings plc v Smith [1990] IRLR 377 .... 38.2, 38.9

T

T v North Yorkshire County Council. See Trotman v North Yorkshire County Council
TSB Bank plc v Harris [2000] IRLR 157, EAT 37.4, 45.19, 50.7
TSC Europe (UK) Ltd v Massey [1999] IRLR 22 .... 38.14
Tagro v Cafane [1991] 2 All ER 235, [1991] 1 WLR 378, 23 HLR 250, [1991] 1 EGLR
    279, CA 40.3
Talbot v Cadge [1995] 2 AC 394, [1995] 2 WLR 312, [1995] ICR 1100, sub nom Re Leyland
    DAF Ltd, [1994] 4 All ER 300, [1994] NLJR 1311; sub nom Re Leyland DAF Ltd
    (No 2) [1994] 2 BCLC 760, sub nom Re Leyland Daf Ltd, Talbot v Cadge [1994] BCC
    658; on appeal sub nom Talbot v Grundy [1995] 2 AC 394, [1995] 2 WLR 312,
    [1995] ICR 1100, [1995] IRLR 269, [1995] 17 LS Gaz R 47, sub nom Re Leyland
    DAF Ltd [1995] 2 All ER 65, [1995] NLJR 449, sub nom Re Leyland DAF Ltd (No 2)
    [1995] 1 BCLC 386, sub nom Talbot v Cadge (Leyland DAF Ltd) [1995] BCC 319,
    HL 8.28, 29.10
Tanks and Drums Ltd v Transport and General Workers' Union [1992] ICR 1; affd [1992]
    ICR 1, [1991] IRLR 372, 135 Sol Jo LB 68, CA 42.15
Tanna v Post Office [1981] ICR 374, EAT 11.12
Tanner v D T Kean Ltd [1978] IRLR 110, EAT 55.5
Taplin v C Shippam Ltd [1978] ICR 1068, [1978] IRLR 450, 13 ITR 532, EAT 52.21
Tarling v Wisdom Toothbrushes Ltd (COIT 1500148/97) (24 June 1997, unreported) 9.14
Tarmac Roadstone Holdings Ltd v Peacock [1973] 2 All ER 485, [1973] 1 WLR 594,
    [1973] ICR 273, [1973] IRLR 157, 14 KIR 277, 8 ITR 300, 117 Sol Jo 186, CA 31.36
Tattari v Private Patients Plan Ltd [1998] ICR 106, [1997] IRLR 586, 38 BMLR 24,
    CA 12.27
Taupo Totara Timber Co Ltd v Rowe [1978] AC 537, [1977] 3 All ER 123, [1977] 3
    WLR 466, 121 Sol Jo 692, [1977] 2 NZLR 453, PC 8.28
Taylor v Connex South Eastern Ltd IDS Brief No 670 .... 49.20
Taylor v East Midlands Offender Employment [2000] IRLR 760, EAT 7.24
Taylor v Lowe [2000] IRLR 760, EAT 27.8
Taylor v National Union of Mineworkers (Derbyshire Area) [1984] IRLR 440 .... 48.15
Taylor v Secretary of State for Scotland. See Secretary of State for Scotland v Taylor
Taylor v Serviceteam Ltd, IDS Brief No 602 .... 49.14
Taylor Gordon & Co Ltd (t/a Plan Personnel) v Timmons [2004] IRLR 180, [2003] 44
    LS Gaz R 32, (2003) Times, 7 November, [2003] All ER (D) 05 (Oct), EAT 18.11,
                                                                                                              31.6, 41.8
Taylor Stuart & Co v Croft (9 April 1997, unreported) 38.6
Taylorplan Services Ltd v Jackson [1996] IRLR 184, EAT 18.31, 31.8
Tehrani v United Kingdom Central Council for Nursing, Midwifery and Health Visiting
    [2001] IRLR 208, 2001 SLT 879, Ct of Sess 28.7
Teinaz v Wandsworth London Borough Council [2002] EWCA Civ 1040, [2002] ICR 1471,
    [2002] IRLR 721, (2002) Times, 21 August, [2002] All ER (D) 238 (Jul) 19.54, 28.7
Tejani v Superintendent Registrar for the District of Peterborough [1986] IRLR 502, CA .. 11.6
Tele Danmark A/S v Handels- og Kontorfunktionærernes Forbund i Danmark (HK): C-
    109/00 [2001] All ER (EC) 941, [2001] ECR I-6993, [2002] 1 CMLR 105, [2004]
    ICR 610, [2001] IRLR 853, [2001] All ER (D) 37 (Oct), ECJ 11.5
Tele-Trading Ltd v Jenkins [1990] IRLR 430, CA 52.13
Telephone Information Services Ltd v Wilkinson [1991] IRLR 148, EAT 19.17, 52.1
Temco Service Industries SA v Imzilyen: C-51/00 [2002] ECR I-969, [2004] 1 CMLR
    877, [2002] IRLR 214, [2002] All ER (D) 199 (Jan), ECJ 49.4
Ten Oever v Stichting Bedrijfspensioenfonds voor het Glazenwassers- en Schoonmaakbedrijf:
    C-109/91 [1993] ECR I-4879, [1995] 2 CMLR 357, [1995] ICR 74, [1993] IRLR
    601, [1995] 42 LS Gaz R 23, ECJ 22.18

Table of cases

PARA

Terry v East Sussex County Council [1977] 1 All ER 567, 75 LGR 111, [1976] ICR 536, [1976] IRLR 332, 12 ITR 265, EAT 44.7, 51.14

Tesco Stores Ltd v Pook [2003] EWHC 823 (Ch), [2004] IRLR 618, [2003] All ER (D) 233 (Apr) 7.13

Tesco Supermarkets Ltd v Nattrass [1972] AC 153, [1971] 2 All ER 127, [1971] 2 WLR 1166, 69 LGR 403, 135 JP 289, 115 Sol Jo 285, HL 25.38

Thames Water Utilities v Reynolds [1996] IRLR 186, EAT 7.24, 27.8, 31.14, 31.22

Thibault v Caisse Nationale d'Assurance Viellesse des Travailleurs Salaries (CNAVTS). See Caisse Nationale d'Assurance Vieillesse des Travailleurs Salaries v Thibault

Thomas v Bristol Aeroplane Co Ltd [1954] 2 All ER 1, [1954] 1 WLR 694, 52 LGR 292, 98 Sol Jo 302, CA 25.3

Thomas v National Coal Board [1987] ICR 757, [1987] IRLR 451, [1987] LS Gaz R 2045, EAT 22.6

Thomas v National Union of Mineworkers (South Wales Area) [1986] Ch 20, [1985] 2 All ER 1, [1985] 2 WLR 1081, [1985] ICR 886, [1985] IRLR 136, 129 Sol Jo 416, [1985] LS Gaz R 1938 .... 4.5, 42.2, 42.12

Thomas & Betts Manufacturing Ltd v Harding [1980] IRLR 255, CA 51.11

Thompson v SCS Consulting Ltd [2001] IRLR 801, [2001] All ER (D) 03 (Sep), EAT 49.20

Thompson v Walon Car Delivery [1997] IRLR 343, EAT 50.20

Thomson (D C) & Co Ltd v Deakin [1952] Ch 646, [1952] 2 All ER 361, [1952] 2 TLR 105, CA 42.2

Thorpe v Dul [2003] ICR 1556, [2003] All ER (D) 14 (Jul), EAT 14.2, 15.3

Tice v Cartwright [1999] ICR 769, EAT 6.9

Ticehurst and Thompson v British Telecommunications plc. See British Telecommunications plc v Ticehurst

Timeplan Education Group Ltd v National Union of Teachers [1997] IRLR 457, CA 42.2

Tipper v Roofdec Ltd [1989] IRLR 419, EAT 6.5

Titchener v Secretary of State for Trade and Industry [2002] ICR 225, [2002] IRLR 195, [2001] All ER (D) 93 (Sep), EAT 29.5

Tocher v General Motors Scotland Ltd [1981] IRLR 55, EAT 5.3

Todd v British Midland Airways Ltd [1978] ICR 959, [1978] IRLR 370, 13 ITR 553, 122 Sol Jo 661, CA 50.15

Toffel v London Underground Ltd IDS Brief No 609 .... 9.12

Tomlinson v Dick Evans U Drive Ltd [1978] ICR 639, [1978] IRLR 77, EAT 7.15

Torquay Hotel Co Ltd v Cousins [1969] 2 Ch 106, [1968] 3 All ER 43, [1968] 3 WLR 540, 4 KIR 635, 112 Sol Jo 688; affd [1969] 2 Ch 106, [1969] 1 All ER 522, [1969] 2 WLR 289, 6 KIR 15, 113 Sol Jo 52, CA 42.2

Tottenham Green Under Fives' Centre v Marshall [1989] ICR 214, [1989] IRLR 147, [1989] 15 LS Gaz R 39, EAT 12.4

Tottenham Green Under Fives' Centre v Marshall (No 2) [1991] ICR 320, [1991] IRLR 162, EAT 12.4

Tower Hamlets Health Authority v Anthony [1989] ICR 656, [1989] IRLR 394, CA 51.9

Tower Hamlets London Borough Council v Qayyum [1987] ICR 729, EAT 11.8

Tracey v Crosville Wales Ltd [1998] AC 167, [1997] 4 All ER 449, [1997] 3 WLR 800, [1997] ICR 862, [1997] 41 LS Gaz R 28, [1997] NLJR 1582, sub nom Crosville Wales Ltd v Tracey (No 2) [1997] IRLR 691, HL 52.13

Tradewinds Airways Ltd v Fletcher [1981] IRLR 272, EAT 52.12

Trafford v Sharpe & Fisher (Building Supplies) Ltd [1994] IRLR 325, EAT 49.20

Trafford Carpets Ltd v Barker IDS Brief No 440 .... 2.4

Transco plc (formerly BG plc) v O'Brien [2002] EWCA Civ 379, [2002] ICR 721, [2002] IRLR 444 .... 7.13

Transport and General Workers' Union v Howard [1992] ICR 106, [1992] IRLR 170, EAT 48.7, 52.19

Transport and General Workers' Union v Ledbury Preserves (1928) Ltd [1985] IRLR 412, EAT 36.4

Transport and General Workers' Union v Ledbury Preserves (1928) Ltd [1986] ICR 855, [1986] IRLR 492, EAT 36.6

Transport and General Workers' Union v McKinnon [2001] ICR 1281, [2001] IRLR 597, [2001] All ER (D) 275 (Jun) 36.6, 49.18

PARA

Travers v Planning Inspectorate (9 December 2002, unreported) 22.10
Treganowan v Robert Knee & Co Ltd [1975] ICR 405, [1975] IRLR 247, 10 ITR 121,
    119 Sol Jo 490 .... 45.5, 55.1
Trevelyans (Birmingham) Ltd v Norton [1991] ICR 488, EAT 18.25
Trico-Folberth Ltd v Devonshire. See Devonshire v Trico-Folberth Ltd
Trimble v Supertravel Ltd [1982] ICR 440, [1982] IRLR 451, EAT 18.14, 19.75,
                                                                                                         52.13
Trotman v North Yorkshire County Council [1999] LGR 584, [1998] 32 LS Gaz R 29,
    142 Sol Jo LB 218, sub nom ST v North Yorkshire County Council [1999] IRLR 98,
    sub nom T v North Yorkshire County Council 49 BMLR 150, CA 53.2
Trotter v Forth Ports Authority [1991] IRLR 419, Ct of Sess 45.7
Trussed Steel Concrete Co Ltd v Green [1946] Ch 115, 44 LGR 263, 110 JP 144, 115 LJ
    Ch 123, 90 Sol Jo 80, 174 LT 122, 62 TLR 128 .... 8.3
Trustees of Uppingham School Retirement Benefit Scheme for Non-Teaching Staff v
    Shillcock [2002] EWHC 641 (Ch), [2002] IRLR 702, [2002] All ER (D) 147
    (Apr) 22.17, 22.18
Tuck (A & G) Ltd v Bartlett [1994] ICR 379, [1994] IRLR 162, EAT 49.10
Tucker v British Leyland Motor Corpn Ltd [1978] IRLR 493, Cty Ct 27.8
Tunstall v Condon [1980] ICR 786, EAT 55.8
Turner v Commonwealth and British Minerals Ltd [2000] IRLR 114, [1999] All ER (D)
    1097, CA 38.16
Turner v Grovit: C-159/02 [2004] All ER (EC) 485, [2004] 2 All ER (Comm) 381, [2004]
    2 Lloyd's Rep 169, [2004] IRLR 899, (2004) Times, 29 April, [2004] All ER (D)
    259 (Apr), ECJ 24.11
Turner v Labour Party and Labour Party Superannuation Society [1987] IRLR 101,
    CA 11.9
Turvey v C W Cheyney & Son Ltd [1979] ICR 341, [1979] IRLR 105, EAT 35.12
Tyagi v BBC World Service [2001] EWCA Civ 549, [2001] IRLR 465 .... 13.3, 18.29
Tyldesley v TML Plastics Ltd [1996] ICR 356, [1996] IRLR 395, EAT 22.11

U

UK Waste Control Ltd v Wren [1995] ICR 974, EAT 49.3
UNECTEF v Heylens. See Union Nationale des Entraîneurs et Cadres Techniques Pro-
    fessionnels du Football (UNECTEF) v Heylens
UNIFI v Union Bank of Nigeria [2001] IRLR 713 .... 47.47
Ulsterbus Ltd v Henderson [1989] IRLR 251, NICA 51.4, 51.9
Uniform Star, The. See Shipping Co Uniform Inc v International Transport Workers'
    Federation, The Uniform Star
Union Nationale des Entraîneurs et Cadres Techniques Professionnels du Football (UNECTEF)
    v Heylens: 222/86 [1987] ECR 4097, [1989] 1 CMLR 901, ECJ 23.4
Union Traffic Ltd v Transport and General Workers' Union [1989] ICR 98, [1989] IRLR
    127, CA 42.2, 42.9,
                                                                                                         42.16
UNISON v United Kingdom [2002] IRLR 497, ECtHR 28.4, 42.4
United Arab Emirates v Abdelghafar [1995] ICR 65, [1995] IRLR 243, EAT 20.6
United Bank Ltd v Akhtar [1989] IRLR 507, EAT 7.13, 55.22
United Kingdom v EU Council: C-84/94 [1996] All ER (EC) 877, [1996] ECR I-5755,
    [1996] 3 CMLR 671, [1997] ICR 443, [1997] IRLR 30, ECJ 23.11, 54.1
University College London Hospital NHS Trust v UNISON [1999] ICR 204, [1999] IRLR
    31, [1998] 41 LS Gaz R 45, 142 Sol Jo LB 270, [1998] All ER (D) 450, CA ... 42.4
University College of Swansea v Cornelius [1988] ICR 735, EAT 19.50
University of Cambridge v Murray [1993] ICR 460, EAT 18.18
University of Central England v National and Local Government Officers' Association
    [1993] IRLR 81 .... 42.14
University of Nottingham v Eyett [1999] 2 All ER 437, [1999] 1 WLR 594, [1999] ICR
    721, [1999] IRLR 87, [1999] ELR 141, [1999] 01 LS Gaz R 24, [1998] All ER (D)
    584 .... 7.13, 39.11
University of Oxford (Chancellor, Master and Scholars) v Humphreys [2000] 1 All ER
    996, [2000] 1 CMLR 647, [2000] ICR 405, [2000] IRLR 183, CA 49.12, 49.20

Table of cases

V

Vakante v Addey and Stanhope School [2004] ICR 279, [2003] All ER (D) 352 (Dec),
EAT; affd [2004] EWCA Civ 1065, [2004] 36 LS Gaz R 33, [2004] All ER (D) 561
(Jul) 12.16
Vauxhall Motors Ltd v Ghafoor [1993] ICR 376, EAT 51.10
Venables v Hornby (Inspector of Taxes) [2003] UKHL 65, [2004] 1 All ER 627, [2003]
1 WLR 3022, [2004] STC 84, [2004] ICR 42, (2003) Times, 5 December, 147 Sol
Jo LB 1431, [2003] All ER (D) 86 (Dec) 39.1
Vento v Chief Constable of West Yorkshire Police. See Chief Constable of West Yorkshire
Police v Vento
Verholen v Sociale Versekeringsbank Amsterdam: C-87/90, C-99/90, and C-89/90 [1991]
ECR I-3757, [1994] 1 CMLR 157, [1992] IRLR 38, ECJ 23.2
Vicary v British Telecommunications plc [1999] IRLR 680, EAT 9.4, 9.7
Vidal (Francisco Hernandez) SA v Perez: C-127/96, C-229/96 and C-74/97 [1998] ECR
I-8179, [1999] IRLR 132, ECJ 49.5
Viggosdottir v Islandspostur HF [2002] IRLR 425, EFTA Ct 34.2
Villella v MFI Furniture Centres Ltd [1999] IRLR 468 .... 7.13, 39.11, 41.14, 45.19, 55.19
Virgin Net Ltd v Harper (9 July 2003, unreported), EAT 55.33
Virgo Fidelis Senior School v Boyle [2004] ICR 1210, [2004] IRLR 268, (2004) Times,
26 February, [2004] All ER (D) 214 (Jan), EAT 10.18
Visa International Service Association v Paul [2004] IRLR 42, [2003] All ER (D) 265
(May), EAT 13.8
Vogt v Germany (Application 17851/91) (1995) 21 EHRR 205, [1996] ELR 232, ECtHR 28.4
Vokes Ltd v Bear [1974] ICR 1, [1973] IRLR 363, 15 KIR 302, 9 ITR 85, NIRC 51.11
Von Horn v Cinnamond: C-163/95 [1998] QB 214, [1997] All ER (EC) 913, [1998] 2
WLR 104, [1997] ECR I-5451, ECJ 24.11
Voteforce Associates Ltd v Quinn [2002] ICR 1, [2001] All ER (D) 483 (Jul), EAT 27.2
Vroege v NCIV Institut voor Volkshuisvesting BV: C-57/93 [1995] All ER (EC) 193,
[1994] ECR I-4541, [1995] 1 CMLR 881, [1995] ICR 635, [1994] IRLR 651, ECJ 22.10

W

Wadcock v London Borough of Brent [1990] IRLR 223 .... 7.23
Waddington v Leicester Council for Voluntary Services [1977] 2 All ER 633, [1977] 1
WLR 544, [1977] ICR 266, [1977] IRLR 32, 12 ITR 65, 121 Sol Jo 84, EAT 22.6
Wadman v Carpenter Farrer Partnership [1993] 3 CMLR 93, [1993] IRLR 374, EAT 11.12,
23.1
Waite v Government Communications Headquarters [1983] 2 AC 714, [1983] 2 All ER
1013, [1983] 3 WLR 389, 81 LGR 769, [1983] ICR 653, [1983] IRLR 341, 127 Sol
Jo 536, [1983] LS Gaz R 2516, 133 NLJ 745, HL 50.14
Wakeman v Quick Corpn [1999] IRLR 424, [1999] All ER (D) 158, CA 11.5
Walden Engineering Co Ltd v Warrener [1993] 3 CMLR 179, [1993] ICR 967, [1993]
IRLR 420, [1992] OPLR 1, EAT 49.15
Walker v Josiah Wedgwood & Sons Ltd [1978] ICR 744, [1978] IRLR 105, 13 ITR 271,
EAT 50.7
Walker v Northumberland County Council [1995] 1 All ER 737, [1995] ICR 702, [1995]
IRLR 35, [1995] ELR 231, [1994] NLJR 1659 .... 7.13, 25.8, 26.24
Walker (J H) Ltd v Hussain [1996] ICR 291, [1996] IRLR 11, EAT 13.8
Wall v British Compressed Air Society [2003] EWCA Civ 1762, [2004] ICR 408, [2004]
IRLR 147, [2004] 05 LS Gaz R 28, [2003] NLJR 1903, (2004) Times, 9 January,
[2003] All ER (D) 169 (Dec) 39.2, 50.14
Wallace v C A Roofing Services Ltd [1996] IRLR 435 .... 14.2, 55.44
Wallace Bogan & Co v Cove [1997] IRLR 453, CA 38.5
Walls Meat Co Ltd v Khan [1979] ICR 52, [1978] IRLR 499, 122 Sol Jo 759, CA 18.25
Walls Meat Co Ltd v Selby [1989] ICR 601, CA 51.11
Walmsley v C & R Ferguson Ltd [1989] IRLR 112, 1989 SLT 258, Ct of Sess 45.16
Walter v Secretary of State for Social Security [2001] EWCA Civ 1913, [2002] ICR 540,
(2001) Times, 13 December, [2001] All ER (D) 71 (Dec) 11.5
Walton v Airtours plc [2002] EWCA Civ 1659, [2004] Lloyd's Rep IR 69, [2003] IRLR
161, [2002] All ER (D) 34 (Nov) 41.17

PARA

Walton v Independent Living Organisation [2003] EWCA Civ 199, [2003] ICR 688, [2003]
    IRLR 469, (2003) Times, 27 February, 147 Sol Jo LB 266, [2003] All ER (D) 373
    (Feb) 31.12
Waltons and Morse v Dorrington [1997] IRLR 488, EAT 7.13, 26.23, 50.7
Wandsworth London Borough Council v D'Silva [1998] IRLR 193, CA 7.11, 7.22
Wandsworth London Borough Council v National Association of Schoolmasters/Union of
    Women Teachers (1994) 92 LGR 91, [1994] ICR 81, [1993] IRLR 344, [1994] ELR
    170, [1993] NLJR 655n, CA 34.2, 42.20
Ward Evans Financial Services Ltd v Fox [2001] EWCA Civ 1243, [2002] IRLR 120,
    [2001] All ER (D) 415 (Jul) 38.11
Warner v Adnet Ltd [1998] ICR 1056, [1998] IRLR 394, CA 49.20, 51.11
Warnes v Trustees of Cheriton Oddfellows Social Club [1993] IRLR 58, EAT 50.5, 50.7
Warnock v Scarborough Football Club [1989] ICR 489, EAT 18.26, 19.22
Warren v Mendy [1989] 3 All ER 103, [1989] 1 WLR 853, [1989] ICR 525, [1989]
    IRLR 210, CA 7.13, 7.24
Waters v Metropolitan Police Comr [1997] ICR 1073, [1997] IRLR 589, CA; revsd [2000]
    4 All ER 934, [2000] 1 WLR 1607, [2000] ICR 1064, [000] IRLR 720, HL 7.13, 11.10,
                                                                                                          11.13, 12.35, 34.2
Weathersfield Ltd (t/a Van and Truck Rentals) v Sargent [1999] ICR 425, [1999] IRLR
    94, 143 Sol Jo LB 39, CA 11.6, 11.13, 12.40, 45.19
Webb v EMO Air Cargo (UK) Ltd [1992] 4 All ER 929, [1993] 1 WLR 49, [1993] 1
    CMLR 259, [1993] ICR 175, [1993] IRLR 27, [1993] 9 LS Gaz R 44, 137 Sol Jo
    LB 48, HL; refd C-32/93: [1994] QB 718, [1994] 4 All ER 115, [1994] 3 WLR 941,
    [1994] ECR I-3567, [1994] 2 CMLR 729, [1994] ICR 770, [1994] IRLR 482, [1994]
    NLJR 1278, ECJ; apld sub nom Webb v EMO Air Cargo (UK) Ltd (No 2) [1995] 4
    All ER 577, [1995] 1 WLR 1454, [1996] 2 CMLR 990, [1995] ICR 1021, [1995]
    IRLR 645, [1995] 42 LS Gaz R 24, 140 Sol Jo LB 9, HL 11.5, 22.22, 23.2
Weber v Universal Ogden Services Ltd: C-37/00 [2002] QB 1189, [2002] All ER (EC)
    397, [2002] 3 WLR 931, [2002] ECR I-2013, [2002] ICR 979, [2002] IRLR 365,
    [2002] All ER (D) 377 (Feb), ECJ 24.11
Weddel (W) & Co Ltd v Tepper [1980] ICR 286, [1980] IRLR 96, 124 Sol Jo 80, CA 51.9
Weir v Bettison (sued as Chief Constable of Merseyside Police) [2003] EWCA Civ 111,
    [2003] ICR 708, [2003] 12 LS Gaz R 32, (2003) Times, 4 February, 147 Sol Jo LB
    145, [2003] All ER (D) 273 (Jan) 53.2
Wellcome Foundation v Darby [1996] IRLR 538, EAT 18.18
West v Kneels Ltd [1987] ICR 146, [1986] IRLR 430, [1986] LS Gaz R 2488, EAT 50.13,
                                                                                                                  55.5
West Dunbartonshire Council v Wallace. See Strathclyde Regional Council v Wallace
West Midland Co-operative Society Ltd v Tipton [1986] AC 536, [1986] 1 All ER 513,
    [1986] 2 WLR 306, [1986] ICR 192, [1986] IRLR 112, 130 Sol Jo 143, [1986] LS
    Gaz R 780, [1986] NLJ Rep 163, HL 50.13, 51.4, 51.10
West Midlands Passenger Executive v Singh [1988] 2 All ER 873, sub nom West Midlands
    Passenger Transport Executive v Singh [1988] 1 WLR 730, [1988] ICR 614, [1988]
    IRLR 186, 132 Sol Jo 933, CA 13.5, 19.12
West Midlands Travel Ltd v Transport and General Workers' Union [1994] ICR 978,
    [1994] IRLR 578, CA 42.14
Western Excavating (ECC) Ltd v Sharp [1978] QB 761, [1978] 1 All ER 713, [1978] 2
    WLR 344, [1978] ICR 221, [1978] IRLR 27, 121 Sol Jo 814, CA 50.7
Westminster City Council v Cabaj [1996] ICR 960, [1996] IRLR 399, CA 51.10, 55.1
Westminster City Council v Haywood [1998] Ch 377, [1997] 2 All ER 84, [1997] 3 WLR
    641, [1998] ICR 920, CA 39.12
Westminster City Council v UNISON [2001] EWCA Civ 443, [2001] LGR 378, [2001]
    ICR 1046, [2001] IRLR 524, [2001] 20 LS Gaz R 41, [2001] All ER (D) 250 (Mar) . 42.4,
                                                                                                          42.14, 42.15
Weston v Vega Space Systems Engineering Ltd [1989] IRLR 429, EAT 50.15
Westwood v Secretary of State for Employment [1985] AC 20, [1984] 1 All ER 874, [1984]
    2 WLR 418, [1985] ICR 209, [1984] IRLR 209, 128 Sol Jo 221, HL ... 29.5, 55.27, 55.30
Wheeler v Patel [1987] ICR 631, [1987] IRLR 211, [1987] LS Gaz R 1240, EAT 49.8, 49.20
Whelan (t/a Cheers Off Licence) v Richardson [1998] ICR 318, [1998] IRLR 114, EAT 52.12

Table of cases

PARA

Whent v T Cartledge Ltd [1997] IRLR 153, EAT 5.4, 49.16
Whiffen v Milham Ford Girls' School [2001] EWCA Civ 385, [2001] LGR 309, [2001]
    ICR 1023, [2001] IRLR 468, [2001] All ER (D) 256 (Mar) 12.8
Whitbread & Co plc v Mills [1988] ICR 776, [1988] IRLR 501, EAT 51.9, 51.10
Whitbread & Co plc v Thomas [1988] ICR 135, [1988] IRLR 43, [1987] LS Gaz R 3500,
    EAT 51.9
Whitbread plc (t/a Whitbread Medway Inns) v Hall [2001] EWCA Civ 268, [2001] ICR
    699, [2001] IRLR 275, [2001] 16 LS Gaz R 32, 145 Sol Jo LB 77, [2001] All ER
    (D) 338 (Feb) 51.4
Whitbread West Pennines Ltd v Reedy [1988] ICR 807, 20 HLR 642, CA 40.4
White v Bristol Rugby Ltd [2002] IRLR 204 .... 45.19
White v Chief Constable of South Yorkshire Police. See Frost v Chief Constable of South
    Yorkshire Police
White v Holbrook Precision Castings [1985] IRLR 215, CA 25.2
White v Reflecting Roadstuds Ltd [1991] ICR 733, [1991] IRLR 331, EAT 7.13
White v South London Transport Ltd [1998] ICR 293, EAT 51.4, 51.11
Whitefield v General Medical Council [2002] UKPC 62, [2003] IRLR 39, 72 BMLR 7,
    (2002) Times, 29 November, [2002] All ER (D) 220 (Nov) 28.7
Whitehouse v Blatchford & Sons Ltd [2000] ICR 542 .... 49.20
Whitely v Marton Electrical Ltd [2003] ICR 495, [2003] IRLR 197, (2003) Times, 2
    January, [2002] All ER (D) 370 (Nov), EAT 14.2
Whitewater Leisure Management Ltd v Barnes [2000] ICR 1049, [2000] IRLR 456, [2000]
    All ER (D) 568, EAT 49.5
Whittaker v Watson and Watson (t/a P & M Watson Haulage) [2002] ICR 1244, 67 BMLR
    28, [2002] All ER (D) 424 (Feb), EAT 18.13, 20.1, 28.7
Wickens v Champion Employment [1984] ICR 365, 134 NLJ 544, EAT 44.2
Wigan Borough Council v Davies [1979] ICR 411, [1979] IRLR 127, EAT 50.7
Wignall v British Gas Corpn [1984] ICR 716, [1984] IRLR 493, EAT 46.2
Wilding v British Telecommunications plc [2002] EWCA Civ 349, [2002] ICR 1079,
    [2002] IRLR 524, [2002] All ER (D) 278 (Mar) 52.5, 52.13
Wileman v Minilec Engineering Ltd [1988] ICR 318, [1988] IRLR 144, EAT 13.8, 19.75,
    20.16
Williams v Channel 5 Engineering Services Ltd IDS Brief No 609 .... 9.14
Williams v Compair Maxam Ltd [1982] ICR 156, [1982] IRLR 83, EAT 51.11
Williams v Ferrosan Ltd [2004] IRLR 607, [2004] All ER (D) 272 (May), EAT 18.14, 19.75
Williams v Watsons Luxury Coaches Ltd [1990] ICR 536, [1990] IRLR 164, EAT 45.3
Willment Bros Ltd v Oliver [1979] ICR 378 .... 52.13
Wilsher v Essex Area Health Authority [1988] AC 1074, [1988] 1 All ER 871, [1988] 2
    WLR 557, 132 Sol Jo 418, [1988] 15 LS Gaz R 37, [1988] NLJR 78, HL 25.8
Wilson (Inspector of Taxes) v Clayton [2004] EWHC 898 (Ch), [2004] STC 1022, [2004]
    IRLR 611, [2004] 19 LS Gaz R 29, (2004) Times, 7 June, [2004] All ER (D) 313
    (Apr) 52.22
Wilson v Ethicon Ltd [2000] IRLR 4, EAT 51.4
Wilson v Maynard Shipbuilding Consultants AB [1978] QB 665, [1978] 2 All ER 78, [1978]
    2 WLR 466, [1978] ICR 376, [1977] IRLR 491, 13 ITR 23, 121 Sol Jo 792, CA 50.15
Wilson v Post Office [2000] IRLR 834 .... 51.2
Wilson v Racher [1974] ICR 428, [1974] IRLR 114, 16 KIR 212, CA 55.17
Wilson v St Helens Borough Council [1999] 2 AC 52, [1998] 4 All ER 609, [1998] 3
    WLR 1070, [1999] 1 CMLR 918, [1999] LGR 255, [1998] ICR 1141, [1998] IRLR
    706, [1998] All ER (D) 516, HL 49.20
Wilson v United Kingdom (Applications 30668/96, 30679/61 and 30678/96) [2002] IRLR
    568, 13 BHRC 39, (2002) Times, 5 July, [2002] All ER (D) 35 (Jul), ECtHR 47.19,
    48.18
Wilson (Joshua) & Bros Ltd v Union of Shop, Distributive and Allied Workers [1978] 3
    All ER 4, [1978] ICR 614, [1978] IRLR 120, 13 ITR 229, EAT 47.20
Wilson (Paal) & Co A/S v Partenreederei Hannah Blumenthal, The Hannah Blumenthal
    [1983] 1 AC 854, [1982] 3 All ER 394, [1982] 3 WLR 49, [1982] 1 Lloyd's Rep 582,
    126 Sol Jo 292, CA; varied [1983] 1 AC 854, [1983] 1 All ER 34, [1982] 3 WLR
    1149, [1983] 1 Lloyd's Rep 103, 126 Sol Jo 835, HL 45.3

PARA

24/85: Spijkers v Gebroeders Benedik Abbatoir CV and Alfred Benedik en Zonen BV [1986] ECR 1119, [1986] 2 CMLR 296, ECJ 49.5
66/85: Lawrie-Blum v Land Baden-Württemberg [1986] ECR 2121, [1987] 3 CMLR 389, [1987] ICR 483, ECJ 22.4
186/85: Family Benefits for Community Civil Servants, Re, EC Commission v Belgium [1987] ECR 2029, [1988] 2 CMLR 759, ECJ 34.8
225/85: Employees of the Consiglio Nazionale delle Ricerche, Re, EC Commisison v Italy [1988] ECR 2271, [1988] 3 CMLR 635, ECJ 34.7
237/85: Rummler v Dato-Druck GmbH [1987] ICR 774, [1987] IRLR 32, ECJ 22.7
111/86: Delauche v EC Commission [1987] ECR 5345, [1989] 2 CMLR 565, ECJ 34.8
157/86: Murphy v Bord Telecom Eireann [1988] ECR 673, [1988] 1 CMLR 879, [1988] ICR 445, [1988] IRLR 267, ECJ 22.6, 22.8
222/86: Union Nationale des Entraîneurs et Cadres Techniques Professionnels du Football (UNECTEF) v Heylens [1987] ECR 4097, [1989] 1 CMLR 901, ECJ 23.4
287/86: Landsorganisationen i Danmark v Ny Molle Kro [1987] ECR 5465, [1989] ICR 330, [1989] IRLR 37, ECJ 49.4
324/86: Foreningen af Arbejdsledere i Danmark v Daddy's Dance Hall A/S [1988] ECR 739, [1989] 2 CMLR 517, [1988] IRLR 315, ECJ 38.22, 49.4, 49.24
101/87: P Bork International A/S v Foreningen af Arbejdsledere i Danmark [1988] ECR 3057, [1990] 3 CMLR 701, [1989] IRLR 41, ECJ 49.4, 49.10
144/87 and 145/87: Berg and Busschers v Besselsen [1988] ECR 2559, [1989] 3 CMLR 817, [1990] ICR 396, [1989] IRLR 447, ECJ 49.4, 49.14
180/87: Hamill v EC Commission [1990] 1 All ER 982, [1988] ECR 6141, [1990] 1 CMLR 982, ECJ 34.8
193/87: Maurissen and European Public Service Union v Court of Auditors of the European Communities [1989] ECR 1045, ECJ 34.8
33/88: Allué and Coonan v Università degli Studi di Venezia [1989] ECR 1591, [1991] 1 CMLR 283, ECJ 34.7
109/88: Handels-og Kontorfunktionaerernes Forbund i Danmark v Dansk Arbejdsgiver-forening, acting on behalf of Danfoss [1989] ECR 3199, [1991] 1 CMLR 8, [1991] ICR 74, [1989] IRLR 532, ECJ 22.11
171/88: Rinner-Kühn v FWW Spezial-Gebäudereinigung GmbH & Co KG [1989] ECR 2743, [1993] 2 CMLR 932, [1989] IRLR 493, ECJ 22.3
177/88: Dekker v Stichting Vormingscentrum voor Jong Volwassenen (VJV - Centrum) Plus [1990] ECR I-3941, [1992] ICR 325, [1991] IRLR 27, ECJ 11.5
322/88: Grimaldi v Fonds des Maladies Professionnelles [1989] ECR 4407, [1991] 2 CMLR 265, [1990] IRLR 400, ECJ 23.1
C-262/88: Barber v Guardian Royal Exchange Assurance Group [1991] 1 QB 344, [1990] 2 All ER 660, [1991] 2 WLR 72, [1990] ECR I-1889, [1990] 2 CMLR 513, [1990] ICR 616, [1990] IRLR 240, [1990] NLJR 925, ECJ 22.3, 22.5, 22.16, 23.2, 39.1, 39.4
C-33/89: Kowalska v Freie und Hansestadt Hamburg [1990] ECR I-2591, [1992] ICR 29, [1990] IRLR 447, ECJ 22.24, 22.25
C-106/89: Marleasing SA v La Comercial Internacional de Alimentacion SA [1990] ECR I-4135, [1992] 1 CMLR 305, [1993] BCC 421, 135 Sol Jo 15, ECJ 23.2
C-184/89: Nimz v Freie und Hansestadt Hamburg [1991] ECR I-297, [1992] 3 CMLR 699, [1991] IRLR 222, ECJ 5.6, 22.3, 22.11, 22.24, 22.25
C-188/89: Foster v British Gas plc [1991] 1 QB 405, [1990] 3 All ER 897, [1991] 2 WLR 258, [1990] ECR I-3313, [1990] 2 CMLR 833, [1991] ICR 84, [1990] IRLR 353, ECJ; apld [1991] 2 AC 306, [1991] 2 All ER 705, [1991] 2 WLR 1075, [1991] 2 CMLR 217, [1991] ICR 463, [1991] IRLR 268, [1991] 18 LS Gaz R 34, HL 23.2, 34.7
C-192/89: Sevince v Staatssecretaris van Justitie [1990] ECR I-3461, [1992] 2 CMLR 57, ECJ 24.2
C-229/89: EC Commission v Belgium [1991] ECR I-2205, [1993] 2 CMLR 403, [1991] IRLR 393, ECJ 12.8
C-362/89: d'Urso v Ercole Marelli Elettromeccanica Generale SpA [1991] ECR I-4105, [1993] 3 CMLR 513, [1992] IRLR 136, ECJ 49.20, 49.23
C-6/90 and C-9/90: Francovich and Bonifaci v Italy [1991] ECR I-5357, [1993] 2 CMLR 66, [1995] ICR 722, [1992] IRLR 84, ECJ 23.2

Table of cases

PARA

C-87/90, C-99/90, and C-89/90: Verholen v Sociale Versekeringsbank Amsterdam [1991]
ECR I-3757, [1994] 1 CMLR 157, [1992] IRLR 38, ECJ 23.2
C-208/90: Emmott v Minister for Social Welfare and A-G [1991] ECR I-4269, [1991] 3
CMLR 894, [1993] ICR 8, [1991] IRLR 387, ECJ 18.33, 23.2
C-360/90: Arbeiterwohlfahrt der Stadt Berlin e V v Bötel [1992] ECR I-3589, [1992] 3
CMLR 446, [1992] IRLR 423, [1993] 21 LS Gaz R 45, ECJ 22.3, 22.10
C-29/91: Redmond (Dr Sophie) Stichting v Bartol [1992] ECR I-3189, [1994] 3 CMLR
265, [1992] IRLR 366, ECJ 49.3, 49.5
C-109/91: Ten Oever v Stichting Bedrijfspensioenfonds voor het Glazenwassers- en
Schoonmaakbedrijf [1993] ECR I-4879, [1995] 2 CMLR 357, [1995] ICR 74, [1993]
IRLR 601, [1995] 42 LS Gaz R 23, ECJ 22.18
C-110/91: Moroni v Collo GmbH [1993] ECR I-6591, [1995] 2 CMLR 357, [1995] ICR
137, [1994] IRLR 130, [1995] 42 LS Gaz R 23, ECJ 22.18
C-132/91, C-138/91 and C-139/91: Katsikas v Konstantinidis [1992] ECR I-6577, [1993]
1 CMLR 845, [1993] IRLR 179, ECJ 49.12
C-140/91, C-141/91, C-278/91 and C-279/91: Suffritti v Istituto Nazionale della Previdenza
Sociale (INPS) [1992] ECR I-6337, [1993] IRLR 289, ECJ 23.2
C-152/91: Neath v Hugh Steeper Ltd [1994] 1 All ER 929, [1993] ECR I-6935, [1995] 2
CMLR 357, [1995] ICR 158, [1994] IRLR 91, [1995] 42 LS Gaz R 23, ECJ 20.27,
22.18
C-173/91: EC Commission v Belgium [1993] IRLR 404, ECJ 22.3
C-200/91: Coloroll Pension Trustees Ltd v Russell [1995] All ER (EC) 23, [1994] ECR
I-4389, [1995] 2 CMLR 357, [1995] ICR 179, [1994] IRLR 586, [1995] 42 LS Gaz
R 23, (1994) Times, 30 November, ECJ 22.18, 39.6
C-209/91: Rask and Christensen v ISS Kantineservice A/S [1992] ECR I-5755, [1993]
IRLR 133, ECJ 49.5
C-271/91: Marshall v Southampton and South West Hampshire Area Health Authority
(No 2) [1994] QB 126, [1993] 4 All ER 586, [1993] 3 WLR 1054, [1993] ECR
I-4367, [1993] 3 CMLR 293, [1993] ICR 893, [1993] IRLR 445, ECJ; apld sub nom
Marshall v Southampton and South-West Hampshire Area Health Authority (Teaching)
(No 2) [1994] 1 AC 530n, [1994] 1 All ER 736n, [1994] 2 WLR 392, [1994] ICR
242n, HL 13.8, 18.12, 19.67, 23.5
C-338/91: Steenhorst-Neerings v Bestuur van de Bedrijfsvereniging voor Detailhandel,
Ambachten en Huisvrouwen [1993] ECR I-5475, [1995] 3 CMLR 323, [1994] IRLR
244, ECJ 23.2
C-91/92: Faccini Dori v Recreb Srl [1995] All ER (EC) 1, [1994] ECR I-3325, [1995] 1
CMLR 665, ECJ 23.2
C-125/92: Mulox IBC Ltd v Geels [1993] ECR I-4075, [1994] IRLR 422, ECJ 24.11
C-127/92: Enderby v Frenchay Health Authority [1994] 1 All ER 495, [1993] ECR I-5535,
[1994] 1 CMLR 8, [1994] ICR 112, [1993] IRLR 591, ECJ 20.27, 22.10,
22.11
C-132/92: Birds Eye Walls Ltd v Roberts [1993] ECR I-5579, [1993] 3 CMLR 822, [1994]
IRLR 29, sub nom Roberts v Birds Eye Walls Ltd [1994] ICR 338, ECJ 22.12, 22.17,
22.18
C-382/92: EC Commission v United Kingdom [1994] ECR I-2435, [1995] 1 CMLR 345,
[1994] ICR 664, [1994] IRLR 392, ECJ 16.12, 23.2, 49.18
C-383/92: EC Commission v United Kingdom [1994] ECR I-2479, [1995] 1 CMLR 345,
[1994] ICR 664, [1994] IRLR 412, ECJ 23.8, 23.9
C-392/92: Schmidt v Spar und Leihkasse der früheren Amter Bordesholm, Kiel und Cronshagen [1994] ECR I-1311, [1995] 2 CMLR 331, [1995] ICR 237, [1994] IRLR 302,
ECJ 49.5
C-399/92, C-409/92, C-425/92, C-34/93, C-50/93, and C-78/93: Stadt Lengerich v Helmig
[1994] ECR I-5727, [1995] 2 CMLR 261, [1996] ICR 35, [1995] IRLR 216, ECJ ... 22.11
C-408/92: Smith v Avdel Systems Ltd [1995] All ER (EC) 132, [1994] ECR I-4435, [1995]
3 CMLR 543, [1995] ICR 596, [1994] IRLR 602, ECJ 20.27, 22.18, 39.4
C-410/92: Johnson v Chief Adjudication Officer (No 2) [1995] All ER (EC) 258, [1994]
ECR I-5483, [1995] 1 CMLR 725, [1995] ICR 375, [1995] IRLR 157, ECJ 23.2
C-7/93: Bestuur van het Algemeen Burgerlijk Pensioenfonds v Beune [1995] All ER (EC)
97, [1994] ECR I-4471, [1995] 3 CMLR 30, [1995] IRLR 103, ECJ 22.18

PARA

C-32/93: Webb v EMO Air Cargo (UK) Ltd [1994] QB 718, [1994] 4 All ER 115, [1994] 3 WLR 941, [1994] ECR I-3567, [1994] 2 CMLR 729, [1994] ICR 770, [1994] IRLR 482, [1994] NLJR 1278, ECJ; apld sub nom Webb v EMO Air Cargo (UK) Ltd (No 2) [1995] 4 All ER 577, [1995] 1 WLR 1454, [1996] 2 CMLR 990, [1995] ICR 1021, [1995] IRLR 645, [1995] 42 LS Gaz R 24, 140 Sol Jo LB 9, HL 11.5, 22.22, 23.2

C-46/93: Brasserie du Pecheur SA v Germany [1996] QB 404, [1996] All ER (EC) 301, [1996] 2 WLR 506, [1996] ECR I-1029, [1996] 1 CMLR 889, [1996] IRLR 267, ECJ 23.2

C-48/93: R v Secretary of State for Transport, ex p Factortame Ltd [1996] QB 404, [1996] All ER (EC) 301, [1996] 2 WLR 506, [1996] ECR I-1029, [1996] 1 CMLR 889, [1996] IRLR 267, ECJ; apld [1998] 1 All ER 736n, [1998] 3 CMLR 192, [1998] NPC 68, [1998] Eu LR 456, CA; affd [2000] 1 AC 524, [1999] 4 All ER 906, [1999] 3 WLR 1062, [1999] 3 CMLR 597, [1999] 43 LS Gaz R 32, HL 23.2

C-57/93: Vroege v NCIV Instituut voor Volkshuisvesting BV [1995] All ER (EC) 193, [1994] ECR I-4541, [1995] 1 CMLR 881, [1995] ICR 635, [1994] IRLR 651, ECJ 22.10

C-128/93: Fisscher v Voorhuis Hengelo BV [1995] All ER (EC) 193, [1994] ECR I-4583, [1995] 1 CMLR 881, [1995] ICR 635, [1994] IRLR 662, ECJ 18.12, 22.18, 23.2

C-317/93: Nolte v Landesversicherungsanstalt Hannover [1996] All ER (EC) 212, [1995] ECR I-4625, [1996] IRLR 225, ECJ 23.2

C-342/93: Gillespie v Northern Health and Social Services Board [1996] All ER (EC) 284, [1996] ECR I-475, [1996] 2 CMLR 969, [1996] ICR 498, [1996] IRLR 214, ECJ 22.9, 22.14, 30.14, 39.8

C-435/93: Dietz v Stichting Thuiszorg Rotterdam [1996] ECR I-5223, [1997] 1 CMLR 199, [1996] IRLR 692, 563 IRLB 13, ECJ 22.17, 22.18

C-444/93: Megner and Scheffel v Innungskrankenkasse Vorderpfalz [1996] All ER (EC) 212, [1995] ECR I-4741, [1996] IRLR 236, ECJ 23.2

C-449/93: Rockfon A/S v Specialarbejderforbundet i Danmark [1995] ECR I-4291, [1996] ICR 673, [1996] IRLR 168, ECJ 36.4

C-450/93: Kalanke v Freie Hansestadt Bremen [1996] All ER (EC) 66, [1995] ECR I-3051, [1996] 1 CMLR 175, [1996] ICR 314, [1995] IRLR 660, ECJ 11.5, 11.12, 12.9, 34.2

C-457/93: Kuratorium für Dialyse und Nierentransplantation eV v Lewark [1996] ECR I-243, [1996] IRLR 637, ECJ 22.3, 46.4

C-472/93: Spano v Fiat Geotech SpA and Fiat Hitachi Excavators SpA [1995] ECR I-4321, ECJ 49.23

C-13/94: P v S [1996] All ER (EC) 397, [1996] ECR I-2143, [1996] 2 CMLR 247, [1996] ICR 795, [1996] IRLR 347, [1997] 2 FCR 180, [1996] 2 FLR 347, ECJ 11.2, 11.6, 20.27, 22.2

C-48/94: Ledernes Hovedorganisation (acting for Rygard) v Dansk Arbejdsgiverforening (acting for Sto Molle Akustik A/S) [1995] ECR I-2745, [1996] 3 CMLR 45, [1996] ICR 333, [1996] IRLR 51, ECJ 49.5

C-84/94: United Kingdom v EU Council [1996] All ER (EC) 877, [1996] ECR I-5755, [1996] 3 CMLR 671, [1997] ICR 443, [1997] IRLR 30, ECJ 23.11, 54.1

C-116/94: Meyers v Adjudication Officer [1995] All ER (EC) 705, [1995] ECR I-2131, [1996] 1 CMLR 461, [1995] IRLR 498, ECJ 23.5

C-171/94 and C-172/94: Merckx v Ford Motors Co Belgium SA [1996] All ER (EC) 667, [1996] ECR I-1253, [1997] ICR 352, [1996] IRLR 467, ECJ 49.5, 49.12

C-178/94, C-179/94, C-188/94, C-189/94 and C-190/94: Dillenkofer v Germany [1997] QB 259, [1996] All ER (EC) 917, [1997] 2 WLR 253, [1996] ECR I-4845, [1996] 3 CMLR 469, [1997] IRLR 60, ECJ 23.2

C-194/94: CIA Security International SA v Signalson [1996] All ER (EC) 557, [1996] ECR I-2201, [1996] 2 CMLR 781, ECJ 23.2

C-298/94: Henke v Gemeinde Schierke and Verwaltungsgemeinschaft Brocken [1997] All ER (EC) 173, [1996] ECR I-4989, [1997] 1 CMLR 373, [1997] ICR 746, [1996] IRLR 701, ECJ 34.2, 49.3

C-305/94: Hertaing v Benoidt [1997] All ER (EC) 40, [1996] ECR I-5927, [1997] 1 CMLR 329, [1997] IRLR 127, ECJ 49.9

C-319/94: Dethier (Jules) Equipement SA v Dassy and Sovam SPRL (in liquidation) [1998] All ER (EC) 346, [1998] ECR I-1061, [1998] 2 CMLR 611, [1998] ICR 541, [1998] IRLR 266, ECJ 49.7, 49.20

Table of cases

PARA

C-1/95: Gerster v Freistaat Bayern [1997] ECR I-5253, [1998] 1 CMLR 303, [1998] ICR 327, [1997] IRLR 699, ECJ 22.3, 22.11

C-13/95: Suzen v Zehnacker Gebaudereinigung GmbH Krankenhausservice [1997] All ER (EC) 289, [1997] ECR I-1259, [1997] 1 CMLR 768, [1997] ICR 662, [1997] IRLR 255, ECJ 49.5

C-100/95: Kording v Senator für Finanzen [1997] ECR I-5289, [1998] 1 CMLR 395, [1997] IRLR 710, ECJ 22.3

C-136/95: Caisse Nationale d'Assurance Vieillesse des Travailleurs Salaries v Thibault [1998] All ER (EC) 385, [1998] ECR I-2011, [1998] 2 CMLR 516, [1998] IRLR 399, [1998] All ER (D) 167, sub nom Thibault v Caisse Nationale d'Assurance Viellesse des Travailleurs Salaries (CNAVTS) [1999] ICR 160, ECJ 11.5

C-163/95: Von Horn v Cinnamond [1998] QB 214, [1997] All ER (EC) 913, [1998] 2 WLR 104, [1997] ECR I-5451, ECJ 24.11

C-188/95: Fantask A/S v Industriministeriet (Erhvervsministeriet) [1998] All ER (EC) 1, [1997] ECR I-6783, [1998] 1 CMLR 473, ECJ 23.2

C-243/95: Hill v Revenue Comrs [1998] All ER (EC) 722, [1998] ECR I-3739, [1998] 3 CMLR 81, [1999] ICR 48, [1998] IRLR 466, [1998] 34 LS Gaz R 33, [1998] All ER (D) 277, ECJ 22.3

C-374/95: Barker v Service Children's Schools (unreported), ECJ 11.12

C-383/95: Rutten v Cross Medical Ltd [1997] All ER (EC) 121, [1997] ECR I-57, [1997] ICR 715, [1997] IRLR 249, ECJ 24.11

C-409/95: Marschall v Land Nordrhein-Westfalen [1997] All ER (EC) 865, [1997] ECR I-6363, [1998] 1 CMLR 547, [2001] ICR 45, [1998] IRLR 39, ECJ 11.12, 12.9

C-15/96: Schöning-Kougebetopoulou v Freie und Hansestadt Hamburg: [1998] All ER (EC) 97, [1998] 1 CMLR 931, sub nom Kalliope Schöning-Kougebetopoulou v Freie und Hansestadt Hamburg [1998] ECR I-47, ECJ 24.2

C-50/96: Deutsche Telekom AG v Schröder [2000] ECR I-743, [2002] 2 CMLR 583, [2000] IRLR 353, ECJ 22.18

C-66/96: Handels-og Kontorfunktionaerernes Forbund i Danmark (acting on behalf of Hoj Pedersen) v Faellesforeningen for Danmarks Brugsforeninger (acting on behalf of Kvickly Skive) [1998] ECR I-7327, [1999] 2 CMLR 326, [1999] IRLR 55, sub nom Pedersen v Kvickly Skive [1999] All ER (EC) 138, [1998] All ER (D) 614, ECJ 22.14

C-127/96, C-229/96 and C-74/97: Vidal (Francisco Hernandez) SA v Perez [1998] ECR I-8179, [1999] IRLR 132, ECJ 49.5

C-173/96: Hidalgo v Asociacion de Servicios Aser and Sociedad Cooperativa Minerva [1998] ECR I-8237, [2002] ICR 73, [1999] IRLR 136, ECJ 49.5

C-246/96: Magorrian v Eastern Health and Social Services Board [1998] All ER (EC) 38, [1997] ECR I-7153, [1998] ICR 979, [1998] IRLR 86, ECJ 18.12

C-249/96: Grant v South-West Trains Ltd [1998] All ER (EC) 193, [1998] ECR I-621, [1998] 1 CMLR 993, [1998] ICR 449, [1998] IRLR 206, [1998] 1 FCR 377, [1998] 1 FLR 839, [1998] Fam Law 392, 3 BHRC 578, ECJ 28.5

C-326/96: Levez v TH Jennings (Harlow Pools) Ltd [1999] All ER (EC) 1, [1998] ECR I-7835, [1999] 2 CMLR 363, [1999] ICR 521, [1999] IRLR 36, 608 IRLB 3, [1998] All ER (D) 662, ECJ 18.12

C-394/96: Brown v Rentokil Ltd [1998] All ER (EC) 791, [1998] ECR I-4185, [1998] 2 CMLR 1049, [1998] ICR 790, [1998] IRLR 445, [1999] 1 FCR 49, [1998] 2 FLR 649, [1998] Fam Law 597, 48 BMLR 126, [1998] 34 LS Gaz R 34, [1998] All ER (D) 313, ECJ 11.5

C-411/96: Boyle v Equal Opportunities Commission [1998] All ER (EC) 879, [1998] ECR I-6401, [1998] 3 CMLR 1133, [1999] ICR 360, [1998] IRLR 717, [1999] 1 FCR 581, [1999] 1 FLR 119, 608 IRLB 5, [1998] All ER (D) 500, ECJ 22.14, 39.8

C-125/97: AGR Regeling v Bestuur van der Bedrijfsvereniging voor de Metaallnijverheid [1998] ECR I-4493, [1999] 1 CMLR 1410, [1999] ICR 605, [1999] IRLR 379, [1998] All ER (D) 336, ECJ 29.5

C-167/97: R v Secretary of State for Employment, ex p Seymour-Smith [1999] 2 AC 554, [1999] All ER (EC) 97, [1999] 3 WLR 460, [1999] ECR I-623, [1999] 2 CMLR 273, [1999] ICR 447, [1999] IRLR 253, ECJ; apld sub nom R v Secretary of State for Employment, ex p Seymour-Smith (No 2) [2000] 1 All ER 857, [2000] 1 WLR 435, [2000] 1 CMLR 770, [2000] ICR 244, [2000] IRLR 263, [2000] 09 LS Gaz R 40, HL 6.1, 11.8, 12.8, 22.3, 22.10, 23.2, 50.11